Integral Dreaming

SUNY series in Dream Studies

Robert L. Van de Castle, editor

INTEGRAL DREAMING

A Holistic Approach to Dreams

Fariba Bogzaran and Daniel Deslauriers

SUNY
PRESS

Cover art designed by the authors and illustrated by Gwendolyn Jones.

Published by
STATE UNIVERSITY OF NEW YORK PRESS
Albany

Printed in the United States of America

For information, contact
State University of New York Press
www.sunypress.edu

Production, Laurie Searl
Marketing, Kate McDonnell

Library of Congress Cataloging-in-Publication Data

Bogzaran, Fariba, 1958–
Integral dreaming : a holistic approach to dreams / Fariba Bogzaran and Daniel Deslauriers.
p. cm. — (SUNY series in dream studies)
Includes bibliographical references and index.
ISBN 978-1-4384-4237-2 (hbk. : alk. paper) 978-1-4384-4238-9 (pb : alk. paper)
1. Dreams. I. Deslauriers, Daniel, 1958– II. Title.

BF1091.B62 2012
154.6'3—dc23 2011027894

10 9 8 7 6 5 4 3 2 1

To the memory of our mothers
for their support of our creative endeavors
and of the pursuit of our dreams.

Contents

Figures

Acknowledgments

We are grateful to many people who have helped us while writing this book. We jointly thank Bob Van de Castle, editor of SUNY Press's series in Dream Studies, and Jane Bunker, former associate director and editor-in-chief at SUNY Press. Both were enthusiastic about this book and waited patiently for several years. We thank SUNY Press senior editor Nancy Ellegate and senior production editor Laurie Searl for working with us throughout the process.

We want to thank our editor, Nancy Adess, and our colleagues Elizabeth Shaver, Kimmy Johnson, and Karen Jaenke whose feedback were invaluable. We thank Gwen Jones for helping us in designing the illustrations that grace this book and Monika Tomaszewska, Ezra and Anna Mikeda for technical assistance. We are deeply appreciative of Lynne Ehlers for her participation in this book: through countless hours of interviews, her willingness to share her process brought heart and meaning to our philosophy of practice.

We each individually want to thank special people in our lives. From Fariba: I honor my early mentors in consciousness studies from whom I learned science, phenomenology, and integral studies: Daniel Kortenkamp and Hamid Hekmat (University of Wisconsin); Bill Wynne (University of Regina, Canada); Yi Wu, James Kidd, and Ralph Metzner (California

Institute of Integral Studies); and Stephen LaBerge (Stanford University). I give my heartfelt gratitude to my mentors who taught me the art of practice: T'ai Chi master Pi Lu Fei; shaman Joska Soos; Reichian Ed Jackson; Dzogchen master Lama Tharchin Rinpoche; painters Gordon Onslow Ford, John Anderson, and Matta. My appreciation reaches out to the graduates of the Dream Studies Program at John F. Kennedy University: my reward is to be the witness of your blossoming. Three colleagues at JFKU were pillars of support while I created the program: David Goldberg, Vernice Solimar, and Nancy Slocum. Thank you for believing in my vision and for the gift of our deep friendship.

From Daniel: I wish to acknowledge and thank my mentor George W. Baylor for his teachings, sometimes unbearable, on how to lead life with joyful purpose. One day I will find the best recipe for Sauce Aurore! I also wish to thank the late Alan Moffitt and his associates at the Chronopsychology Lab at the University of Carleton, Ottawa for opening their doors to me in order to "pay my dues" to science. Those forty nights inverting my sleep pattern were like crossing the desert of consciousness! I am also indebted to my colleagues in the East-West Psychology and Transformative Studies Programs at the California Institute of Integral Studies (CIIS) and especially all my students who put their trust in their dreams. Their openness and deep questioning allowed all of us to enter the mystery of dreams together. I wish to thank Judie Wexler, dean of faculty at CIIS, for providing the right atmosphere for scholarship. Merci à Apela Colorado for her fervent and subtle support and prayers on this journey. And to my friends in Quebec who supported me in many ways, and who demanded regular progress reports, especially Dominique Major, Marie-Ève Pelletier, Laurette Dupuis, and Marc Valois, I say "merci infiniment"!

We give our gratitude to late James Hillman, late Montie Ullman, Harry Hunt, Gordon Globus and Ken Wilber whose works have been an intellectual inspiration for both of us.

Many friends and colleagues listened to our process for years while we were writing this book: thank you to Patricia Garfield, Jayne Gackenbach, Rita Dwyer, Stan Krippner, Tore Nielsen, Don Kuiken, Barbara and Denis Tedlock, Mary Dombeck, Elizabeth Zarlengo, Yalda Kamrani, Runa Gustafsson, Emily Anderson, Christiam Nabadon, Carol Sipper, Daniel Rybold, Marilyn Fowler, Atom Patten, Barbara de Franco, Keelin, Robert Snyder, Sharon Kehoe, the late Vicki Helms, Ngawang Zangpo, Zayra Yves, and many others. Esta Feedora, Badri, Nima, and George provided the best encouragement: they constantly insisted we should just go out and play rather than write. They teased us to the brink of completion! Our colleague and friend Marc Barasch once told us writing a book is an isolating affair—one can disappear for years. We now understand what you meant, Marc!

We want to acknowledge the support of our brothers Faramarz, François, Guy, Louis-Jean, and Ramin who were, along with their families, very patient with us for our lack of participation in family functions while working on this project. Thank you for your understanding.

Finally, during the process of writing this book we had two major losses: Daniel's mother and Fariba's father passed. They constantly heard us talking about this book. We wish they were with us today—we know well that they would have rejoiced the most.

Introduction

Dreaming is the art of the mind. Every dream is intrinsically a creative experience. As the artists of the night, we are co-participants in weaving new creations from the complexity of our entire being. Dreaming forms an integral part of who we are. Becoming familiar with our dreaming life becomes increasingly important to a life of self-inquiry and self-understanding. Not only do dreams spur insight and personal growth, they also help us understand the creative nature of the mind.

The emerging field of dream studies has formed from many coalescing strands: the analytical power of science, the cumulative knowledge of wisdom traditions, the insights of modern psychology, and the renewed interest in human consciousness. Several competing theories and approaches have tried to explain the nature, functions, and creative use of dreaming. With so many exciting avenues of inquiry, the amount of information and the wide range of perspectives on dreams can be overwhelming. How does it all connect?

Integral Dreaming brings a connective voice and an expansive approach to the field of dream studies. Its holistic perspective springs from the idea that we are multidimensional beings, that dreams are multidimensional events, and that there are multiple ways of viewing and gaining insights into dreams.

We use the word *integral* to convey a deep personal and professional affinity with the concept of unity in diversity, and conversely, diversity in unity.[1] Our philosophical view is rooted in the core belief that human beings, with their complex nature, share a common ground in dreaming. Dreaming is an inner phenomenon open to us all, regardless of age, gender, race, religion, culture, or social status.

While it addresses a diversity of disciplines, *Integral Dreaming* also fosters an attitude of deep inquiry. Like our own dreams, the book asks us to question our assumptions about dreams and to challenge our habitual perspectives. It invites us to open the aperture of our perception to include new ways of viewing dreams: scientific, phenomenological, cultural, ancestral, artistic, and integrative. This broader approach can lead to a wider range of creative choices in understanding dreams. *Integral Dreaming* addresses the creative function of dreams as understood through various research methodologies.

THE ORIGINS OF INTEGRAL DREAMING

The concept of *Integral Dreaming* evolved out of our thirty years of participation in the "movement" of dream studies. As with most movements, divergent viewpoints among those studying dreams create tension between and among theoretical approaches and applications. Rather than privileging one discipline or one theory, the integral approach takes an inclusive position. It brings different paradigms into dialogue in order to develop a comprehensive view of the multiplicity of approaches.

To offer a theory of wholeness and search for an overarching model is a weighty task, and one that we approach with humility. This book is by no means an exhaustive review of the field of dream studies. Others have made invaluable contributions, including Robert Van de Castle's extensive historical overview, *Our Dreaming Mind* (1994); Barbara Tedlock's cross-cultural anthology, *Dreaming* (1987); Anthony Shafton's comprehensive history of contemporary methods, *The Dream Reader* (1995); *Extraordinary Dreams* (2002), by Stanley Krippner, Fariba Bogzaran, and André de Carvalho; the three-volume theoretical and scientific compendium, *The New Science of Dreaming* (2007), edited by Deirdre Barrett and Patrick McNamara; and

Kelly Bulkeley's *Dreaming in the World's Religions* (2008). From our perspective, these important works cover the foundational ground for dream studies.

Still, crucial questions remain that frame the present work:

- Is it possible to conceive of a holistic approach to exploring dreams, one that incorporates the rigors of science and also respects the wholeness of our being and our process of becoming?

- What comes to light when we look at dreams and the dreaming process from an integrative perspective?

- How can we include multiple disciplines and perspectives in a larger dialogue, in order to advance the field of dream studies?

OVERVIEW

This book consists of three parts: Part I introduces the field of integral studies in relation to dream studies; Part II explores the science, phenomenology, and sociocultural aspects of dreaming; Part III discusses assumptions about dream meaning and introduces our philosophy of Integral Dream Practice.

Part I sets the philosophical foundation. In chapter 1 we discuss the meaning of the term *integral*, showing how the term is currently applied and understood, and discuss the integral philosophy of Sri Aurobindo, Haridas Chaudhuri, and Ken Wilber. In chapter 2, we propose the core principles of *Integral Dreaming*, addressing the multiplicity of the self and ways of viewing dreams from a multidimensional perspective.

Part II uses Ken Wilber's four-quadrant model as a framework to explore the existing multidisciplinary knowledge about dreams and dreaming. The four-quadrant model sets out different aspects of existence within four main ways of knowing: the objective aspect captured by science; the subjective aspect captured by phenomenology; the intersubjective aspect captured by clinical practice and cultural studies; and the interobjective or socio-environmental aspect captured by social history, anthropology, and sociology. We illustrate and situate important contributions from various disciplines within the field of dream studies within this model while recognizing that each area of study expands into overlapping disciplines.

In chapter 3 we address the third-person approach to dreams: the scientific theories concerning the nature, physiology, and function of dreaming. In particular, we examine one night of sleep as it moves through different stages and propose a novel way of looking at the sleep experience by exploring its regenerative and integrative aspects. Chapter 4 examines the connections between dreams, memory, and creative insight, and shows how dreaming is an embodied state of consciousness essential to human maturation. In chapter 5, we explore the inner realm of dreams and its phenomenology. In chapter 6 we look at the variety of dreams that inhabit our night life and those that affect us most deeply. In chapter 7 we look at the various strategies for how the self makes sense of its oneiric, or dream-related, creations. In chapter 8, we address dreams and intersubjectivity, examining how our concerns for others form the fertile ground of dream life. Chapter 9 discusses cultural influences on dreams and how dreams, in turn, contribute to cultural renewal. Chapter 10 concludes Part II by exploring how social systems and the environment affect the dreaming world. We look at the social role that dreams have played across time and throughout cultures, including how dreaming interfaces with social issues such as identity, power, and legitimization.

Part III focuses on dream practices and explores how to integrate various ways of approaching dreams. Here we discuss the framework of an integral philosophy of practice. In chapter 11 we introduce a variety of general assumptions concerning ways of being and working with dreams, then present the creative roots of Integral Dream Practice.

In chapter 12, drawing from a biblical story, we discuss the interpretive approach, which is still a predominant way of working with dreams. In chapter 13 we contrast this approach with the noninterpretive approach to dreams, based on an Eastern philosophical view. Next, we introduce our particular approach, the Integral Dream Practice, in chapter 14, discussing its philosophy and how it has evolved. Chapter 15 goes in depth into the process of Integral Dream Practice. Finally, we conclude the book with an extensive and embodied example.

Keeping the integrity of the dreamer's own voice, the chapter illustrates how a dream can be explored through different modalities of the Integral Dream Practice method.

The subject of dreaming is vast. Countless personal and professional discoveries and years of teaching experience have not abated the awe we feel toward the creative power of the dreaming mind. We constructed this book like a vessel containing a host of ideas, approaches, and practices side by side. Like a living system, this vessel is both open-ended and finite (it obviously cannot include everything!). We hope that it will help others navigate the ocean of knowledge and explore the shores of new inquiries in dream studies.

AUTHORS' BACKGROUND

For over twenty years, we have been teaching in academic institutions where the words *integral* and *holism* are root concepts feeding a unique pedagogical direction. The two universities where we teach—California Institute of Integral Studies in San Francisco and the Graduate School for Holistic Studies at John F. Kennedy University in Berkeley—have been cradles for our decades-long inquiry about dreams. In these institutions, teachers and students alike are challenged to develop and refine a holistic perspective within their particular discipline.

Our individual paths have also allowed us to explore a diversity of viewpoints by living in different cultures, learning other languages, and experimenting creatively with the multilayered reality of dreams. We began paying attention to our dreams from a young age; eventually, this interest led us to investigate the topic in our graduate work and later in our professional life. Our background spans scientific, clinical, theoretical, and artistic perspectives. A brief excursion into our personal narratives will contextualize how we came to an integral view as part of our personal and professional quests.

We met at the inaugural congress of the International Association for the Study of Dreams in 1984 in San Francisco. We were both graduate students and perhaps the youngest members and attendees at this conference. At the time, Daniel was studying cognitive psychology at the University of Montreal and researching the nature of dream understanding. He was writing a book on dreams with his mentor, George Baylor (Baylor & Deslauriers, 1987). His early research focused on the cognitive process of dream understanding, based on data from psychology students at the University of Auckland, New Zealand. Fariba was studying clinical psychology at the University of Regina, Canada and teaching undergraduate students the psychology of sleep and dreams as an experimental section of the course Psychology of Consciousness. With her students, she was experimenting in finding diverse, creative methodologies to address dreams.

We each continued our graduate work on dream research, using both quantitative and qualitative approaches. In the 1980s, we worked as dream researchers in sleep laboratories. Daniel's research at the Chronopsychology and Sleep Laboratory headed by the late researcher Alan Moffitt at Carleton University was the basis for his doctoral dissertation on dream narratives and dream bizarreness (Deslauriers, 1990). Fariba worked with psychophysiologist and lucid dream researcher Stephen LaBerge exploring scientifically the phenomena of lucid dreaming at the Stanford Sleep Laboratory. Her thesis used quantitative analysis to understand the spiritual dimensions of lucid dreaming (Bogzaran, 1989).

Perhaps the depth of our integral viewpoint and practice arises out of our training in other disciplines. Since the mid-1970s, we have both trained in the arts as well as in psychospiritual and contemplative practices. Fariba was trained academically in Eastern philosophy and Western psychology and has received in-depth training in somatic psychology and shamanic studies. She is a painter, longtime meditator, and authorized T'ai Chi teacher. She also has an in-depth background in rhythmic and sonic entrainment.

Daniel was exposed to Eastern culture from the age of eighteen; as part of a Canadian youth exchange program, he lived in a village in Sumatra in the 1970s. He later traveled extensively in Bali in the 1980s and 1990s to learn the Indonesian language and receive training in Balinese-style dancing. He performed for ritual events in Bali and in dance performances in the United States and Canada. He practices yoga, meditation, Aikido, and other body-based spiritual practices.

In 1989, we jointly developed a graduate course called Theory and Practice of Dreams that became the first comprehensive course on dreams taught at John F. Kennedy University. The course surveyed the history and science of dream studies and a variety of approaches to dreams, including scientific, clinical, archetypal, lucid, creative, somatic, shamanic, and cross-cultural. The class laid the groundwork for developing an integral approach to dreams.

Our diverse backgrounds in the field of dream studies have led to a rich dialogue between us. Individually and together, we have developed research programs, pedagogical courses, and graduate-level curricula, workshops/retreats and works of art, all focused on dreams. These experiences made us appreciate each field's perspective and knowledge and the value each offers to an integral approach.

Most important to us was our acceptance of each other as *integral beings.* Even though idealistically and theoretically there is a striving for holistic living, many times, this aspect of our being is not recognized nor well understood. Too often we have encountered the tendency from others to compartmentalize us into one discipline or another. In some circles, we are known as the researchers, teachers, or counselors and it is hard to be seen as artists. In other circles, we experience the reverse. Early on we decided not to subscribe to that tendency and vowed to follow the inner calling to grow multidimensionally and holistically.

Perhaps our hardest project has been writing this book jointly. We have learned that coauthoring a book is no small challenge: doing so surfaced each of our views, our creative predilections and philosophical preferences; how they differ and how they relate. One approaches dreams more theoretically and the other more philosophically. Eventually, our philosophical views gave form to theory, and both theory and philosophy yielded an organizing frame to the applied dream practice that we have been developing for years.

Dream creativity and lucidity were the guiding principles about which we most easily agreed. They have a central place within *Integral Dreaming.* By entering the epistemic uncertainty within the process of writing, we began integrating and bridging our respective worlds. Still holding our individuality, we allowed the integral framework to inform our larger aspirations.

In a sense, we are asking the reader to do the same: to consider other views and paradigms in dream studies and remain open to personal change in the process. Our aspiration is that this book be the starting point of new insights for its readers, and that it expands the horizon of knowledge called forth by *Integral Dreaming*.

Part I

HISTORY AND CONTEXT

CHAPTER ONE

A Larger Calling

The Field of Integral Studies

At any moment, half of the globe, animals and humans included, is engaged in sleeping and dreaming. As the Earth's rotation in space brings about the night, sleep and dreaming slowly pass from one time zone to the next. Given that dreams are such an important part of our life, a simple question lies at the heart of this book: How do dreams participate in our process of becoming the whole of who we are? To try to answer this question we turn to the concept of *integralism*.

The integral paradigm is still emerging, stimulated by a growing need to make sense of the interconnectedness of the various dimensions of our life, from the cellular to the individual, and all the way to global living systems. In this chapter we explore briefly the context and history of integral philosophy (see also McIntosh, 2007) and some of its applications within psychology.

THE INTEGRAL MEME: THREE MAIN STREAMS

We have identified three main streams of thought woven into the meaning of the term *integral* (see figure 1). The first stream is *holism* and general systems theory. Holism derives from the insight that both the forms in nature and organization within human cultures became progressively more complex with time

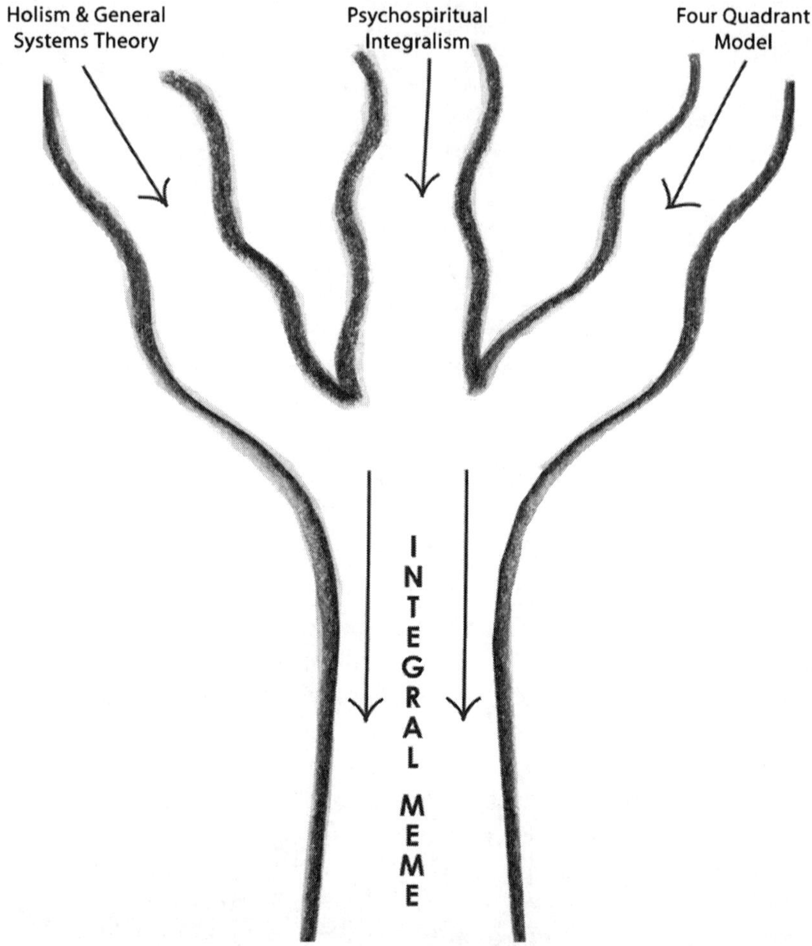

FIGURE 1. THE THREE STREAMS OF INTEGRAL.

and evolution. This insight has fueled an interdisciplinary focus in life and social sciences that has stimulated development of a general systems theory and the science of complexity. The influences and applications of these lines of thought have reached many other fields, including psychology.

The second stream is *integralism*, a term used in the psycho-spiritual context. Founded within philosophy and psychology, integralism focuses on the development of the whole person with a view toward unfolding its fullest potential, at both an individual and collective level.

The third stream speaks of integralism within an *epistemological* context. This view takes into account the fact that different types of human expertise are connected to different ways of acquiring knowledge. These diverse areas of knowledge often compete in claiming the best forms of truth. When viewed from an integral perspective, however, their inherent complementarity becomes more apparent.

This book arises at the confluence of these three streams as we attempt to integrate them into an expanded understanding. Although these streams of ideas have their origins in the premodern era, their current configuration started to take shape in the early twentieth century and matured into the work of several authors at the end the century. By now, the integral *meme* (understood as a self-reproducing idea that informs the behaviors and beliefs of individuals and groups) is playing out in the global cultural sphere. An integral movement is emerging whose cultural importance is still cresting. What follows is an introduction to each of these three streams that anchor the foundation of our inquiry.

THE FIRST STREAM: HOLISM AND GENERAL SYSTEMS THEORY

The idea of *integral* conveys comprehensiveness, or the search for an all-inclusive model that helps us find and understand the diverse contributions and recognizable patterns in the workings of the universe and human consciousness. In particular, it relates to the general idea of holism, or nondual thinking, resists any kind of oppositional thinking, and avoids reducing a complex system to the sum of its parts by valuing the creative synergy that is present in any whole.

Dutch philosopher Baruch Spinoza introduced the idea of holism (1963/1677) in the seventeenth century in opposition to reductionism and in reaction to Descartes' mind-body dualism

(Bennett, 1984; Della Rocca, 1996; Koistinen & Biro, 2002). Cognizant of Spinoza and his dialectics, the eighteenth-century German philosopher Georg Wilhelm Friedrich Hegel (1770–1831) used the idea of unity also as a form of anti-reductionism.[1] "The 'reality' to Hegel is only in the 'whole,' and nothing less than whole is real" (Razali, 2003). Hegel's dialectic idealism has had a broad influence in social philosophy across many systems including existentialism and socialism.

However, the actual word *holism* was proposed by South African philosopher Jan Smuts in his book *Holism and Evolution* (1926). He defines holism as follows:

> [Holism is] the ultimate synthetic, ordering, organizing, regulative activity in the universe which accounts for all the structural groupings and syntheses in it, from the atom and physico-chemical structures, through the cell and organisms, through Mind in animals, to Personality in man. The all-pervading and ever increasing character of synthetic unity or wholeness in these structures leads to the concept of Holism as the fundamental activity underlying and co-ordinating [*sic*] all others, and to the view of the universe as a Holistic Universe. (317)

An alternative formulation of the same idea is that of a system, defined as a set of interacting or interdependent entities forming an integrated whole. From the 1930s through the 1950s, in particular with the work of Austrian biologist Karl Ludwig von Bertalanffy (1951), a creative explosion led to the development of a general systems theory with applications in many fields, including ecology, cybernetics, psychology, medicine, anthropology, and organizational theory.

From a general systems perspective, phenomena can be viewed as a web of relationships. All systems—whether informational, biological, or social—share common patterns, behaviors, and properties. Understanding these patterns brings insight into complex phenomena. As physicist Fritjof Capra explains, "There is something else to life, something nonmaterial and irreducible—a pattern of organization" (Capra, 1996: 81). Capra continues, the "pattern of life, we might say, is a network pattern capable of self-organization" (83). Systems theory has enabled a dialogue toward a unity of science. One of the most prevalent examples today is seen in the field of health care with the movement toward holistic medicine. Such an approach fosters practices that deal with health problems in their many dimensions—physical, psychological, social, cultural, and existential (spiritual)—and in which different preventive and healing modalities are used in an integrative manner.

Applied to human life and evolution, the core idea of systems theory is that humans are open systems. We participate in and are influenced by many other systems simultaneously. Human life is coextensive with nature (our biology), nurture (our unique developmental journey), and culture (our cultural matrix). For example, our brain reflects our biological and hereditary origins and autonomous programs (one of which is the sleep-wake cycle), but it is also connected to our cognitive-emotional functions that accumulate experience and developmentally make sense of it. In addition, through language and other creative forms (in particular the arts and technology), an extended social consciousness connects our personal awareness to larger social and cultural processes.

Holistic models consider the mind not as a simple property that emerged from the evolution of a more complex brain but as the site of a dynamic interplay among many levels and scales of a complex system. These are characterized by the presence of multiple interacting components whose connections, far from being fixed, vary dynamically. For example, within the human personality, we could speak of conscious awareness flowing through not only our bodily self, but also our emotional self, our relational/intersubjective self, our intellectual self (cognition), and our spiritual self (morality, faith). Each of these elements dynamically coalesces with the others to give rise to experience at the fluid border between inner and outer life. Within this holistic view, we bring dream studies as an essential phenomenon of the mind.

Holism and general systems theory arose within the context of the secular humanism of the Enlightenment, where spiritual concerns are confined to personal beliefs and choice. Because of this historical limitation, the theory tends to fall short in one serious way, as Ken Wilber (1995) has pointed out: holism seems overly reliant on "horizontal" (material) explanations and leaves out the aspects that would give it "vertical" (existential or spiritual) depth. The second stream addresses this lack from a profoundly radical perspective.

THE SECOND STREAM: INTEGRALISM IN THE PSYCHOSPIRITUAL CONTEXT

The second stream informing the meaning of integralism connects the insights of complexity, dynamism, and evolution to a deeper, larger, and more encompassing ground. This stream is rooted in the integral philosophy and lifework of Indian philosopher Aurobindo Ghose (known as Sri Aurobindo) early in the twentieth century (Aurobindo, 1970). It was further developed by Haridas Chaudhuri (1965, 1974, 1977) and later on by Ken Wilber (2000). Their views assert that the material universe (the preoccupation of science) unfolds as an expression of a boundless spirit, and evolution is seen as an intelligent process that relies on our conscious human participation—a view that is absent in the purely material rendition of holism.

Integralism originated in the philosophy of *purna* (full, complete, integral) *yoga* (meaning to unite or bind), translated as "integral yoga," a practice that points toward an integration among the material, psychological, and spiritual spheres of knowledge and being. "For integral yoga the ultimate goal of life is complete self-integration" (Chaudhuri, 1965: 77). This philosophy also considers the evolution of consciousness, both individual and collective, as one of its central concerns.

Sri Aurobindo, a philosopher and yoga practitioner, was born in India in 1872, educated in England, and developed his philosophical ideas out of several Western and Eastern philosophical thought systems. When he returned to India at the turn of the twentieth century, he became embroiled in the fight for India's independence. While a political prisoner, he underwent a profound spiritual opening. Being familiar with both Eastern and Western traditions at a time when the colonial era was coming to an end, his thinking expressed a form of cultural integration that was unprecedented and contained keen foresight of the global awareness that would emerge decades later.

Aurobindo was familiar with the philosophy of Kant and Hegel and the evolutionary theory of Darwin and Spencer.

Philosopher Steve Odin (1981) states that Hegel appropriates Kant's "impersonal unity of self-consciousness" and develops his metaphysical system of "universal consciousness" or "Absolute Spirit." Within the Eastern system of Indian philosophy, Aurobindo relied on Vedanta (a set of philosophical traditions, based on the Hindu Vedas and concerned with the self-realization by which one understands the ultimate nature of reality or Brahman) and the complex spiritual system known as the Yoga Sutras of Patanjali. Aurobindo attempts to create a synthesis among these different East-West philosophical systems.

In *The Meeting of the East and the West in Sri Aurobindo's Philosophy*, Indian scholar S. K. Maitra (1968) shows the commonality and differences between Hegel and Aurobindo in their views of spiritual evolution. Aurobindo disagreed with Hegel in identifying Spirit with Reason. Maitra views Aurobindo's evolutionary philosophy as a "new idea, which is not found in any system, either ancient or modern." Maitra goes on:

> This is the idea of integration. Evolution is not merely an ascent from a lower to a higher state. It is also an integration of the higher with the lower ones. This means when a higher principle emerges, it descends into the lower ones causing a transformation of them. Thus when Mind emerges, not only does a new principle appear on the scene, but the lower principles of matter and life also undergo a transformation, so that they become different from what they were before the emergence of this new principle. (38–39)

Aurobindo's evolutionary model considers spiritual nature as an important aspect of an integral view. Chaudhuri and Spiegelberg (1960) state that Aurobindo's philosophy is "integral nondualism." Aurobindo acknowledges that Eastern philosophy in general promotes the idea of nondualism, which is "an intuitive approach to life and existence—an approach which seeks to understand reality in its undivided wholeness and fundamental oneness" (19).

Originally, non-Western approaches to an integral philosophy meant almost exclusively "Eastern" approaches.[2] Since then, the integral approach has grown to encompass other wisdom traditions, including mystical and indigenous or Earth-based spirituality as well as insights from new spiritual movements, such as that sparked by Aurobindo himself. Chaudhuri and Spiegelberg offer an interpretation of the concept of integral nondualism within Aurobindo's philosophy: "Integral nondualism integrates the significant distinctions of ethics, religion, logic and metaphysics in its nondualistic philosophical outlook, without deprecating their value and importance. It reconciles the dualities of thought and existence in the unity of integral experience, integral living, and the integral sweep of cosmic evolution" (19).

The *integral* concept has also been applied within the field of psychology. For some, it relates principally to the psychology derived from the integral philosophy of Aurobindo (e.g., Sen, 1986; Cortright, 2007). For others (e.g., Shirazi, 2001; Chaudhuri, 1977; Combs, 2002), integral psychology takes its inspiration from Aurobindo but remains an open-ended inquiry into human wholeness and incorporates the findings of science.

Shirazi (2001) speaks of four general postulates that form the essence of the integral worldview:

1. Nonduality: the nonseparability of body-mind and spirit.
2. Multidimensionality: the spectrum of qualities and characteristics that is the outer manifestation of the unified self.
3. Holism: a potential state of integration of our multifaceted self, actualized through a process of self-realization.
4. Evolution: the transitional nature of being, engaged in participatory movement toward a personal and collective transformation of consciousness.

Shirazi's main work has been to expound on the writings of Chaudhuri. In particular, he uses Chaudhuri's simple but profound triadic principle of uniqueness (each individual has a particular signature and contribution), relatedness (we learn who we are through our being with others), and transcendence (our relationship with something larger than the self or community), to capture the complexities of human self-realization. The views described by Chaudhuri question the assumptions of dualistic mind at all levels of discourse and foster the ultimate philosophical principle of unity: "A thoroughly integrated person seems somehow to go beyond all striving and straining and to touch the bedrock of timeless Being. . . . The conflict and tension of becoming are replaced within him by the profound peace of being. The anguish of ethical struggle is overcome with the joy and love of union with the infinite" (Chaudhuri, 1965: 102).

Chaudhuri and Shirazi propose a psychology that integrates and acknowledges the spiritual nature of the human experience. In the same vein, and following the insights of Aurobindo, Cortright (2007) describes how integral psychology addresses the growth and transformation of consciousness as a central feature of psychological life. Within its maturational arc, human development eventually discloses the existence of a psychic being, a "soul aspect" that is open to evolutionary changes. The maturation process, combined with spiritual practice, can bring about a refinement of consciousness through opening the heart, quieting the mind, and nurturing authentic relationships (Cortright, 2007). Transpersonal psychologists Almaas (1986, 2000), Ferrer (2002), Grof (1988, 1998), Walsh and Vaughan (1993), Washburn (1994), and Wilber (2000) have given similar accounts of these realms of experience as delineated by integral psychology (see also Caplan et al., 2003 and Hartelius et al., 2007). In the past decade, research in the emerging field of "positive psychology" has begun to provide empirical evidence of what it calls *psychological flourishing* (Fredrickson et al., 2005).

In integral psychology, the Western and Eastern configurations of psychology are viewed as complementary. Western psychology fosters the healing of psychological fragmentation that results from psychological wounding, as well as the relational deficits and defensive structures that make up the unconscious. Eastern psychology, on the other hand, helps us "find our psychic center so it becomes a guiding influence in our life" (Cortright, 2007: 72). Aurobindo called the latter process *psychic transformation.* Integral psychology thus sees the two movements—psychological healing and psychic transformation—as interconnected and inseparable.

To summarize, the notion of integralism has been used in a psychospiritual context in the following ways:

- As valuing cultural diversity, syncretism, and reciprocal integration of Western and non-Western approaches to the self and being.
- As understanding psychological development and moral/spiritual advancement as complementary and interconnected.
- As fostering a diversity of practices that address the multiplicity of our being.

THE THIRD STREAM: INTEGRALISM IN AN EPISTEMOLOGICAL CONTEXT—WILBER'S FOUR-QUADRANT MODEL

Wilber (2000) addresses integral psychology as an important subset of his own formulation of an integral philosophy. He attempts to substantiate a synthesis of developmental research by comparing a number of developmental theories and models proposed over the past fifty years in the West and borrowing aspects of Eastern philosophy, such as Buddhist and Vedantic ideas of human development and Aurobindo's evolutionary schema.

Wilber's main contribution to the notion of integralism has been to explain the diversity of the various fields of knowledge by mapping them in a simple epistemological framework: the four-quadrant model. This section looks at Wilber's philosophy in some detail.

Wilber's integral psychology (2000) borrows from holism and systems theories in viewing humans as *holons* (i.e., units of reality). Each human holon is composed of smaller holons (e.g., organs, cells, genes, etc.) and is nested within larger sociocultural (family, affiliative groups, nation-state), ecological, and cosmological holons. In his theory of nested holons, Wilber echoes the dialectics of Hegel in proposing that more complex holons include more fundamental ones as well as presenting new properties at each level of complexity.

Wilber acknowledges an equal inclusion of three main epistemological approaches: "first-person" phenomenal accounts—that is, the subjective stance of "I"; "second-person" accounts—the intersubjective view from the collective stance of "we"; and "third-person" accounts of physical systems given by objective science (2000: 183). Wilber colloquially calls these approaches the "Big Three." Within his model, he postulates that phenomena (in particular, human consciousness) can be understood by looking at the intersection of two main orthogonal dimensions: 1) the interior/exterior dimension and 2) the individual/collective dimension. Together, these constitute the classical four-quadrant cells:

Individual + Interior	Individual + Exterior
Collective + Interior	Collective + Exterior

In its most simple expression, the upper half looks at the individual holon, the bottom half looks at collective holons. The right half deals with exterior knowledge (objective, material) seen in the dispassionate observer stance, the left half deals with interior knowledge (subjective consciousness) unfolded from a participative stance. For Wilber, human phenomena, in particular human consciousness, unfolds as a "mesh" involving the four quadrants simultaneously. Different aspects of consciousness and human phenomena are disclosed when looked at from the vantage point of each quadrant.

In approaching dream studies from the larger context of integralism, we have found Wilber's model useful for locating diverse theories and methods about the process of dreaming and the understanding of dreams. The four-quadrant map incorporates what can be understood as four epistemological perspectives or four broad categories of knowledge, as presented as follows.

Upper-Left Quadrant (UL)—Individual Interior: Subjective Modes of Knowing (e.g., phenomenology, psychotherapy).

The upper-left quadrant concerns internal and subjective knowledge. It includes the various ways that we know ourselves through experience. Thus, we can understand this quadrant as dealing with self and consciousness as we all experience it. It includes the realm of meaning and aesthetics and how they inform our actions in the world. Psychological models of the self and spiritual inquiry practices generally fall within this quadrant.

Upper-Right Quadrant (UR)—Individual Exterior: Objective Modes of Knowing (e.g., biology, physiology, and cognitive neuroscience).

The upper-right quadrant represents scientific knowledge about objects. It includes the study of the organism at all levels, and in particular, of brain functions. For example, all biologically based models explaining consciousness and experience fall into this mode. It also includes third-person approaches to dream text, such as content analysis (Hall & Van de Castle, 1966).

Lower-Left Quadrant (LL)—Collective Interior: Intersubjective Modes of Knowing (e.g., hermeneutics, social anthropology).

The lower-left quadrant concerns interpersonal, linguistic, and cultural knowledge. It includes the realms of values and morals that regulate our familial and collective life. Generally speaking, it could be construed as the realm of culture and worldview, disclosing collective and normative meanings, attitudes, ethics, aesthetics, and cultural practices that shape our experience.

Lower-Right Quadrant (LR)—Collective Exterior: Interobjective Modes of Knowing (e.g., critical theory, general systems theory, history).

The lower-right quadrant represents objective knowledge about groups, including social systems and the ecological environment. It focuses on material, economic, and social factors and is best equipped to disclose social structure and design (including their inequities) and how socioeconomic factors affect human experience (including learning).

The mapping of these modes of knowing is further refined when combined with the developmental stages (or structures of consciousness) that mark the human maturational process. Wilber follows Piaget's argument that each stage of cognitive development will be accompanied with shifts in cognitive understanding of the world. The connection between ontogeny (the arc of structural changes within the development of an individual) and epistemological sophistication (the acquisition of more encompassing cognitive functions and capacities) also finds expression in each higher stage of maturation. Not only do particular dimensions of consciousness get disclosed by each mode of apprehending reality (the four quadrants): subjective, objective, intersubjective, among others, but deeper, more comprehensive, and possibly more refined dimensions of our experience get disclosed as we mature and engage with transformative practices such as meditation and working with dreams. Developmental phases are seen as progressive stages. We can only understand and explain our experience from the place of our highest achievement along any developmental lines described by Wilber and other developmental theorists.

Beyond the developmental stages described by Piaget for the first two decades of the human life cycle, Wilber explains subsequent, more advanced stages—sometimes called *post-formal* or *post-conventional* stages. Aurobindo has also described these stages and cross-cultural views of human development found in contemplative religious systems such as Buddhism, Vedanta, or even mystical Christianity. Following the principle of "include and transcend," each developmental phase includes earlier achievements and transcends them, affording a new perspective on earlier capacities and knowledge.

Evolutionary thinking as well as the idea of holism pervades Wilber's approach. He finds it necessary to account for the developmental arc traced by individuals along several maturational lines—including cognitive, moral, emotional, and spiritual. His emphasis is on mapping broad structural stages rather than understanding the more fine-grain, micro-developmental processes that define day-to-day adaptation. The latter, however, are more likely to be the scale at which ordinary dreams operate. Perhaps this is why Wilber makes very little mention of dreaming in his own work. When he does, he considers that we understand reality from the perspective of particular states of consciousness. In his view, advanced and possibly mystical states of consciousness (unitive experiences, meditative absorption) derive from (or show refinement of) the three basic states of consciousness available to healthy individuals, no matter their age: waking, dreamless sleep, and dreaming. How one interprets these experiences, he concludes, depends on the maturational level of each individual (Combs, 2002, 2009).

In summary, Wilber emphasizes an epistemological context in understanding the concept of *integral,* from modes of knowing (corresponding to the four quadrants) to levels of development. He has coined the acronym AQAL (short for "All Quadrants, All Levels") to summarize this complex idea in one word.

THE CONCEPT OF INTEGRAL

The word *integral* is thus used in three senses: the strict Aurobindonian sense, the Wilberian sense, and in a more generic sense. Wilber's work was strongly influenced by Aurobindo at first. However, over the years, Wilber's usage of the term has changed as his philosophy evolved. He states that his current model supersedes that of Aurobindo.

In the marketplace of current ideas, the term *integral* has acquired a strong Wilberian overtone, following his published works to signify a holistic, comprehensive, and all-encompassing map framed around the AQAL model. We can't blame Wilber for adopting the word *integral* as the best qualifier for his all-encompassing philosophy. The popularity of his writing has served as a strong attractor that has, for many, become equated with the word's usage and meaning. For many others, however, who have been in the integral movement for decades, to find the word *integral* equated to the AQAL model seems restrictive. Many scholars have used the word *integral* without strictly associating themselves with a particular philosophy (e.g., Ferrer, 2002; Schlitz et al., 2008). For them, the word has become almost synonymous with *holistic* or *wholeness*. Others have presented ideas that are consonant with the notion of integrality without necessarily adopting the term. In this book we claim the use of the word in a way that reflects both Wilber's and Aurobindo's meanings but is not entirely Wilberian nor Aurobindonian.

SUMMARY

In this chapter we have reviewed the different meanings of the integral meme. We use the word *integral* in a broad and nondenominational way. Our approach seeks to explore and understand the multiplicity of human experience. In the next chapter we will explore how the concept of *integral* applies to dreams. Within dream studies, an integral approach to dreams would foster multidisciplinary awareness, embrace the complexity of dreaming phenomena, and recognize that dream practices engage countless forms of creative participation in the ongoing mystery of life. We also explore different epistemological approaches to dreams and apply the four-quadrant model to situate the many disciplines within the field of dream studies.

CHAPTER TWO

An Integral Approach to Dreaming

No single theory can contain the array of facets that make dreams so compelling. Our aim is to come close to the most inclusive perspective, which we call *Integral Dreaming*. We are aware this is an ambitious agenda: inclusiveness asks everyone to stretch beyond familiar modes of understanding. For example, it asks scientists to see beyond the biophysiological or cognitive aspects of dreaming to consider how dreams affect individuals in their daily life. Likewise, it asks dream practitioners to consider not only the psychological nature of dreams but also their biological underpinnings as understood by science.

An integral view asks us to take a larger perspective across time: from the distant past to the future. If we follow the long and culturally diverse history of dreaming, we eventually connect back to our ancestral roots. Evolutionary psychology looks even further back to our predecessors as a means to understand our present biological makeup. Conversely, if evolution is still ongoing, we should also ask ourselves, what role does dreaming play in the evolutionary process?

The field of dream studies is diverse, having attracted the attention not only of psychologists and clinicians, but also of anthropologists, neuroscientists, philosophers, theologians, and artists, among others. We hope to articulate a framework large enough to unite disparate views into a coherent whole, without losing sight of the rich and nuanced knowledge embedded in each niche where dreams are studied.

In this chapter, we first discuss the core principles of Integral Dreaming, which serve as the pillars of this approach. Then, to organize the seemingly separate modes of inquiries under the umbrella of holism, we apply Wilber's four-quadrant model to the field of dream studies. Finally, we ask what binds these separate parts together. We close the chapter by discussing how awareness (here understood as "presence to what is") and creativity give cohesion to this multidisciplinary approach.

THREE CORE PRINCIPLES

An integral approach is, by design, *inclusive, holistic,* and *multidisciplinary*; in practice, it is *eclectic.* Derived from our personal dream experience, our professional work with students and clients, and from our study of psychology, comparative religion, and the arts, we have distilled three core principles. We present them as a set of simple but articulated assertions:

1. We are multidimensional beings.
2. Dreams are multidimensional.
3. Working with dreams requires a multidimensional approach.

1. Multidimensionality of Being

This first principle points to the fact of the totality of who we are as physical, emotional, mental, and spiritual beings engaged in a multidimensional world. We render symbolically this multidimensionality in figure 2. Looking across time and cultures, we find a multitude of maps that speak to the multidimensional aspects of our experience. Religious images, for example, are often attempts at conveying the paradox that links multiplicity to a larger unifying whole.[1] Human experience, either in dreaming or waking, is always multidimensional. Maturing from infancy through adulthood, our sphere of experiences becomes increasingly more encompassing. Adult development

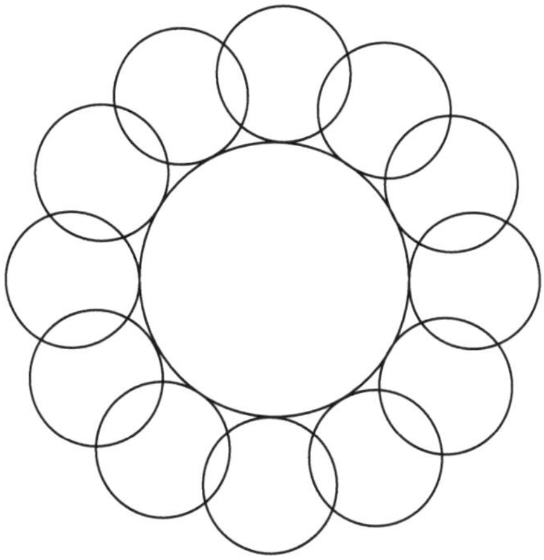

FIGURE 2. THE MULTIPLICITY OF BEING.

can be seen as a journey of discovery of the multiplicity of our being (Brunton, 2009). This process takes on a particular coherence and orientation based on our intentions, aspirations, and even our sense of calling. Ideally, we find resonance within the groups we belong to and in our culture (Schweder, 1991); the absence of such resonance often leads to a sense of alienation or estrangement, a theme that often surfaces in dreams (Busink & Kuiken, 1996).

The ancient dictate to "know thyself" is as fresh now as when written at the Greek temple in Delphi. Dreams play a crucial role in this process. Science shows that human development becomes increasingly unhinged from biology at the end of adolescence, and the responsibility shifts to the intentional (or conscious) self in its quest for maturity. Learning that takes place through direct experience is amplified by the process of self-inquiry. Engaging with dreams is predicated on learning basic awareness skills that relate to, but are not limited by, self-inquiry.

Our waking consciousness focuses on only a fraction of what is available to it. The interplay between the narrowing and the expansion of consciousness is at the core of how we may perceive the multiplicity of our being at any given moment.[2]

The world is so complex that living organisms—including humans—naturally adjust the "bandwidth" of their experience in order to meet their immediate concerns. But a broader spectrum of experience may be available to us by the power of our reflective consciousness, ready to be unfolded with proper practice and intention.

Experiences in consciousness, including dreams, are organized around the same principles that regulate living processes in any complex ecosystem. Theorists Allan Combs and Stanley Krippner (1998) have begun to apply chaos theory to dreaming. Like similar attempts to understand the intricacies of the living psyche, newer theories (such as chaos theory and complexity theory) continue to intimate the presence of an unconscious mind. Departing from orthodox psychoanalysis however, contemporary views of the unconscious recast it in neurocognitive terms: implicit cognitions are overlearned habits or functions of the brain/mind that occur below the threshold of awareness (Fosshage, 1997).

A comparable reframing is being applied to Jung's idea of a collective unconscious and its putative content, archetypes. Understood through the framework of nonlinear dynamics, archetypes are cast as *psychological strange attractors*, that is, objective patterns of organization that exist at every layer of a living system, including the psychological layer of human consciousness (Bütz, 1997; Conforti, 2003; McDowell, 2001). In these models, experiences like dreams are viewed as one would a landscape: a territory of consciousness in which paths and networks gradually form as a result of prior learning. Not unlike the outside landscape, this "landscape of consciousness" is constantly changing. Somewhat in contrast to the physical landscape however, the topography of consciousness takes shape and transforms *as we explore it*.

One of the paradoxes of the integral approach is found in the efforts we make to apply language to the various dimensions of being. In naming the dimensions of the self, we can innocently mistake them as "things," as if each dimension was entirely distinct and separate from the others. In reality, all dimensions of the self are interconnected or nested. Experience unfolds in the physical or somatic space enfolded within our body. Human experience contains an emotional aspect that gives it its color and texture, from the passion of excitement to the blandness of boredom. Our experience also has a cognitive aspect. All experience is held within the support of an ecosystem and can be colored by our sociocultural framework. With insight, experience eventually can be perceived in continuity with a putative core essence common to all that is. Each of these dimensions is a particular *gateway to the self,* and a potential point of inception for its transformation and that of the world. However, habits of the body, emotional and mental tendencies, and even spiritual habits, will often have us consciously or unconsciously identifying and relating to some facets of our being at the expense of others.

Dreams are often a way of reminding us to acknowledge the wider spectrum of our being. In this perspective, self-actualization could be understood as the integration of the multiplicity of being. If multidimensionality relates structurally to the facets of the self, it also pertains to its psychological and spiritual development. From a developmental perspective, one should question the relationship of self-actualization to self-realization. Self-actualization may be the process of living an authentic life that draws upon our unique and signature strengths, where the different facets of self find coherent expression. Self-realization, in contrast, is often used within a spiritual context to point out a gradual or sudden letting go of personal representations, beliefs, and self-centeredness in order to be fully present to a larger view (Welwood, 2000). Of course, this explanation begs the question of "who" it is that is aware of this multiplex of experiences and of its incipient unity.[3] The process of maturation is such that each stage of development filters the particular understanding of our psychological (and spiritual) experiences. In this way, the interplay of self-actualization and self-realization sets the stage for the multidimensional self[4] to unfold developmentally, in which each subsequent phase always transcends and includes the previous one (Wilber, 1995).

2. Dreams Are Multidimensional

Dreams present occasions of experience that reflect the multidimensional aspects of being. Memory, sensations, and emotional patterns from the experience of the dreamer blend with perception and spontaneous creative imagination to form dreams. According to Harry Hunt (1989), dreams are in the business of translation: translating felt experience into meaningful and possibly comprehensible events; translating embodied sensations into visual events, metaphorical or metonymic imagery; or translating linguistic or semantic knowledge into more abstract perceptual experience. Within the multidimensional plenum of being, dreams creatively translate one type of experience into another. To attend to our own dreams only amplifies this work of creative translation and integration.

Dreams unfold believable worlds. By themselves, and especially when viewed in contrast to waking, they offer us a felt sense of other dimensions of being. Verbal dream reports rarely capture the complexity of the dreaming experience. Unfortunately, this often leads to some gaps in recall or in reporting or sharing dreams. The linearity of language gets overlaid onto the description of an experience that is in essence nonlinear and somatically felt. More encompassing types of expression, image-based perhaps, can help in this regard. Jung illustrated many of his experiences through symbolic imagery: the complexity of abstraction through geometric forms could render the felt sense of the dreams he had and his imaginal journeys (Jung, 2009).

Art hints at the multidimensionality of dream experiences. The surrealists, in particular, attempted to capture dreams in artworks. Salvador Dali and René Magritte, for example, were among many who have shown the creative aspects of the dream narrative. Others who wished to stay true to the complex nature of the dreaming mind (such as surrealists Wolfgang Paalen, Roberto Matta, and Gordon Onslow Ford) found that it is extremely difficult, if not impossible, to confine the dimensionality of dreams in words or images (Bogzaran, 2007). But these limitations have not stopped artists trying their best. Many in the contemporary movement of "dream art" continue to be inspired and to innovatively express the multifaceted aspects of oneiric life (see examples in Gamwell, 2000). If we take seriously the notion that dreams are creative by nature, they are then canvasses or better, perhaps, open stages: ever ready for the spontaneous display of the multidimensional mind.

In recent decades we have witnessed a number of major movies depicting complex dream imagery, such as *Waking Up*, *Avatar*, and *Inception*. Furthermore, with the advance of virtual games and animation, vivid imagery combined with sound might come closest to capturing the complexity of the felt sense and the ecology of dreams. Not surprising, research has shown that virtual games, with their complex visual-spatial participatory immersion, show similarities to dream environments. Jayne Gackenbach and her team have demonstrated a correlation between regular video game players and the frequency of lucid dreaming (Gackenbach, 2012; Gackenbach & Reiter, 2006).

In *The Multiplicity of Dreams*, Harry Hunt (1989) discusses the multifaceted intricacy of dream experiences. This includes a complex narrative, a somatic and energetic felt sense, verbal aspects, visual-spatial metaphors (including mandalic and light phenomena), prospective intuitions, and insightful problem-solving. "All dream episodes, like all waking situations, vary in terms of the complexity of the story narrative (sequential structure) and complexity of setting (simultaneous or spatial structure)" (96). Adding to these structural dimensions, we also find the role of the self within the dream—varying from actively self-initiated participation to observation to, ultimately, detached receptivity. In figure 3, we try to capture the

FIGURE 3. THE MULTIPLICITY OF DREAMING EXPERIENCES.

multiplicity of the dreaming experience. Multidimensionality has also been shown using numerical methods. Research using content analysis[5] shows "differences and similarities between the dreamer's scores and the norms . . . and [helps] define an individual's uniqueness with considerable precision" (Van de Castle, 1994: 304).

The ecology of dreams is complex: various types of dreams, each with its own phenomenology, involve their own subset of levels or layers of intricacies. Although one of the most stable dimensions in dreaming lies in its story form, extraordinary dream experiences often break open the linear narrative sequence. Certain categories of extraordinary dreams—such as telepathic, clairvoyant, mutual, out-of-body dreams of sleep paralysis, and lucid dreams—have the potential to move away from the normal confines of the narrative schema. These types of dreams lead the dreamer to touch the boundaries of nonlinear, transpersonal experiences (Bogzaran, 2003; Bulkeley, 1995, 2000; Garfield, 1979; Krippner et al., 2002).

Grasping the multidimensionality of dreams raises existential questions: Who are we? What is the relation between inner and outer life? Many authors and spiritual leaders encourage inward orientation as one of the strategies of transformative integration. "We get scattered into multiplicity because our attention is directed toward outer things and events in an imbalanced manner; whereas by turning within, we find the single source of wholeness" (Metzner, 1998: 111). The inner world of dreams and its multilayered nature can be as overwhelming as the outer. How does the self reconcile the outer complexities with the inner multiplicities? A. H. Almaas, author and founder of the Diamond Heart Approach, has written extensively on spiritual psychology through the lens of an East-West philosophical perspective. "Being or Essence or Spirit," he writes, "could be described as a multidimensional aliveness that also has a dimension of emptiness and awareness" (Peay, 1999: n.p.). Within the kaleidoscope of experience, Almaas enjoins us to discern "Essential Qualities," or ways in which "Being . . . differentiates itself through our particular experience in life. These Essential Qualities are necessary for integrating a personal life with the spirit" (Peay, n.p.). Perhaps through creativity, our dream experiences carry these "essential qualities." Cultivating awareness of these qualities can assist us with integrating the complexity of the multidimensional nature within our being.

3. Working with Dreams Is Multidimensional

If we are multidimensional beings and dreams express complex and varied forms of experiences and dimensionalities, then working with dreams must also address those aspects in depth and in a multidimensional way. Concerns over how to approach dreams have been recorded historically as well as cross-culturally. A number of anthologies have tried to bring to light the rich cultural history of dreaming, among them the following: *The New World of Dreams* (Woods & Greenhouse, 1974); *Dreamtime, Dreamwork* (Krippner, 1990); *Dreaming* (Tedlock, 1992), *Dreaming in the World's Religions* (Bulkeley, 2008), *On Dreams and Dreaming* (Kakar, 2011). Seeking meaning in dreams continues to evolve, just as we do. Contemporary dream practitioners endorse creative methods of dream understanding or conduct research on them (Castonguay & Hill, 2007; Pesant & Zadra, 2004). While anticipation for new methods abounds at professional conferences, other methods are passed on over extended periods, as long as they are seen as effective. Eventually, they may become part of a tradition. Within Tibetan Buddhism for example, following a certain lineage implies not changing the context or the nature of practice in the hope of transmitting it to the next generation as faithfully as possible.

A tension often exists between tradition and experimentation. Based on systematic observation and research, our work includes integrative methods combining creativity, embodiment, cognitive inquiry, and other modalities. As we will see in Part III, with skillful attunement, these methods can be adapted to the particular needs of a group or an individual.

From an integral point of view, dreams call for practices that address the whole being throughout the whole spectrum of the dream experience.[6] Paradoxically, with such a view we cannot fix an integral approach as *a* method that is permanent and unchangeable. In Part III, we introduce Integral Dream Practice (IDP) as an example of how different disciplines and methods can find synergy when we understand the potential of multidisciplinarity. With the knowledge that no single approach to working with dreams addresses the whole being, we would like to pose a few friendly challenges to practitioners. If a practitioner is mainly cognitively oriented, how does she/he deal with the somatic ways of unfolding dreams? If the practitioner is involved in somatic understanding, how does she/he understand the creative aspects of approaching dreams? If one addresses dreams interpretively, how would it be to approach them non-interpretively? And so on.[7] The integral approach challenges us to open and expand our horizons of methods, not so much to introduce more interpretive approaches to dreams, but to ask a larger question: How does the complexity of dreams, and the range of impressions they leave in their wake, relate to dimensions of the self and the world? How are these dimensions addressed in the methods of dream awareness?

We advocate for the value of holding an integral view to explore the many aspects of dreams, the dreaming self, and the process of working with dreams. We attempt to represent this view in figure 4 as an overlap between the two earlier figures. If we enter the field of dream studies with an integral view, suddenly we invite a different picture to form within our awareness.

FIGURE 4. THE MULTIPLICITY OF DREAM PRACTICES.

DREAM STUDIES: AN INTEGRAL PERSPECTIVE

In the following pages we have invited seemingly different perspectives under the same umbrella for a dialogue. Like a tower of Babel, the knowledge about dreaming seems to be built around each specialty speaking its own language. To try to overcome the parochialism that can come with specialization, an integral approach searches for a perspective that helps make sense of the diversity of views. A measure of success would be to show how the fields of knowledge not only complement each other but also cohere even within their differences.

In the mid-1990s, when Wilber refined his four-quadrant model, we began exploring how his model can give a cohesive organization to the seemingly separated disciplines within the field of dream studies. Out of this dialogue, we developed a structural application of the quadrant model to dream studies.[8]

Beyond its organizational benefit, the four-quadrant structure became a helpful tool to view different approaches to dreams and the explicit and implicit connections between them. To sound out our model, we presented it to a diverse group of scientists, clinicians, and researchers at the International Association for the Study of Dreams conference in Copenhagen, Denmark (Bogzaran & Deslauriers, 2004). It became apparent that through applying the model, scientists and researchers gained a better understanding and appreciation of other ways of approaching dreams. Clinicians and people from other fields felt their own approaches validated.[9] We became convinced that this structure, despite its limitations,[10] can serve as a guide to understanding how different ways of knowing dreams cohere in their complementarity.

Within our own holistic view, we were not satisfied compartmentalizing ways of knowledge as per each quadrant, so we began to examine the connective and overlapping areas. The quadrant model became an initial platform to dive deeper into the complexities of the self, dreaming, and ways of viewing dreams. The diagram in figure 5 is simply used as a structural guiding map. It lays out the major inquiry in the field of dream studies and situates a number of disciplines and inquiries through the particular lenses of the type of inquiry they

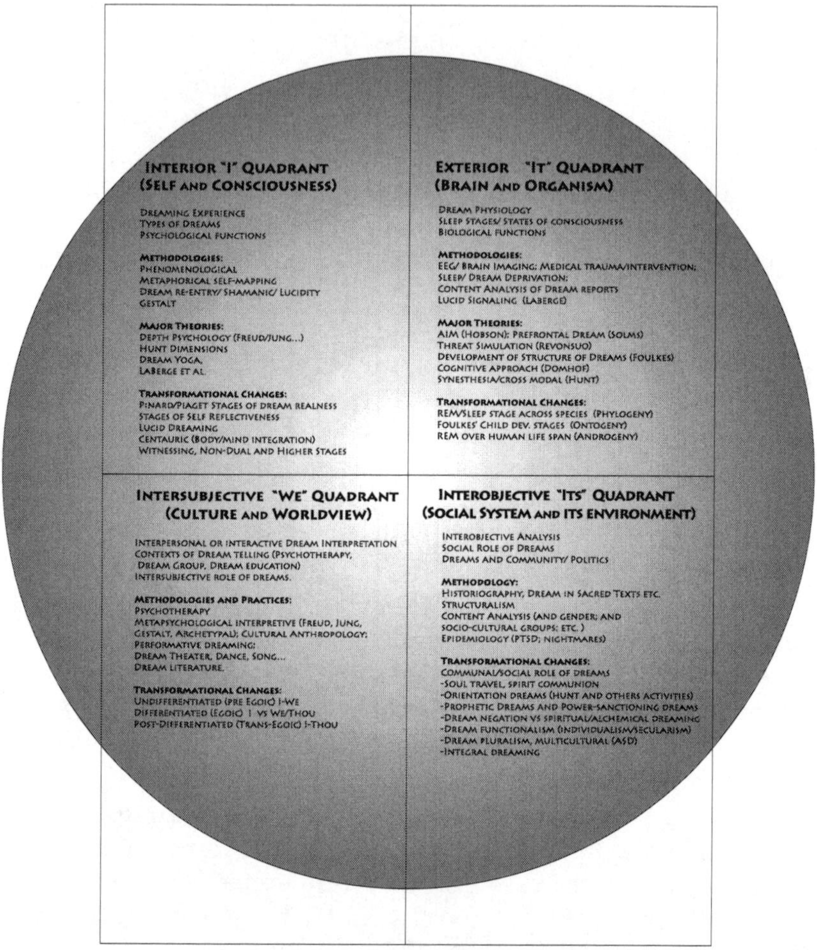

FIGURE 5. THE FOUR QUADRANTS OF DREAMING.

favor. Within each quadrant we highlighted methods, major theories, and developmental frame.

To view dreaming within the quadrant model is like taking hold of a natural environment by looking at a map. One needs to bear in mind that no single discipline (or model) can encompass the complexity of the entire field. The premise of the quadrant map is epistemological inclusivity: every discipline within dream studies has intrinsic validity. However, truth claims are best judged from within the paradigmatic framework from which they emerge. Their validity, or explanatory power, may not necessarily extend from one quadrant to another. Furthermore, some "dream quadrants" have been explored and validated more than others. Some quadrants may be more familiar to readers while others might be a source of surprise. The premise of inclusivity is best met with an open mind and critical appreciation, guided by a healthy dose of curiosity. Finally, it is also important to remember that a map (including the present one), however accurate and informative it may be, remains essentially a representation. It brings integrative order to a complex field. But even an integral map that makes us appreciate the nuanced contours of the territory of dreaming should not be mistaken with the lived expression of this complex state of consciousness.

CREATIVITY AND AWARENESS

As an interdisciplinary field, dream studies brings together different points of view and approaches. With this arise some challenges. First, in an amalgam without a fixed center, what binds the field together? Second, how does the vast knowledge of the different quadrants, as described in Part II, connect with the application of an Integral Dream Practice as described in Part III? Reflecting on these questions led us to identify two main essential qualities that pervade our theoretical and practical inquiry: creativity and awareness.

Philosophically, these two qualities speak to a dynamic tension between two poles inherent in Being. The first, creativity, speaks to a spontaneous, emergent, organic aspect that is the very ground of all creation, either in nature and personal experience or in culture and society. The second, awareness, speaks to an intentional, reflective, lucid attention that can be brought to bear to the first quality; an essential quality that characterizes human conscious experience.

We believe that in every discipline, a creative spark leads to the advancement of the field, while the dimension of conscious awareness refines, modulates, and gives directionality to this emergent quality. The cognizance and appreciation of one another's work helps people connect within their own discipline and between disciplines. Part II gathers evidence from different research that particularly addresses the importance of both poles of creativity and awareness in the dreaming experience.

In relationship to practice, we believe that *paying attention to and exploring dreams is, in its essence, a practice of awareness and creativity.* Exploring dreams, either by oneself or with others, fosters greater awareness of the nuances of our interior world. Integral Dream Practice puts special emphasis on the creative nature of dreams, as it guides dreamers to unfold aspects of their multidimensional self. As part of this practice, the dreamer ideally finds the vibrant meeting place between lucid awareness and emergent creative unfolding.

From an integral perspective, *dream awareness* is the practice of being present to one's inner life in its full integrity. The simple but powerful act of being present to one's dreams helps dreamers perceive aspects of their selves that are perhaps the growing tip of their own being. Often, this perception reinforces the dreamer's wish to know him- or herself better, thus helping to overcome self-limitations. Dreams become a potent vehicle for creative insight connecting seemingly divided or unfamiliar parts, or even discarded ones, into a more complex, interconnected whole.

Each of the basic dimensions of being (physical, mental, emotional, spiritual) is a distinct and powerful portal of experience, and each is connected to the others in various degrees of integration. For some individuals, for example, a set of beliefs might keep ideas of sexuality and spirituality completely separate in a way that does not foster their natural integration. For others, it would be unthinkable to have a spiritual experience that is not embodied in one way or another, including through sexuality. Although there is no right or wrong way of looking at experience, we recognize that mental habits (especially deep beliefs about the body or about the nature of spiritual reality) shape our experience in a way that either fosters or hinders the integration of the different dimensions of the self.

The notion of process has an important place in an integral approach. At any moment we are faced with the challenge of understanding our state of being, which is composed of multiple flowing streams of experiences and open-ended processes. The integral approach sensitizes us to the fact that, by becoming an aware and creative participant in these processes, we have a transforming influence on our own self as well as on the larger ecological and sociocultural systems in which we are embedded.

It may be hard to override the habit of seeing ourselves as stable and unchanging. When we wake up each morning, we seem to spontaneously reenter a fairly stable pattern of being that we recognize as ourselves. If we take a closer look, however, what we see is a constant process of change that includes processes of growth, regeneration, and, alas, eventual decay.

As much as possible, an integral approach fosters awareness of experience as it arises, encouraging unconditional acceptance and creating new connections among experiences by finding novel and expanded ways to relate to them. We share with Aurobindo the life-affirming insight that spirituality needs to inform and infuse material processes, and that the principal evolutionary role of humanity is to act as a catalyst for this process. The ancient interlocking image of the Flower of Life (figure 6) is perhaps the closest image to the concept of Integral Dreaming. The center, the self, is expressed and nourished by

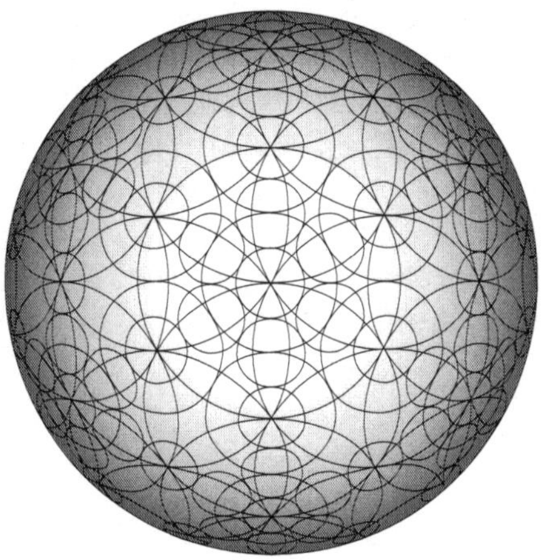

FIGURE 6. SYMBOLIC REPRESENTATION OF INTEGRAL DREAMING.

different aspects. By becoming aware of its different sides and facets through dreams, the self expands to its fullest potential, which is itself contained within a larger reality.

SUMMARY

In this chapter, we have located dreaming as a spontaneous expression of life. We introduced an integrative model affirming the multidimensionality of our being, of dream life, and of the ways of being with dreams. Because dreams are at once complex and mysterious, their exploration calls for methods that are commensurate with their open-ended nature. To give perspective to the diversity of dream understanding, we broadly applied the four-quadrant model of Wilber to offer an inclusive view of the field and to show how dialogue between different paradigms helps us perceive the complexity of what we call *Integral Dreaming*.

Focusing on different paradigms in the quadrants of dream studies, the next part of the book explores the multidimensionality of dreaming through different but connected epistemological strategies. First, the scientific knowledge about the mechanism of sleep and dreams (chapter 3) gives way to an exploration of the creative brain through enactive psychology (chapter 4). Second, we enter the realm of phenomenology to inquiry on the dream experience itself (chapter 5), the multiple types of dreams (chapter 6), and the different ways we explore them subjectively (chapter 7). Third, we take a look at dreams from the perspective of intersubjectivity to explore how our dreams connect us to others (chapter 8) or speak to our social-cultural affiliations and identities (chapter 9). Finally, we look at larger patterns of change in dreaming life that are connected to societal transformations (chapter 10).

Part II

DREAMING FROM AN INTEGRAL PERSPECTIVE

Research and Theory

CHAPTER THREE

The Creative Brain and the Science of Sleep and Dreams

This chapter explores scientific approaches[1] to dreams and sleep. Essential within the integral model, third-person (scientific) approaches provide an objective map of the different states of consciousness across the sleep-wake cycle. The course of a night's sleep has a known and observable structure, well described by science. Each of us, however, has a personal sleep signature—a unique pattern that varies with our life habits. Because lifestyle choices affect sleep and dreams, getting to know the phenomenology of "one night of sleep" can help us achieve, or even restore, healthy sleep habits and strengthen dream recall. With dreams as the fruit of slumber, a good night's sleep[2] is necessary to obtain an abundant harvest.

The goal of this chapter is to generate familiarity with scientific ideas about sleep and dreams.[3] The nightly cycle may have been discovered more than half a century ago but new findings continue to shed light on the potential functions of sleep and dreaming. In particular, evidence is mounting that sleeping and dreaming creatively participate in the maintenance of physiological and psychological health. Research also shows a strong connection between sleep and neuroplasticity: the architecture of one night of sleep is deemed essential to the formation of new memories.

Before discussing further the various scientific approaches, we wish to put at ease the readers who may not be versed in science. We respect that science is one of the main cultural forces of the contemporary world. Research into sleep and dreaming has made tremendous gains over the last century, providing a growing body of insights. However every good scientist is able to show humility, knowing that scientific views always remain partial and change over time as new evidence comes to light. It is after all the nature of science to be open to new findings, where new discoveries constantly reshape older views of dreaming.[4]

What makes dreams meaningful is hard to capture with scientific and quantitative methods. The subjective aspects of dreaming, which are so central to phenomenologists and clinicians, has presented the most difficult challenge to scientists. Being researchers ourselves, we have studied dreams both quantitatively and qualitatively. We are aware of the tensions between the views of science and those with a more experiential orientation when it comes to dreams. While staying true to the scientific method and findings, we try in this chapter to build bridges between different approaches in the hope of opening new avenues for convergence and integration. For us, the findings of science are a source of awe: science has helped explain how the brain, in unique and creative ways, illuminates the multidimensionality of being. This is, in itself, an astonishing reality!

THE NEUROPHENOMENOLOGY OF SLEEP AND DREAMS: ONE NIGHT OF SLEEP

The sleep-wake cycle is the product of a long evolutionary process and is a core part of our biological makeup. As consciousness shifts from waking to sleeping, we experience dramatic changes in our physiology, inner experience, and sense of self. The same is true when we shift from one type of sleep to another, for example from deep sleep to REM sleep.

Brain researchers assume that any fluctuations in the brain, either metabolic, structural, or neurochemical are correlated with changes in our experience. Conversely, what we experience as the texture of life is also linked to particular brain states: the experience of moods, feelings, emotions, fatigue, rest, contemplation, anticipation, planning, and insights can all be correlated to changes in the brain and connected to the entire body. Thus, when compared to waking, sleeping and dreaming are naturally induced altered states of consciousness (Tart, 1968; Hobson, 2000).

Sleep and dreaming are not only a *result* of brain activity; they are also major *determinants* of brain function. We spend nearly one-third of our life in these states of consciousness and they are essential to our quality of life. Productivity, health, and effective learning all depend on the brain conditions that are associated with good sleep and regular dreaming (Dement & Vaughan, 1999).

On a daily basis, sleep patterns are finely tuned to our life habits or any disturbances of those habits. The quality of sleep (and incidentally dreams) is in direct response to the amount of stress we face, especially if it involves emotional upheaval. Changes in sleep pattern are observed when we are engaged in learning or enhanced cognitive activity. Exposure to natural daylight and regular physical exercise are two of the best known regulators of sleep, and any changes to our normal rhythms, such as long-distance travel and night-shift work, can severely impact sleep.

The amount of sleep we need shifts over our life span: humans require more of it in infancy and adolescence and somewhat less during adulthood and old age. Sleep is deeply affected by pregnancy and by the presence and care of infants whose different sleep patterns impinge on their parents. At midlife, sleep is affected by menopause, and old age brings yet another different pattern of sleep. Sleep is responsive to medications we take, and to alcohol or drug use. Furthermore, illness and trauma are known to profoundly affect sleep and dreams, sometimes in a chronic manner; for example, there exists a connection between obesity, sleep apnea, and impaired sleep that, if left untreated, can become life threatening.

Observing sleep with the help of a laboratory polygraph has yielded a clear map of the various stages of sleep. Each stage is associated with discernable patterns of brain activation, heart rate, breathing, and muscle tone. The discovery of the regularity of Rapid Eye Movement sleep (or REM sleep) by Aserinsky and Kleitman in 1953 prompted a revolution in sleep and dream studies. By mapping brain activation throughout the night, research revealed that sleep is organized according to repeating cycles of approximately ninety minutes. In a full night's sleep, a person may experience four or more complete cycles depending on their sleep signature. Each cycle moves through different stages of REM and non-REM (NREM) sleep. REM sleep is highly activated and desynchronized[5] sleep accompanied by rapid saccadic eye movements, after which it is named. NREM sleep is comprised of three sub-stages, also called *slow-wave sleep*. During slow-wave sleep, brain activation (quantified by electrical surface measurements also known also as brain waves) becomes lower in frequency and more synchronous. The three sub-stages of non-REM sleep (stages 2, 3, and 4) vary according to an increasing percentage of slow-wave activation.

People experience dreams *both* in REM (Aserinsky & Kleitman, 1953) and NREM sleep (Foulkes, 1962). A larger preponderance of dreaming occurs during REM sleep. When awakened from REM sleep, approximately 80 percent of people will report a dream compared to 30 to 50 percent, awakened from NREM sleep. Most NREM dreams occur predominantly at sleep onset and during stage 2 sleep. In stage 3 and, in particular, stage 4, the brain produces low-frequency high-amplitude (delta) waves, which appear to inhibit the dreamer from either having or recalling vivid dreams.

THE FOUR PHASES OF SLEEP

Sleep cycles show a regular pattern, and the cyclic progression of stages of sleep has been well documented (Dement, 1972). We find it useful to condense the complex architecture of sleep into two boundary states between waking and sleeping, and two overarching segments with sleep, namely:

1. *Sleep onset* or the *hypnagogic* phase when we fall asleep.
2. *Regenerative sleep*, during the first half of the night, when slow-wave brain activation patterns dominate sleep. This stage has also been called *restorative sleep* (Staner, 2002).

3. *Integrative sleep* takes place during the second half of the night and is dominated by REM and stage 2 sleep. This is when we most likely experience dreaming. Psychological regulation occurs during this stage of the night involving affect, memories, and the schemas associated with self-experience.
4. *Hypnopompic* phase where sleep comes to an end. This is a short-sleep offset period when we gradually (or abruptly) emerge from sleep and reenter waking consciousness.

In order to understand the wider spectrum of the sleep-dream cycle from both objective and subjective viewpoints, it is crucial to understand the cohesive sequence of that cycle. Even though we are speaking of the mechanical aspects of this process, its phenomenology remains deeply poetic. In the next section we briefly describe each of the four segments of one night of sleep, followed by a more in-depth delineation of scientific thinking about the nature and functions of dreaming.

1. Sleep Onset: The Hypnagogic Phase

Every night we partake of an internal theater through sleep. Perhaps one of the most creative and exciting stages of sleep is the onset of sleep, known as hypnagogia. This first stage is associated with rich dreams or "dream-like" experiences (Foulkes & Vogel, 1965). The word *hypnagogia* is derived from the Greek words *Hypnos* (the Greek god of sleep) and *agogeus* (conductor, leader). Numerous expressions have been used to describe this state, including anthypnic sensations (visions of half-sleep), oneirogogic images (borderland of sleep), praedormitium (half-dream state), and sleep-onset dreams. Occurring within a highly variable period of time, sleep onset can last between a few minutes to more than thirty minutes or even longer for those who have problems falling asleep (Mavromatis, 1987).

As we close our eyes and enter the world of sleep, first our brain activation decreases from the waking state (characterized by beta waves, which occur in twelve to forty cycles per second) to alpha waves (brain waves of eight to twelve cycles per second, indicative of relaxation). Soon after, brain activation decreases further to a still slower wave pattern called theta (four to eight cycles per second).[6] We eventually experience a feeling of drifting away, as our perceptual focus softens and eventually disappears when consciousness enters sleep. During this phase, we gradually begin to lose the sense of self that is present when awake. This is a natural, but quite profound experience of letting go, made more difficult if one feels unsafe, anxious, or agitated. A drop in muscle tone naturally happens as we relax. Muscle twitches (called *hypnagogic* or *myoclonic jerks*) are common. These spasms can be associated with feelings of falling or with dreams of "missteps," often leading to a sudden and abrupt awakening.

Typical hypnagogic visual experiences include flashes of light, fading colors, and entoptic phenomena—visual effects whose source is within the eye itself. Fading awareness of touch and sounds permeate our experience. Abstract verbal thinking gives way to dreamlike imagery, loosely connected. As this loosening occurs, the content of the sleep-onset dreams can be quite creative, although not always strongly bounded by a narrative plot (Mavromatis, 1987). Many individuals have purposely used the hypnagogic state for creative problem-solving and artistic creativity. As a particular state of consciousness, it is also a significant threshold in the practice of dream lucidity (Bogzaran, 2003; Wallace, 2006).

2. Regenerative Sleep: Slow-Wave-Dominated Sleep during Early Night

After sleep onset, the brain's priority is to progressively reach a deep-sleep state, also known as slow-wave sleep, delta sleep, or synchronized sleep. Slow-wave sleep is essential for body rejuvenation and plays a crucial role in boosting and preserving the immune system (Vgontzas, 2002). For this reason, slow-wave sleep can also be called *regenerative sleep*. Without adequate sleep, the immune system may become weak and the body more vulnerable to infection and disease (Zager et al., 2007). Growth hormones are also released during this stage of sleep, and slow-wave sleep seems to serve a vital function in proper physical and mental development (Van Cauter et al., 2000). For example, hormones essential to the development of secondary sex characteristics that are produced in the hypothalamus and stored in the pituitary gland are released during slow-wave sleep.

A progressive descent through stage 2 sleep changes the frequency of brain waves from theta to the slower delta wave pattern (0.5 to 4 cycles per second). Simultaneously, the heart rate slows and body temperature decreases. Brain activation progressively decreases as it moves from stage 2 to stage 3 and on to stage 4 sleep. Stages 3 and 4 are distinguishable only by the amount of high-amplitude, low-frequency delta waves: in stage 3 fewer than half the brain waves are delta waves; in stage 4 more than half are. While the brain exhibits high-amplitude/low-frequency wave patterns in stages 3 and 4, it is more difficult to wake up. If awakened during these stages, we often feel groggy and disoriented for several minutes. In one study, fewer than 20 percent of people awakened at this point in the sleep cycle reported coherent thinking (see Nielsen, 2000 for review).

Failure to get enough deep sleep on any given night results in sleep deprivation and shorter sleep and a need for more sleep. If sleep is regained the following night, stronger, slower waves are observed, a process scientifically known as *sleep pressure*. In humans and other mammals, sleep deprivation eventually causes weight gains and obesity (Cappuccio et al., 2008), hunger, irritation, and other symptoms that can lead to serious illness if loss of sleep is prolonged. Animal experiments have shown that rats will eventually die of exhaustion if deprived of sleep for extended period.

Edelman and Tononi (2000) argue that consciousness is lost[7] in slow-wave sleep, because, as the brain is producing high-amplitude low-frequency brain waves, the firing neurons are highly *synchronized*. Not only do neurons fire more slowly in deep sleep than in REM sleep, they fire in *synchrony*, and this is perhaps one of the reasons for lack of dream activity during this stage. By comparison, during waking consciousness and REM sleep, the brain produces a mixed frequency of brain waves, showing diversified activity in many parts of the brain.

During the synchronous slow-wave sleep, neuronal connections undergo another important change, consolidating new memories formed in the previous day. A series of studies show that the quality and intensity of the day's wakefulness can affect slow-wave activity during subsequent sleep (Cirelli, 2007). People placed in a cognitively enriched environment during the day, with high levels of exploratory activity, are more likely to experience increased synaptic potentiation[8] during waking. This is followed by increased slow-wave activity in sleep. It has been hypothesized that such enhanced cognitive activity triggers and sustains changes in the brain called *neuronal plasticity*, that is, transformations in the brain consisting of adding or reinforcing neural connections, or the addition of new cells (and associated with learning).

Furthermore a connection exists between what we do during the day and the mechanism in sleep that helps recalibrate our neural circuits. Tononi and Cirelli (2006) call this neural recalibration process "synaptic homeostasis." These researchers hypothesize that neurons used during the day may go through a process of "unloading" during sleep, so that we can be ready to face the new day without the accumulation of days past. According to this hypothesis, in order to recalibrate synaptic activity to sustainable levels, we need an off-line period (sleep) or downtime when we are not exposed to the external environment. This may be one of the main functions of sleep. Without sleep, the brain reaches a "saturation point that taxes its energy budget, its store of supplies and its ability to learn further" (University of Wisconsin-Madison, 2008). As our brain circuits get progressively stronger during wakefulness with active learning, this is associated with increased delta sleep activity (or, in scientific parlance, stronger sleep pressure).

Slow-wave sleep enables the consolidation of memories, with the transfer from short-term to long-term memory centers in the brain—that is, from the hippocampus to cortical areas (Lee & Wilson, 2002; Maquet, 2001). This happens simultaneously as the brain goes through a recalibration process regarding its neuronal load (Tononi & Cirelli, 2006). The recalibration hypothesis, which emphasizes the unloading of neuronal circuitry, and the consolidation hypothesis, which emphasizes the strengthening of neuro pathways in the formation of new memories, are seemingly contradictory. To us, however, it appears that a double action may be taking place in deep sleep more akin to pruning a tree: certain branches are encouraged to grow more fully (consolidation), while at the same time there is a paring down of the overall network of leaves and branches (recalibration).

Returning to the timeline of the night: the first two slow-wave-dominated cycles end with short crests of REM sleep, usually lasting just a few minutes. For most individuals, there is very little recall from these early-night REM cycles, even if awakened.[9] As the night progresses, the proportion of slow-wave sleep decreases while REM sleep and stage 2 progressively increases.

3. Integrative Sleep: REM and Stage 2-Dominated Sleep

The second half of the night unfolds very differently than the first half. As the night progresses, the preponderance of slow-wave sleep (stages 3 and 4) is gradually replaced by a pattern alternating between stage 2 and REM sleep. After each REM there are very short periods of micro-awakening when the body tosses and turns, creating an opportunity to bring awareness to the dream experience before cycling back into stage 2 sleep.

Dreaming mostly occurs in REM sleep, but it can also take place in stage 2 sleep. Since the second half of the night is mainly comprised of these two stages, it is not surprising that dream recall takes place most frequently at that time. Awakenings in stage 2 sleep yield different kinds of dream reports than in REM. These NREM dreams are less intense, showing fewer emotions, often with a kind of prosaic recollection and rumination of the events of the day (Hobson et al., 2000; Nielsen, 2000). This contrasts with REM dreams, which present more vivid and creative imagery, often emotionally laden and linked together by plot.

While in the first half of the night REM periods are shorter in length (five to ten minutes), toward the end of the night they can extend to thirty to forty minutes (Dement, 1972). The level of brain activation in REM approaches or even surpasses that of waking, but even so, recalling dreams is not assured. Most of us quickly forget our dreams if we don't write them down or reenact or rehearse them mentally, unless of course we happen to have a highly memorable and impactful dream (see also chapter 5).

REM sleep is also called *paradoxical sleep* because it brings together high brain activation—the strongest brain activation in sleep—with the lowest muscle activation, associated with the inhibition of all major muscle groups. This normal state of semi-paralysis, called *atonia*, blocks motor activity from the brain. Although in dreams we feel as though we are moving, our physical body is not fully engaged in any willful movement (eye movements, breathing, and twitches make up most motor activity during that stage).

While in REM, the brain actively inhibits sensory input from the environment. But a host of physiological changes often occur in synchrony with dream imagery. Anxiety dreams and nightmares are often associated with a racing heartbeat and faster breathing. In sexual dreams, dreamers often find themselves aroused, even to the point of physical orgasm. Conversely, bodily reactions are not necessarily expressed in the dream content. For example, in both men and women, REM sleep is connected with genital arousal, but this is only rarely translated into sexual content in dreams. In contrast to Freud's view of psychic release, research has found that sexual arousal tends to *increase* in REM *after* sexual activity (Van de Castle, 1994).

Many dream theorists believe dreaming contributes to connecting various registers of memory, integrating more recent events within long-term memories. Dream content is often organized around emotions: it is assumed that dreaming helps us sort through what may be most important and relevant to our well-being (Antrobus, 1991, 2000; Cartwright, 1992; Combs & Krippner, 1998; Fosshage, 1997, 2007; Hartmann, 1999; Kramer, 2007; McNamara, 2004). For these reasons, we term the second part of the night integrative sleep. After describing the last phase of sleep, we will come back to this idea in more detail.

4. Hypnopompic Stage: Waking Up

The night journey comes to closure by either a gradual or sudden awakening, called the *hypnopompic stage*. This stage can be shortened by abrupt interruptions such as those triggered by a strong stimulus (alarm clock) or by being physically awakened. In abrupt awakenings, the dreamer could arouse out of REM or stage 2, where a dream is often broken up in midcourse. Recall of the dream may be lost if the dreamer starts to interact with the outer environment, losing contact with the inner experience he or she is just emerging from. In the natural unfolding of sleep offset, the dreamer gradually exits out of a dreaming state, often from the longest REM period of the night, to enter a waking state (Balkin et al., 2002).

During the gradual hypnopompic period, the sense of self shifts from being subsumed into the "dream ego," or clouded awareness of self in sleep, to becoming a self-reflecting, awake self. A kind of twilight state pervades as we gradually regain sensation and awareness of our identity.[10] Physiologically, the brain's transitory state affects dream recall. In the laboratory, in order to aid dream recall, sleepers are asked not to move and to assume the posture they had while dreaming. It often helps for the dreamer to remain in the same pose, with eyes closed, while attempting to "reenter" or reenact mentally the dream experience.

Often during the hypnopompic state, one is flushed with the emotional impact left by the dream from which one is awakening. Impactful dreams, such as nightmares or even flying dreams are accompanied by strong emotional carryovers (Kuiken & Sikora, 1993). Dreams may sensitize us to some aspects of our waking experience, just as the latter impinges on our dreams. An integral approach to dreams emphasizes the value of this fluid and continual creative interaction between the dreaming and waking states of consciousness.

A CLOSER LOOK AT THE DREAMING BRAIN

Dreaming and waking states of consciousness share important similarities: both states display intentional worlds—the experience of an unfolding space-time continuum within which we move, feel, and act, with the self at the center of experience. From a scientific perspective, the question arises about what truly distinguishes one state from the other.

Hobson (1988, 1994), an ardent defender of the biophysiological approach, has proposed a model explaining the mechanisms of dreaming. He claims that we sleep because of the changing states of the brain. For Hobson, dreaming occurs when the brain assumes specific physiological characteristics:

every night the brain spontaneously stimulates itself four or five times—the REM periods that cycle forth every ninety minutes. In other words, the brain enters REM in order to dream. Relying on this totally automatic and self-regulating biomechanism, Hobson argues—contrary to Freud—that dreaming occurs irrespective of wishes or other desires. For him, REM and dreaming are in part a preprogrammed response to the brain's complex and dynamic regulatory mechanism. Put simply, the brain will enter REM states regardless of psychological motives. Hobson, however, concedes that once dreaming is under way, cognitive and emotional habits may play a role in the dreaming process.

Earlier in his career, Hobson and his colleague McCarley proposed the activation-synthesis model of the dreaming brain, which identified the brain stem as a "dream-state generator" (Hobson & McCarley, 1977). They postulated the presence of powerful bursts of adrenergic stimulation to the visual cortex, arising from the brain stem (in the pontine-geniculate-occipital area or PGO). This high-voltage activation, also known as PGO spikes, stimulates rapid eye movement (REM). During dreaming, these "PGO waves" produce unpatterned (random) activity in the visual cortex, where dream imagery is believed to originate. This corresponds to the "activation phase"[11] of dreaming in his earlier model. In an attempt to organize these visual surges, cortical activity then forms a dream plot (known as "the synthesis phase" of dreaming). This process results in the dreams as we remember them—mainly visually driven, with bizarre or incongruent imagery, and at times discontinuous.

Building on his original activation-synthesis hypothesis, Hobson's revised model, which he calls AIM—for Activation, Input Gating, Modulation—reflects the cyclic pattern of brain neurochemistry and the findings of brain imaging. It encapsulates a complex view of the brain, in which states of consciousness are seen as the result of specific patterns in the brain, exhibited within the three dimensions of the AIM model:

First Dimension: Level of *activation*, Activation level is high in waking, low in slow-wave sleep, and high again in REM sleep.

Second Dimension: The *information flow* (or *input-output gating processes*) refers to how in REM, sensory information is fenced out while physical movement is fenced in. In other words, sensory information does not reach awareness, whereas kinesthetic expression is contained by REM-generated state of paralysis. In REM, the dreaming brain is now responding to its own internal stimulation, as sensation and motor output "goes offline," to use Hobson's expression. In REM, seeing is believing: the brain creates a completely internally generated environment—a form of simulated waking experience that the dreamer fully embodies, no matter how bizarre.

Third Dimension: *Neuro-modulation*. For Hobson, the brain's state is also linked to neurotransmitters that are present at any given moment and in particular structures of the brain. The relative amount of certain kinds of neurotransmitters can have a broad impact in our state of consciousness. Leading up to REM, we see a broad shift from adrenergic (where the secretion of serotonin decreases, thus the name aminergic demodulation) to cholinergic neuromodulation (where acetylcholine dominates). This shift causes the highly activated brain to process information differently in REM. For Hobson (1994), the heightened cholinergic modulation is partly responsible for the creative and bizarre characteristics of REM dreams. Furthermore, REM sleep engages emotional processing, stimulated by the cholinergic stimulation of limbic structures. This increased emotionality in REM is coupled with a gradual decrease in attention, self-reflective processes, working memory, and reasoning. The attenuation of self-reflection and attention is for Hobson the result of aminergic demodulation of prefrontal areas of the brain. Dreams in this model are associated with the disinhibition of cortical networks, resulting in a hyperassociative flow of images, linked to emotions.

Hobson's (1994) formal analysis of dream reports yielded that the dream state contains little or no self-reflection. For him, this lack of self-reflectiveness in dreams, conjunct with visual hallucinations, strong emotionality, and bizarre imagery, renders dreams closer to a state of delirium. Hobson's findings remain contentious however. While his scientific contributions have shaped how dreams are perceived from a scientific perspective, his conclusions linking dreams to a deficient state of consciousness have not been fully embraced on two main fronts; first, in terms of the neuro-correlates of dreaming and second, in terms of the formal qualities he uses to characterize dreaming. In particular, his observations regarding the role of self-reflection in dreams do not take into full account the many ways in which thinking, self-reflection, and metacognition occur in dreaming states. Nor did he seriously consider lucid dreaming until later in his career (Voss et al., 2009). In contrast, many studies (Gackenbach & LaBerge, 1988; Kahan, 1994) have found that self-reflective awareness and metacognition are regular features of the dream experience.

Research has also shown that the brain stem's role as the REM generator is not the sole contributor to dreaming. Other brain structures are at play, in particular the higher cortical functions. Imaging studies have examined in depth the modularity of the brain in relationship to dreaming, showing the relative contribution of different parts of the brain in dreaming.

A MODULAR VIEW OF THE BRAIN DURING REM/DREAMING

The brain is a modular organ, made up of component parts; these distinct parts have been linked to particular functions (vision, audition, proprioception, language, planning, memory, emotional valuing, etc.). Each of the more or less specialized brain modules works simultaneously and in parallel with the others, mostly below the level of conscious awareness. In order to create an increasingly detailed map of the role of various brain sites that affect our consciousness, researchers rely on two main strategies. First using clinical cases, they note how brain traumas is correlated with particular functional deficits in cognition, perception, language, movement, et cetera. Second, using fundamental behavioral research, they ask individuals to perform specific tasks while observing what part of the brain comes online.

With advanced imaging techniques[12] (such as PET scans and functional MRIs), a more refined picture of sleeping and dreaming brain activity emerges: brain metabolism (such as captured by glucose absorption in certain brain areas) and particular centers of activity (indicated by the presence or absence of blood flow in localized brain areas) have begun to fill in the details, supplementing the information and mapping made possible by surface measures through EEGs.

Examining the regions of the brain that are the most and least active during REM sleep, we find correspondences between brain modularity and the experience of dreaming (Braun et al., 1997; Maquet et al., 1996). During REM sleep, there is a preponderance of visual and motor imagery (e.g., walking, driving, swimming, flying) associated with feeling and emotions, which is organized around the self in a relational context and often experienced in a narrative sequence (see figure 7). On the other hand, there is a decrease in brain activity in those regions of the brain generally linked with rational logic, episodic memory, and working memory—also areas associated with diminished self-reflection and critical reasoning during dreaming (see figure 8).

In contrast to Hobson, Solms (1997, 1999, 2000) has argued that the physiologic mechanisms responsible for dreaming are independent of those that produce REM. In particular, he cites strong evidence indicating cortical involvement in the dreaming process (whereas Hobson relies on subcortical activation). His research demonstrates that dreaming completely ceases in people who have lesions on the left or right parietal cortex—areas that are normally connected to the ability to derive abstract concepts from information organized in space (e.g., the capacity to distinguish left from right).

Bosnak (2007), a psychotherapist, draws from Solms' research to link dreaming to sequential presentation of simultaneous patterns in space. Dreaming, Bosnak proposes, forms an embodied story, with the emotional tone organizing the overarching narrative structure. Bosnak reminds us that emotions are "embodied states existing throughout the physical body" (38): we are not just a brain dreaming but actually a whole organism experiencing multiple embodied emotions.

Brain Areas	Function
Visual Associative cortex	Internal imagery constructed from personal association.
Cerebellum, Basal Ganglia	Motion and equilibrium. Perception of physical movement, action imagery and sensation in dreams.
Limbic System, Amygdala	Emotion-image association; social and emotional processing in dreams.
Right inferior parietal cortex	Language of metaphor and imagery. Spatial image construction, images of the self.
Brain stem	Responsible for REM induction.
Thalamocortical network	Associated with global coherence. Consciousness within dreams.

FIGURE 7. BRAIN AREAS SHOWING HIGH ACTIVATION DURING REM.

Brain Areas	Function
Dorsal, Lateral and Parietal Cingulate cortex, Precunius	Associated with rational thinking, episodic memory, working memory, volition and control. In dreams: sudden scene changes and bizarre elements seen as normal; diminished cognizance of one's state of consciousness.
Motor cortex	Atonia, antigravitational muscle inhibition, body paralysis.
Sensory cortex including visual cortex	Minimal sensory input.
Left inferior parietal cortex	Associated with language, words and names. In dreams verbal thinking replaced by imaginal thinking. The visual associative area of the brain works in concert with the emotional areas, as well as with areas that are involved in spatial imagery, self image and imagistic language -- all of which show strong activation in REM.

FIGURE 8. BRAIN AREAS SHOWING LOW ACTIVATION DURING REM.

BRAIN, LEARNING, AND THE METAPHORICAL MIND

Whether awake or dreaming, our brain must meet the demands of the complex human and natural world, and it must do so in a skillful manner. The brain is constantly comparing its current experience at any given moment with experiences of the past, while maintaining an eye toward future goals and intentions. To do this, the brain requires a complex metaphorical and holistic representation of both our inner and outer worlds. The brain is oriented toward novelty, and recognizes it by making a comparison between "now" and "then." Prior learning is composed of neural pathways that have created preferences for how we feel, act, and perceive the world. Perception unfolding in the present moment of experience also replays aspects of past experience. An event will elicit a particular meaning at a given moment because of neural pathways laid out by past experience and connected to related experience. Each moment is an occasion for the brain to bring a fresh response to the experience of "now" while integrating it into experiences of "then."

As a result of the hyperassociative state it generates, dreaming takes this open-ended and creative process even further. Many dream theorists believe dreaming contributes to connecting various registers of memory (long-term memories with more recent events, or semantic and symbolic memory representations) organized around emotions that continuously give value and relevance to our internal states (Antrobus, 2000; Fosse et al., 2003; Fosshage, 1997; Hartmann, 1999; Palombo, 1978). REM sleep is said to play an essential role in constantly updating our experience by forging the neural pathways for new memories. Evidence from animal research has shown that sleep, and REM sleep in particular, contributes to brain plasticity and to the formation of new neurons in the adult brain—a process called *neurogenesis* (American Academy of Sleep Medicine, 2008; Guzman-Marin et al., 2008).

Sleep and dreaming are increasingly seen as playing important roles in the learning process and in memory consolidation—both significant aspects of neuroplasticity. In an experiment, individuals undergoing a French-language immersion course were asked to keep a dream journal and spend some nights in the sleep laboratory. The study showed that those who made significant progress in the new language tended to incorporate

French into their dreams earlier and to have more verbal dialogue in their dreams (De Koninck et al., 1990).

During waking, the brain is gathering and processing large amounts of information below the threshold of awareness. Experimental studies reveal how the overall structure of sleep contributes to the consolidation of different types of learning and memory formation, where different stages of sleep are seen as handling specific types of information (Stickgold, 2007). These kinds of memories consist of procedural memories (e.g., learning an instrument), verbal memories (e.g., learning a new language), and emotional memories (the impact of daily events on us). To help us visualize what the brain may be doing, Carey (2007) proposes the metaphor of a change sorter, where during sleep, the sleeping brain deals with information received in waking, the same way a change sorter sorts and put coins in order.

More specifically, deep sleep and REM (even in naps) seem to benefit the learning process, especially the learning of facts (such as reading this chapter!). On the other hand, there appears to be a strong association between the amount of stage 2 sleep and improvement in learning motor tasks—for instance, mastering a musical instrument or learning a sport or a dance (Smith & MacNeill, 1994). Although all stages of sleep contribute to memory consolidation and retention, different stages of sleep enhance different types of memories. Stickgold (2007) suggests this may be the reason why sleep is composed of different stages, giving us a hint of why mammalian and human sleep evolved this way.

If deep sleep is essential to sorting out and paring down potential input overload, REM processes are seen to assist in sorting out what is most important to us. In dreams we try out various scenarios in an imaginal environment where we can safely explore various consequences.

In this chapter we focused on normal sleep. The healthy and creative integration that takes place in dreaming can nevertheless break down, as we see in people dealing with severe traumas. Clinical cases show that narrative creativity comes to a halt as a result of overwhelming traumatic experience. Victims of trauma are more likely to have repetitive dreams. Distress and severity of symptoms are correlated with how closely the traumatic situation is replayed in recurrent dreams or nightmares (Davis et al., 2007). It is as if the natural creativity that normally helps metabolize human experience and make sense of events becomes impaired, and the organism is overtaken by the automatic replay of traumatic memories.

SUMMARY

In this chapter, we looked at third-person approaches to sleep and dreaming. These approaches situate the main sources of dreaming inside the brain and the organism. Given the fact that humans share with mammals a sleep architecture that includes REM sleep whose importance in consolidation and the sorting of emotional memories is becoming increasingly clear, we can infer that dreaming in part is an important integrative process. Approximately five times a night, the brain will burst into REM. The fact that it does so on its own seems to indicate that, from an evolutionary and physiological standpoint, REM and dreaming are as essential to the health and well-being of the organism as other physiological functions such as hunger. While this rich virtual-world experience of dreaming vanishes when we awake, it often leaves behind important traces, implicit in shaping memory or explicit in the recall of dream content and carryover effects of dreams into waking life. While in this chapter we focused on psychophysiological approaches to dreams, there exist other objective/scientific approaches to dreams. The next chapter, bridging brain science with the question of the self, will introduce research on the content analysis of dreams, dream incorporation, and lucid dreaming to paint a fuller picture of the dreaming mind.

CHAPTER FOUR

Embodied and Purposeful Dreaming

An integral approach not only pays attention to the neurophysiological substrate of dreaming, but also seeks to integrate objective "third-person" perspectives with subjective "first-person" viewpoints. Within this integrative frame, we consider that the brain affords an abundance of creative abilities, and dreaming is among the most significant ones.

The sense of self is an embodied extension of the brain's inherent creativity. Over time, the self develops an increasing sense of participation within the landscape of its own creation, including dreaming. Dreams' creativeness is spontaneous, at times even eruptive. But many researchers question whether dreams possess directionality and purposefulness. For instance, what role do dreams play in the unfolding of human development? In this chapter we examine how dreaming may be considered a purposeful event. We explore how, as an embodied state of consciousness, its creative manifestation is open to reflective awareness.

BRAIN, DREAMS, AND SELF-REGULATION

The human brain is a world-creating organ. Our brains are responsible not only for giving us an experience of the world (through sensation and perception), but also for sustaining the experience of being a self: an embodied agent who stands at the center of his or her world-creation. The brain is a "self-realizable" organ. This means that what are known as "our thoughts," "our feelings," and "our emotions" are the result of a complex set of implicit and explicit processes which, despite being rule-bound, are *not* predetermined. Our brain is an open system. This open-endedness takes widely different forms depending on whether the brain is dreaming, sleeping, or awake and how it creatively combines and ultimately integrates these states.

Perception, emotions, and memory eventually become bound in a complex self-narrative that gives shape to our lived experience. The capacity to reflect on our own experience, to monitor and change our feelings and behaviors, and our sense of being a responsible being (or personal agency) are the fruit of a long maturational process, one that continues throughout our adult years. When diurnal and nocturnal experiences become the subject of reflective self-inquiry, an integrative process is put in motion that can enable conscious self-change.

As self-reflective beings, we can learn to *act* on what our brain "produces." The self, through reflection, mindfulness, and skillful means, can develop the capacity to modulate experience moment by moment. By this we do not mean a restrictive or self-conscious capacity for control. The repertoire for modulation includes, among others, the following: recognizing and facing negative emotions (anger, guilt, jealousy, etc.); attuning to others emotionally, sexually, sensorially (e.g., making music in groups) or empathically; amplifying a sense of the presence through focused attention or meditation; nurturing positive emotions such as loving-kindness and compassion; delaying gratification; influencing future behavior or one's healing response through auto-suggestion; using structured action to accomplish goals, including figuring out our deepest aspirations and trying to live by them amid a changing world; and discerning patterns of behaviors that are self-destructive or negative and moving away from them. These self-modulation practices also include being aware of our dreams, working with them, and even participating lucidly in them.

We believe that dreams play an important part in how the self can learn about itself and creatively engage with the world around it. Creativity—the ability to create new ideas and forms—is a natural extension of the self-organizing nature of our brain-mind. We agree with Krippner and Combs (2000) that the dreaming brain is a complex, self-organizing system. During sleep, free from the pressure of adapting to its outer environment, the dreaming brain relaxes into natural patterns of self-organized activity (see also Kahn et al., 2002). This activity reflects the residual moods, stresses, and concerns of waking life. For Krippner and Combs, the experiential elements of dreams, such as thoughts, perceptions, emotions, and memories, interact to elicit new experiential elements. Dreams are not only *autopoietic* (self-organized), but they can play a crucial role in the *autonoetic* (self-knowing) process: they can lead to insight and increased self-perceptual depth (Kuiken, 1995; Kuiken et al., 2006).

SLEEP, DREAMS, AND INSIGHT

Recent research supports the traditional advice that if we need to find a solution to a problem, we should "sleep on it." This applies to real-life issues just as it does to technical problems relating to one's work, or to more creative problems. Numerous anecdotal accounts suggest that pivotal insights can be gained through sleep and dreaming (Krippner & Dillard, 1988; Barrett, 1993, 2001; Krippner et al., 2002).

A study from University of Lubeck in Germany (Wagner et al., 2004) has provided evidence that sleep and dreaming contribute to problem-solving and to arriving at insights. Participants were given the task to deduce the final digit in a sequence of numbers starting with an initial series of numbers, and a simple rule with which to generate a second string of numbers from the first. Participants could greatly improve their response speed after gaining insight into a hidden abstract rule, but they had to figure out that rule for themselves. People who tackled the problem in the evening and then returned to it after eight hours of sleep were more than twice as likely to recognize the shortcut rule than those who had tried to complete the task in a session without sleep. A third group that tried the problem first in the morning followed by a normal waking interval of eight hours did as poorly in figuring out the rule as those who had stayed awake all night. This showed that poor performance could not simply be attributed to being tired. Sleep is not a magic solution by itself; it did not enhance insight in the absence of initial effort before going to bed.

These findings lend credence to the notion that sleep and dreaming stimulate lateral thinking (lateral thinking is an indirect and creative approach to problem-solving). During sleep, the brain is seen as reorganizing episodic memories—information about specific places, people, conversations, and experiences. Fresh episodic memories are thought to be stored in the hippocampus. Yet long-term memory calls for neocortical activation. Sleep, and REM sleep in particular, seem to facilitate explicit knowledge and insight[1] by restructuring the way memory is stored in the brain.

The fact that dreams participate in the process of insight is central to an integral view of dreaming. In the course of one's life, insights may take different shapes and forms. Dreaming helps us not only to distill (unconsciously or implicitly) what is important to us, but can also help us in a conscious process of discernment. Dreams impart an experiential sense about different states of being.

In the following section we explore, from the perspective of enactive psychology, the way that dreams act in a prospective manner. By this we mean that dreams can give us the occasion to make new experiences: they show us *what it is like*. Because of the importance it places on the embodied confluence of desire (motivation), mentation, and emotions (energetic qualifiers of experience), enactive psychology is a useful framework to explore the dreaming brain in relation to the maturation process.

DREAMS AND ENACTIVE PSYCHOLOGY

Enactive psychology is a recent but critical offshoot of cognitive psychology. It approaches consciousness and learning by emphasizing that we are, first and foremost, embodied organisms wholly embedded in relational and environmental matrices. Enactivism seeks to explain complex human behavior by taking into consideration maturation as an embodied process. For cognitive psychologists, philosophers, and neuroscientists, this approach aims to validate a previously disregarded yet crucial fact: our intelligence is primarily the fruit of our embodied experience in the world, and not merely cognition. Enactive psychology is particularly relevant in helping us bridge the bottom-up model of dream generation (where dreams are seen as the spontaneous product of the brain's self-arousal at night) with a top-down approach that views the self as a creative agent that can participate with the dreaming process.

The notion of an "embodied mind" (Varela et al., 1991) expanded the initial concept of *enactive cognition* first proposed by Maturana and Varela (1987). Enactivism as theory was later amplified by Ellis and Newton (2005). This theory criticizes the purely representational view of the mind, which is found lacking from a developmental perspective. According to Ellis and Newton, our minds don't simply represent the world as it is, but rather our understanding of the world is constantly shaped by our motives and feelings.

From an enactive perspective, the world is something that we grow into as we act within it. The world or the things in themselves are revealed only through our participation with them. Motives and feelings continually change as we mature, and we learn to modulate our experience in relation to the unfolding understanding we have of them. Thus, we don't simply form mental "representations" about a world that exists independently from us. The world constantly changes as we develop, mature, and learn. Along the way, we are always enacting our current understanding of it, hopefully to the best of our capacities (and possibly displaying our ignorance to those who have more experience).

Enactivism applies the epigenetic landscape[2] metaphor to cognitive science. For Burman (2006) what we think and what we do is supported by a "logic of feelings, which affords a landscape of emotional hills and valleys through which the developing organism must travel as it matures" (115). Feelings express how we apprehend the world. Given that no two individuals progress developmentally in the same way, each individual "constructs a 'lens' through which the quality of one's experience is perceived—a kind of internalized felt-approximation of the things-in-themselves" (115). These internal felt senses richly contribute to our best guess at what the world "is" and in turn influence the way we plan our course of action—attempting to meet our needs in the "world" as we perceive it.

> The structures of the world allow the structures of the observer to exist, while the structures of the observer allow the structures of the world to be conceived and perceived. It is this complex interplay between the world and the subject which gives rise to meaning, the understanding of the world. . . . The enactive mind is not a passive recipient of information from the world, but actively engages with its environment. . . . Cognition is not tied into the workings of an "inner mind," some cognitive core, but occurs in directed interaction between the body and the world it inhabits. (McGann & Torrance, 2005: 184)

How we represent the world is just as much related to how we feel about it as to what we think about it. Meanings are enacted by individuals through their actions and feelings, as they configure their lives within the world around them. Burman (2006) writes, "To have a mind means being able to look forward . . . , planning appropriately to end up where 'what it is like' is subjectively good, then undertaking actions to move in that direction" (116).

Of course this begs the question: how do we know that *what it is like* is good? What role do dreams play in how we make sense of a changing world, in how we become more integrated persons? Can dreams help us to "look forward" by providing experiences, albeit virtual ones, of "what it is like"? The sheer variety of dream experiences sensitizes us to a host of feelings that originally may only be implicit and half conscious. While some dreams give us experiences of "what it is like," others may give us experiences of "what it is *not* like," that is, what we wish to avoid. Recurrent dreams for example may alert us to the feeling of being stuck in emotional doldrums or maladaptive patterns, perhaps giving us an opportunity to attend to them.

Enactivism presents an interesting theoretical frame that helps us situate the importance of dreams in personal development. Because "meaning" and "doing" are related through "feeling" and "becoming," feelings and desires enable the organism to act meaningfully in the world. Research presented in the previous chapter disclosed that REM sleep is correlated to the activation of brain centers dealing with emotions. Dreams are a form of emotional metabolization, characterizing what we call the *integrative phase of sleep*.

The perception of meaningfulness,[3] as a form of personal truth, relies on the capacity for the organism to spot regularities in a sea of change. In order to do so, the organism has to be able to make sense of these changes in the context of its own history. This is, in essence an integrative process. Dreams may be particularly useful in this regard.

We have focused until now on the value of REM and NREM sleep in the process of learning, memory consolidation, and insight and have not explored the nature of dream content itself. The assertion that dreams contain *information,* let alone useful information, is still controversial. However, if it could be shown that dreams take on elements of waking life, this may help in validating the relevance of dreams in the process of integration, assimilation, and even maturation. Dreaming is not only essential for health and learning, but it is purposeful in other significant ways. In the next section, we discuss studies that demonstrate how dreams incorporate waking elements, and how this incorporation is subject to a predictable *dream lag* effect (Nielsen et al., 2004). We then go on discussing related approaches that validate dream purposefulness.

DREAM INCORPORATION

Dream incorporation studies provide some of the best experimental evidence that during sleep the brain is spontaneously trying to make sense of markedly strong or intense waking experiences. These studies try to demonstrate how dreams *incorporate* either some selected stimuli (most often presented pre-sleep but sometimes during sleep) or other aspects of the dreamer's lifeworld. Schredl (2003) looked at numerous incorporation studies to evaluate their relative findings. He compared the studies according to the kinds of stimuli presented to the dreamer before sleep: he found that meaningless stimuli—those that did *not* touch the inner world of the dreamer by leaving an emotional impression—were not likely to be incorporated. This finding demonstrates that dream content, rather than being random or easily manipulated, actually addresses what the dreamers care about most. Studies consistently show that while pre-sleep waking thoughts have an influence on dream content, the kind of pre-sleep suggestions most likely to be incorporated are those that address emotional concerns that are real to the dreamer (De Koninck & Brunette, 1991).

During dreaming, the brain/mind may be trying to figure out, or integrate, aspects of experience that are either most salient or meaningful. In contrast to incorporations suggested or manipulated by an experimenter, studies of natural incorporations show that major life events, and especially severe traumas, strongly affect dream contents (Hartmann, 1999). This influence can be very long lasting, and detected even decades after a traumatic event (Kramer, 2007).

Well-known to most laboratory experimenters is the fact that dreams incorporate the experimental settings. People dream about what is happening to them *in* the lab. This effect is even stronger than the experimental manipulation of the presleep situation (Schredl, 2003). This lab-incorporation effect is a clear indication that dreamers are trying to orient themselves within their changing surroundings.

To ascertain the role of dreams as spontaneous meaning-seeking process, researchers have also studied sleep and dreaming disturbance both experimentally and clinically (Cartwright & Wood, 1991; Kramer, 2007). They ask: what happens when dreaming is disrupted? Taking a meta-analytic perspective, Yoo et al. (2007) have found that nearly all psychiatric and neurological disorders indicating sleep disruption present corresponding symptoms of affective imbalance. They estimate that without sleep, the brain reverts back to a more primitive pattern of activation, becoming increasingly unable to put emotional experiences into context and produce appropriate responses. Their research supports the notion that a night of sleep may "reset" the correct brain reactivity to next-day emotional challenges by maintaining "functional integrity of the medial-prefrontal cortex-amygdala circuit" that governs appropriate behavioral repertoires (878).

Dream incorporation and the study of sleep disruption both lend credence to the purposefulness not only of the dreaming process but also of the dreaming content as well. Incorporation studies provide evidence that dreams may help us metabolize significant events, and that dream content resonates with the salient aspects of impactful events over time. Furthermore, incorporation is now known to follow a predictable pattern.

DREAM LAG EFFECT

Nielsen and Powell (1992) have shown that the highest incorporation rates of a self-selected significant event (e.g., a quarrel with a partner) were observed after the first night. Their study also shows a clear tendency for a *lag effect*: incorporation of a specific event slowly decreases after each successive night through the fifth night. Then, a marked peak is noted on the sixth night following the event. Nielsen and his team have replicated the findings of the lag effect in many studies, and it is now considered a solid finding. Nielsen et al. (2004) hypothesize that the lag effect may be a reflection of a two-step memory consolidation process, whose ratio has been well identified in animal models. The hippocampus drives the first step (the first incorporation), whereas the second step (the dream lag incorporation) is propelled by cortical activation.

FURTHER EVIDENCE OF THE PURPOSEFULNESS OF DREAMS

Domhoff (2001, 2003) argues that quantitative studies of dream reports may be the optimal way science can investigate dream meaning and dream purposefulness. The normative categories of a coding system are used to examine dream content objectively: patterns of frequency in a dream series can be juxtaposed to the waking life concerns of the dreamer. Longitudinal studies using content analysis (Hall & Van de Castle, 1966; Domhoff, 2003) to investigate the dream life of individuals show that, over time, dreams tend to consistently address an individual's core psychological issues (Hall & Nordby, 1972).

Among the main dream theories, the *continuity theory* emphasizes the carryover of waking experiences and cognitive abilities into dreaming. The continuity theory was championed by Calvin Hall (Hall, 1953; Hall & Nordby, 1972; Hall & Van de Castle, 1966), who showed that the content of one's dreams reflects the dreamer's waking life interests, activities, and emotional concerns (see also Cartwright & Wood, 1991; Domhoff, 2003; and Schredl, 2003).

Because enactive psychology highlights the orienting, energizing, and meaning-making aspect of emotions, it draws our attention to how and why emotions are such an important factor within dreaming. Content analysis studies focusing on dream emotions show that a higher proportion of negative emotions pervade dreams (Domhoff, 2003; Nielsen et al., 1991; Hall & Van de Castle, 1966). This statistical trend could be interpreted in a number of ways: dreams may be a response to negative emotions or scenarios that have already taken place (incorporation) in waking, as the organism tries to deal with the negative impact of experience. It may be that the dreamer is trying to change the outcome of such events to a more positive one (Kramer, 2007).

Emotions do not just give dreams their dramatic color. From an evolutionary perspective McNamara (2004) considers the limbic activation in dreams, associated with emotions, as a "costly signal." Why should our brain be so emotionally active at night? The payoff could be the fine-tuning of our coping capacities in the face of complex life situations:

> People use information they gather from the ways in which a person "emotes" in various situations to gauge the honesty, trustworthiness, integrity and behavioral competence of that person. Given the stock people put in the value of the information contained in a person's emotional repertoire, there is pressure to fine tune one's emotional capacities as well as one's ability to read the emotions of others . . . REM itself must come under pressure to contribute to that fine-tuning and development

> of emotional signaling and reading abilities. . . . That may be one reason that negative emotion is more often portrayed in dreams than positive emotion. (133–134)

Given that we have limited resources, in dreaming or waking, these resources seem best deployed around threats to personal or collective well-being, those we perceive (and those we may fail to consciously recognize). There are less compelling reasons for dreaming to dwell on what is going well in our life. Revonsuo (2000) made this rationale the linchpin of his "threat rehearsal" theory, postulating an evolutionary function of dreaming in which the organism is prospectively rehearsing possible negative scenarios, and in doing so is better prepared to face them when they to occur in waking.

THE HIGHER STAKES OF PURPOSEFULNESS: DREAM LUCIDITY

Most brain activity is taking place below the threshold of conscious volition. To remember a dream means to break through this threshold. When the dream becomes a conscious memory, we have the opportunity to reflect back on our own emotional state in the dream. Within the framework of psychological self-organization, this can also be an occasion of self-growth. When individuals reflect on their dreams to draw out information about the nature of their own experience, they engage in micro-cycles of learning.

Personal agency can also be cultivated to engage the spontaneous processes of dreaming *within the dream.* This is made possible by the practice of dream lucidity (see LaBerge, 1985). LaBerge (2000) believes that lucid dreaming provides a "test" of the theories of dreaming: simply because dreaming has been associated with the lack of self-reflectiveness does not mean such a lack is either normative or a necessary characteristic of dreaming. Mindful cultivation of cognizance is possible within dreaming—if the dreamer has proper motivation and adequate training.

Experimental studies of lucid dreaming in sleep laboratories have displayed what was once thought impossible: interaction between the lucid dreamer and the experimenter (Dresler et al., 2011; Hearne, 1978; LaBerge, 1980). Lucid dreamers are able to successfully give deliberate eye signals when they consciously recognize that they are "inside" a dream. This intentional and willful act (first-person awareness) combined with third-person objective measurements, provides a very accurate way to match personal reporting and scientific indexing of dream lucidity.

Self-reflection and cognizance (lucidity) can happen spontaneously or be cultivated through practice. Either way, dream lucidity catalyzes an exciting line of inquiry regarding the purposeful role of dreaming from an enactive perspective. In effect, lucidity translates into increased participation by the dreamer inside the dream, opening up a host of choices for creative action or for being witness, within the dream, of the spontaneously arising material. Dreaming shifts from being an unreflective, "take-it-as-we-go" experience to potentially becoming an event for self-reflection, even perhaps changing one's self-perception.

Deslauriers (2000) articulates a version of this process, linking dream cognizance to the development of a series of awareness skills. Bogzaran (1989) offers numerous examples of how lucid dreams present occasions to experience *what it is like* to enter mystical and spiritual states. She also has pointed out that creative fluidity can be refined and expanded whereas the dream's spontaneous, automatic process is complemented with mindful presence. She discussed her own multidimensional experiences of what she calls *hyperspace lucidity* as a paradigmatic exemplar of experiential discoveries enabled by lucid dreaming (Bogzaran, 2003).

If dreams present self-images, what does it mean to wake up and interact with these self-images? Can the self experience transformation through the act of reflection? Does the dream become a mirror of the self in a similar way to a biofeedback device informing individuals on their own autonomic processes? When the dreamer becomes cognizant that a dream is underway, she/he can become aware of the contents of her mind/affect and take an observer stance. The ordinary distance in waking life between the "outer environment" and the landscape of "inner environment" is prone to dissolution within a lucid dream.

What begins as a mental achievement, *this is a dream!*, can flourish into complete autopoietic acts where changes in thinking or feeling patterns translate into new dream experience. When interacting with the dream, dreamers can wake up to the fact that they are experiencing a self-created event. The dreamers have more choice to experiment with *what it is like* to contact aspects of the multidimensional dream space. For example, this opens up new possibilities of emotional self-monitoring to effect new action within the dream if the dreamer chooses to do so: emotions such as fear and anxiety can be mindfully attenuated. When the dreamer becomes less identified with these dream emotions, the dream's imagery usually provides an immediate response to these internal changes. The knowledge that one is now within the safe bounds of a dream experience can have a liberating effect.

Gackenbach (1991) takes this notion even further. She notes that many writers about lucidity draw inspiration from ancient or traditional spiritual views. Translating these views in psychological language, she postulates that lucidity in dreams corresponds to a post-formal stage of development, linking the self to a post-representational, nondual state. She emphasizes the de-embedding of the self from the representational level of the mind:

> A fuller awareness may emerge such that the observer may recognize that the self as dreamer can either continue to actively participate or manipulate the dream world or "step back" in a quite separate fashion. This receptive stance is a witnessing form of consciousness in which awareness itself becomes the dominant feature and consequently, the emotionally impactful quality of the dream fades. (118)

New questions about dream understanding arise from dream lucidity, calling for more expansive ways of relating to dream experiences. For example, self-reflectiveness itself can be viewed as a skill. Dream lucidity can be ephemeral, and the dreamer can lose the thread of this cognizance within the dream, to perhaps reconnect with it at a later time. Upon awakening, dreamers can reflect not only on dream meaning but also on how aware they were during the experience. This can include reflection on how one applies this skill of self-reflectiveness, volition, and witnessing within the dream.

In the past, most practices of self-reflectiveness have been pursued within the context of religious traditions. These in turn provided a spiritual framework to understand the resultant experience and the ultimate goal of such practices. Within the more secular view of Western psychology, the aims of self-reflective practices are not always well understood, nor are the ethical dimensions as developed as within religious traditions. Zaleski (1994) writes: "The training of attention is never simply a matter of using will power to screen out unwelcome thoughts, troubling psychological forces, or the demands of life. . . . Without love, compassion and gratitude, it is a sterile capacity" (106). Dream lucidity inevitably addresses lucidity in waking. The traditional and contemporary induction methods of lucid dreaming begin with self-reflectiveness as a practice for heightened presence in waking. Thus lucidity is a process of maturation that is embodied in both waking and dreaming.

SUMMARY

Within this section, we attempted to show how dreams display purposefulness: by incorporating and metabolizing events and concerns of daytime and by doing so according to a regular pattern stretching over time (dream lag effect). Furthermore, since the psychological lives of individuals are organized around a few core issues, longitudinal numerical studies show that dream content also revolves around these core issues. This may also be a reason why the emotional tone in dreams is likely more negative than positive. Finally, we showed how dream consciousness is amenable to skillful cultivation of cognizance, or dream lucidity. These different lines of evidence point to dreams as an important embodied state of consciousness playing a crucial role in the processes of psychological maturation.

As we close the chapters dealing with objective/scientific views of dreaming, we offer a summary of their main contribution to an integral approach to dreams. Scientific research on the sleep-wake cycle and on the role of dreaming in the process of insight, coupled with the theoretical frame of enactive psychology, converge to consider the brain as a self-creative organ, oscillating between relational consciousness (waking), regenerative sleep (deep sleep), and integrative sleep (dreaming).

Our brain enables both reflexive (emergent and spontaneous) and self-reflective (self-modulating) processes. Dreams contribute significantly in these two different but complementary ways. First, they arise naturally as part of the sleep-wake cycle; whether or not we reflect on them, dreams play a crucial role in the self-regulation of the organism, particularly regarding mood. They also play an essential role in memory consolidation and the learning process. Scientific findings further suggest that the complex processing taking place in dreams pertains to what is emotionally relevant to the dreamer. REM dreaming may be one of the creative ways the brain has found to extract value, find patterns, and compare and contrast emotional memories and rehearse scenarios. In other words, dreaming may help integrate and metabolize experience. Just as virtual reality enables immersive involvement, dreaming can show us "what it is like" to have certain experiences. In this way, dreaming also allows an exploration of possible selves (Kahan, 2011).

Second, dreams are open to the process of self-reflection. By focusing on the mind aspect of the brain-mind equation, the importance of attention awareness comes to light. Varying forms of self-modulation can interact with dream consciousness. By means of self-reflection and self-regulation—either within the dream itself (lucid dreaming), or by working with dreams in the waking state, the dreaming state can help the self to know itself better. In this way, dreams are both autopoietic and autonoetic, generating new patterns of thoughts and potential insights into behavioral patterns wherein the self can understand, transform, and even heal itself.

CHAPTER FIVE

The Subjective Experience of Dreams

From the private confines of the mind sealed by sleep, dreams coalesce as the wondrous display of the inner worlds. There, subjectivity reigns supreme: dreaming is a singular, creative, and utterly personal experience. In philosophical parlance, it is said that we have "privileged access" to our dreams, that is, a direct sensing that becomes the taste of our own experience. Only the dreamer knows what his or her dream really feels like. The exploration of the inner realm of dreaming becomes the foreground in this chapter and the next two.[1] First we focus on the nature of the dream experience itself—its phenomenology—and how the multiplicity of dreams appears in subjective splendor. In the next chapter, we expound on that multiplicity by inquiring into various types of dreams and discussing the powerful carryover that some dreams leave behind. Finally in chapter 7 we discuss the subjective means of dream exploration.

From a first-person perspective, the dreaming state of consciousness is both unique and in close relationship to the waking state. Within the multidimensional self, a circle of reciprocal action is in constant motion, reflecting the recurring ebb and flow of consciousness, from waking to dreaming to waking, and so on (see figure 9).

The inner world revealed in dreams draws from waking experiences. Reciprocally, dreams affect our mood upon waking

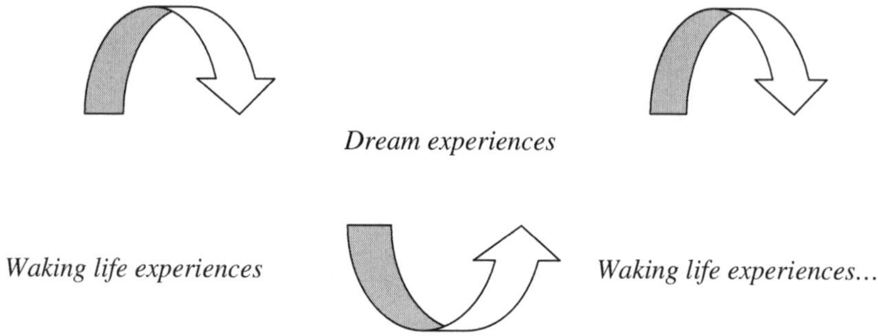

FIGURE 9. CYCLE OF RECIPROCAL INFLUENCE BETWEEN DREAM AND WAKING LIFE EXPERIENCES.

and sensitize us to existential subtleties that can transform waking experience. Insights, creative acts, and new perspectives inspired by dreams have the power to shape the contours of our waking life. In this way, dreams are self-defining.

THE DREAM EXPERIENCE

Let's pretend for a moment that the word *dream* did not exist to describe the phenomenon in question; how would we describe the vivid experiences that we have during sleep? Eliminating this semantic shortcut ("Last night I had a dream . . .") forces us to be more descriptive and brings us closer to the dream experience itself. For instance, people naturally describe their experience as visions: "Last night I saw . . ." or "I had the revelation that . . ." Others tell their experience around the central dream image: "Last night, I was pursued by a stranger . . ." or "I found myself in this majestic mansion . . ." If we closely follow the experience, we realize that our dreaming self was indeed in that "other space," encountering other "selves," wandering in places known and unknown, only for us to "return" upon awakening.

This exercise in imagination also reveals the centrality of embodied visual imagery[2] during dreaming. As we dream, we "see" and "feel"; the dream self "moves about" in "dream space," engaging in myriad activities alongside other people, familiar or unfamiliar. The brain's capacity to present a believable world, one that feels real (to itself!) derives from the tight connection between imagery and feeling (Clément, 2007). Dreams are not only "seen," they are also keenly felt. With considerable range of movement and activities, dream imagery appears in motion: one of the most frequent activities in dream is walking and going to some place.

From the perspective of the dream's main character—the dream ego or the dream self—thoughts, imagery, movement, and feelings fuse to form clusters of experience. Our dream thoughts and emotions are closely connected to the quality of the dream's image and action. Furthermore, these thoughts and feelings combine with action to form the dream plot. Each experience leads to the emergence of the next sequentially, loosely following a set of cognitive or emotional scripts. For example, in a typical anxiety dream, unexamined fear is likely to engender fearful imagery, which in turn can impel action, such as running away. A usual scenario might present the dreamer running faster to get away, only to find the pursuant getting ever closer. This illustrates the intricate and interdependent relationship between emotion (fear), action (running away), and dream imagery (pursuant getting closer) (Rossi, 1985).

Hartmann's (2008) idea of the "central image" underlies the importance of the visual core of the dream. Memorable and significant dreams—the "big dreams"—are characterized by powerful central images, vivid and often bizarre. In the retelling of a dream, the central image is the least likely part of the dream to change, as it is also the most memorable. Hartmann also reports that the emotional intensity of the central image is stronger in "big" dreams: dreams that rate higher in intensity are those that appear the most significant to the dreamer.

Looking further into the central images in "big dreams," Hartmann argues that visual intensity and emotional arousal are closely related and form the emotional core of the dream (see also Davidson et al., 2005). Hartmann treats the central image's intensity as one of most accurate measures of the strength of the emotion in the dream. Connecting back to the phenomenon of dream incorporation, Hartmann found that the intensity of the central image is higher for dreamers who have faced abuse or been the victim of personal or social trauma. On the more positive side, a strong central image also characterizes "breakthrough" dreams, such as those that lead to artistic inspiration or scientific discovery (Hartmann, 2008).

Visual imagery in dreams is not bound by the constraints of waking perception and has a wider range than in waking life. Besides "normal" visual experiences, dreamers have reported experiencing entoptic-like light phenomena (Bogzaran, 1996; Gillespie, 1987; Hunt 1989a); X-ray-type vision; the doubling of perspectives, such as the feeling of being simultaneously in a scene and observing it from a distance; cosmic vision (Bogzaran, 1991; Sparrow, 1976; Kelzer, 1987); intensity or saturation of color; and synaesthetic cross-modal perception, where bodily feeling, sound, and vision merge into a vivid amalgamated experience (Hunt, 1989).

Embodied visual imagery may predominate but other senses also play an important role in dreams.[3] The second-most important sense is that of hearing. The presence of music, sounds, and dialogue form an important part of dreaming. Significant dreams are often accompanied by strong verbal messages either heard from a dream character, "told" or perceived "out loud," or characterized by a memorable "saying" or voice. For instance, visitation dreams (Krippner et al., 2002), in which the dreamer interacts with one who is deceased, often include a soothing or reassuring dialogue, where the deceased figure tells the dreamer everything is okay. Visits by otherworldly beings often bring a verbal message for the dreamer to carry with him or her, or can assist the dreamer in finding meaning in difficult existential situations (Adams & Hyde, 2008).

THE *BIZARRE* IN DREAMS: MEMORY AND NARRATIVIZATION[4]

Dreams are peppered with bizarre intrusions, and these elements are the most puzzling aspects of dreams. Analyzing bizarreness in dream scripts, Deslauriers (1990) suggests that bizarreness is itself a rupture of the habits of meaning. In other words, something is not intrinsically bizarre, but becomes so when it breaks the expectations of the script around which the dream is organized. Bizarreness may be connected to the hyper-associative state that characterizes dreaming.

The intrusion of bizarre elements does not necessarily break the temporal continuity of the dream. Bizarre factors are often woven into the logic of the dream itself, as in the following dream:

Underwater Embrace

> I am in a hotel room with a friend. Someone knocks at the door and I let him in. Not long after he enters, my friend and the visitor start making love on the floor. Suddenly, I cannot see them because the water level has risen to at least a foot, and they became sort of invisible. Then, still standing next to the door, I let them know that I am leaving to take a walk outside. When I open the door, the water recedes and I see them in a full loving embrace.

Putting aside the rapidity of the loving embrace, the most bizarre element of the dream is the floor of the hotel room becoming a body of water. At a script level, there is a break in our general expectation of what a room is: rooms are not supposed to transform within seconds into pools of water. In a temporal sense, the water rises with the arrival of the "other" who becomes the lover (in Jungian terms, this is known as a "constellation" of two elements). One might argue that the bizarre element, when viewed within the framework of a constellation, provides information about the visitor/lover. With the water rising, the couple becomes submerged. The image of a submerged couple may be bizarre but it also can be seen as a rather transparent metaphor, where the rise of the water connotes a rising emotional charge. Also, the couple's embrace, done "under the surface," metaphorically points toward a "covering up" of what shouldn't be seen. Further inferences connect water with what it is covering: pleasure, love, but also denial and guilt. So while there is a break in the dream script (the meeting of a lover in a hotel room) around the water rising, the emotional aspects of the script become metaphorically illumined by the seemingly bizarre element.

Bizarre elements have their own internal consistency that the dream attempts to accommodate. The water element in the aforementioned dream is not only a momentary intrusion, but it continues to inform further actions and images. For instance, the image of water is carried forward when the dreamer's departure results in the water flowing out of the room. This leaving the scene has both a "draining" effect and a revealing one: the couple is now seen in full embrace on the floor! These multivalent meanings call attention to affective elements of the dream. For example: love, guilt, denial, jealousy, and their intensity are metaphorically represented by the rise and fall of the water level, associated within a relational triangle.

During waking, we tend to remember events that are salient or those that break away from the expectations of ordinary life. Could it be that bizarreness in dreams plays a similar anchoring role for long-term memory? Not only are dreams the source of creative novelty; they are also poetic breakthroughs from habitual patterns. In both ways, bizarre elements raise the odds that those dreams will be committed to memory. The central images associated with big dreams are indeed those that stand out by virtue of being especially powerful, vivid, or bizarre.

Memorability and salience, on the other hand, do not always mean that the dreamer is able to understand the dream. Knudson (2007) reports that for many people, the most memorable dreams in their life often do not make sense to them at the moment they had those dreams and that even the passage of time does not always help dreamers find more meaning. For highly memorable and bizarre dreams to make sense, the dream needs to become bonded to the person's waking life story. We call this process *dream narrativization,* which is in itself an integrative act. A memorable dream may mark one person's life indelibly, but for the dream to make sense, the person needs to engage in a process that brings the imagery in a reciprocal dialogue with waking life events. We introduce the idea briefly in the following section to be explored further in Part III.

STORY SCHEMA AND NARRATIVE INTEGRATION

Dream reports, as a textual genre, qualify as "self-referential fiction" (Schwartz, 2004: 28). Dreams are unlike discursive or philosophical thinking. They present us with a world with settings and places, activities and relationships, characters, motivations, feelings and movement. In other words they are the stuff of stories. Dreams are stories organized around the "I" of the dream, a central character that embodies the self of the dreamer and around which the action of the dream mostly revolves or is observed (Deslauriers, 1990; Kahn & Hobson, 2005). The dream ego gives the dream its perspective and the dream "I" holds the subjective consciousness in the dream. He/she can be mere witness to the action, or completely engaged in the dream plot, or moving back and forth between observation and action. In complex dreams, the coherent unfolding of imagery follows a narrative structure, complete with complicating actions (to use a narrative term) within the evolving plot and subplots.

Dreams, in their storied form, offer an integrative way to convey information. The story schema, simple in structure, is open to endless possibilities: stories could be seen as one of the best vehicles for the multidimensional self because they integrate somatic, emotional, cognitive modes of experiencing. The situations we find ourselves in make us see, feel, think, and interact. The story schema enables the multiple dimensions of life to come alive in "one place." The story schema is intricate enough to integrate current concerns with social or interpersonal expectations, historical events, and our connection to place and people.

From the enactive perspective, the self can, through reflection, use dreams to understand aspects of its own experience. Upon awakening, the dream story, in its complexity, can be the starting point for a further inquiry into each of these constituents (Baylor & Deslauriers, 1986, 1989). From an integral perspective, each aspect (such as bodily feelings, sensations, emotions, imagery, etc.) can become the focus of conscious exploration. A dream can set the stage for "playful improvisations" (Knudson, 2007) in which the self is narratively repositioned, restoried, and eventually transformed.

Furthermore by studying the complexity of the dream narrative, dream imagery can be seen as an index of the maturation and psychological growth process (Foulkes, 1999; Rossi, 1985; Van den Daele, 1992). According to Foulkes (1982), dream narrative complexity foretells the emergent cognitive capacities of the developing child. Later in life, structural complexity within dreams may reflect further maturational development beyond the formal operational stage (the highest stage in Piaget's model). Van den Daele (1992) proposes a detailed developmental typology of dream complexity where he identifies two additional maturational stages: *dialectic* and *systemic*. The *dialectic* stage of complexity is evidenced by the presence of multiple perspectives at once within the dream, and where "each reality is portrayed with multiple interdependent facets. At the *systemic* stage, "allegorical, symbolic and general philosophical representations with complex nuances . . . [illuminate] universal patterns that characterize the human condition or the natural order. . . . [This] level allows the comparison of multiple possible worlds (310–311).

Research on the narrative structure of dreams has shown that dreams are often organized around a predictable sequence of events (Deslauriers, 1990). Dream narration generally abides by the following structural framework: orientation, complication, evaluation, resolution, coda (Cariola, 2008). In many dreams, however, the resolution is either not fully explicit or cannot be differentiated from the coda—the ending part of the narrative when the dreamer shifts out of the story mode. It is as if dream endings are left open-ended. This is an important consideration with significant implications for dream practice. In particular, in certain dream methods, it is critical that the dreamer be given the chance to "complete" the dream, as it were, through the process of reentry, to explore alternative endings to the dream, or for the dream to spontaneously resolve itself.

DREAMS AS SOCIAL EVENTS

Dream sociality represents one of the most robust forms of continuity with waking reality. Whereas most aspects of the perceptual field appear fair game for creative or bizarre infringements, the social dimensions of dreams remain fairly exempt. Our relational nature remains mostly intact in dreams. Dreams present us with clear social situations (Hall & Van de Castle, 1966), and aloneness in a dream is more often an anomaly than the norm. Kahn and Hobson (2005) show that individuals encounter at least one character that had feelings toward the dreamer in over 80 percent of dreams; and in more than 90 percent of dreams, dreamers experience feelings associated with other dream characters. Their studies also show that dreamers spend a significant amount of time wondering about the intentions of other dream characters and what they may be thinking or planning (see also Pace-Schott, 2001).

Are these dream experiences simply a reflection of our waking concerns, and/or do they perhaps help prepare us for social encounters in our waking life?

> [T]hinking about the intentions of others is important to survival in a social species. . . . We both live and dream our awareness of the feelings of others. That this awareness cuts across both waking and dreaming consciousness suggests to us that man (and other social animals) have a need for a theory of mind, that is, for knowing what are the intentions of others. Dreaming about the intentions of others could, therefore, prepare us for social encounters when awake. (Kahn & Hobson, 2005: 54–56)

Because of the importance of others in dream life, we later devote an entire chapter (chapter 8) to the relational and intersubjective dimensions of dreams and dreaming.

VOLITION IN DREAMS

In waking life, as self-conscious individuals, freedom and creativity is available to us to a relative degree. Depending on circumstances, this freedom translates into choosing how to act (behavioral choice in the landscape of action) or how to feel or think about something (existential choice in the landscape of consciousness). How much personal choice is available to us in dreams, however, is a matter of debate. Just as in waking life, choice is exercised in dreams along a wide spectrum.

On one side of that spectrum (with little or no volition), we find dreams of paralysis that are particularly difficult and emotionally draining, and in which dreamers experience extreme difficulty in doing the simplest things they want to do, such as running away from a scene. Whether or not these dreams are linked to a carryover of REM atonia (natural state of decreased muscle tone), on a psychological level these dreams can leave a strong impression on the dreamer. It is as if they paradoxically heighten the importance of volition by its negation ("I wanted to move but I could not"), just as dreams of lost loved ones may be those where we feel most strongly the presence of love.

On the other end of the spectrum, self-reflectiveness in dreams is often accompanied by increased volition and choice in dreams. In lucid dreams, dreamers may experience a wider range of possibilities—in particular, greater choice and stronger sense of agency regarding one's own feeling states, actions, or ability to implement changes in the dream environment. In between these two extremes rests most of our dream life. Kahan (2001) has shown that dream life is strangely familiar to waking life in that we get absorbed in waking reality the same way we do in dreams. At the same time, she finds that the display of reflective thought, planning, and self-dialogue is present in dreams almost to the same extent as in waking.

THE REALNESS OF DREAMS: FINE-GRAIN RENDITION

Dreaming is believing. In dreams, we are engaged in something that feels real because we are experiencing it as real. A dream at times may even feel hyperreal: the intensity of experience is so pronounced that waking life pales in comparison, in particular in lucid dreaming. Because the sense of realness can be so strong in a dream, it has led many, including us, to hypothesize that consciousness in both dream and waking states shares many similarities, including a "high definition" rendition of a believable world. Waking consciousness is modulated by the external senses and constrained in large part by the external environment. Dreaming, on the other hand, is modulated by internally generated imagery, an inner perception associated with a sense of reality that can exceed that which we experience in waking, as in the following dream:

Victorian Flight

> I dreamed I was flying over a city. The houses were from the Victorian Era, with fine architectural details. After reflecting on the dream, I was amazed by how I could "produce" such intricate three-dimensional details in "real time." This rendition would take weeks and months for someone to draw, let alone animate. I could not even draw one of these houses if someone was to ask me. However, in the dream, I would be looking at all these fine details at flying speed! Amazing!

Hunt (1989) understands dreams as a complex form of experience. Dreaming, he writes, "is an utterly unique . . . amalgam of remembering, perceiving, thinking, feeling, and imagining. . . . It is a relatively true-to-life reconstruction of our human being-in-the world" (69).

ORGANIZING EXPERIENCE: OSCILLATING BETWEEN THE EMBODIED SENSE AND LANGUAGE

Hunt (1989) articulated a cognitive-transpersonal view of the oneiric experience based on the wide continuum of dreaming experiences. His multifaceted typology accounts for the vast range of dreams: from "cloudy" dreams leaving confused or scant memory traces, to extraordinary, vivid, and intensely numinous dreams, leaving a strong impact on the dreamer. Hunt's model is built on the observation that the mind represents experience in two major ways:

- First, in an imagistic and proprioceptive way, based on immediate felt sense, and generating embodied imagery;

- Second, in a linguistic and propositional way, drawing primarily from semantic memory (including puns), and linguistic representation linked to the story schema.

For Hunt, dreams tend to express one of the two poles. Some are more linguistically organized around story-based imagery, while others are definitely more imagistic-proprioceptive.

Here is an example of a linguistically formed dream. It contains very little action or visual imagery but a lot of verbal reflection. One of the authors (Deslauriers) had the dream while reading and writing about Hunt's theory of dreaming!

The Tail-Tale Dream

> I see the image of the ouroboros [the archetypal image of the snake biting its own tail]. I am hearing the idea that "the tail is the tale." Suddenly I get that the serpent biting its own tail corresponds to the telling of tales: how we make sense of reality through storytelling.

Later he writes:

> By implication, our experience becomes the "tale" when the mouth opens to create it [such as the snake opening its mouth toward its own tail]. In the past I had understood the ouroboros as a snake ingesting itself, some kind of self-referentiality. But the dream is showing me that the snake is creating its own body by "regurgitating" its own self. The same is true when we open our mouth: the self becomes the "tale" it tells about itself. So the "tail is the tale."

One might surmise that this dream presents a response to Hunt's insights, showing how a personal dream provides creative elaboration on someone's theory. To use his own terms, the dream consists of a creative *translation* of the dreamer's comprehension of Hunt's model, moving back and forth between imagistic and linguistic terms. It bears repeating that Hunt's theory of dreaming is centered around the idea of translation as a two-way street: sensory experience translated into linguistic terms and vice versa, linguistic understanding as translated into embodied imagery. The dream is constructed around a play on words that directly expresses the type of transformation that Hunt refers to when he speaks of "cross-modal" translation from one domain (e.g., imagistic experience) into another (e.g., language). In this dream, this abstract idea translates into the double pun of a narrative "tale," represented symbolically through the image of the ouroboros "tail." What was at first a direct symbol (the tail of the snake) is translated linguistically (through its homonym "tale") into an insight about storytelling and self-organization. Both involved references to the "mouth": the mouth that swallows (or regurgitates) the tail is the same mouth that tells the tale. Both speak about the notion of self-referentiality and self-creation. A simplified way of representing the dream insight would be: the transformative act of swallowing/regurgitating one's own tail = the transformative potential of telling one's own tale. The whole dream is creatively structured around a linguistic pun that also conveys a complex idea about translation and meaning. This dream is also an example of the sophisticated cognition that is present in dreams.

By contrast, in the next dream example, the activities unfold across time, forming a tighter plot, following the iterative logic of cause and effect. Most dreams seem to follow this kind of story-like structure.

Out of Control

> I was driving a car down a busy road. The car got out of control, I had a sinking feeling in my tummy as I tried to put on the brakes, but the car would not stop. Finally, I awoke in fear just before I got to a busy intersection.

In this dream, the simple narrative structure intertwines (driving a car, coming to an intersection, car out of control, impeding catastrophe) with salient proprioceptive feelings (feeling out of control, a sinking gut feeling, awakening) to form the plot of the dream. Hunt proposes that most dreams follow this normative interplay between story and bodily felt sense.

The next dream, by contrast, progresses in a way that accentuates transformation, where body feelings and sensation are reciprocally engaged with the visual system. It is not rare for such dreams to take on a spiritual tone. This dream, submitted by one of our students, clearly exemplifies the prevalence of imagistic proprioception. It has a minimal plot, which is itself chiefly organized around the shift in bodily felt sense.

Perfection

> I am a triangle. Actually, I am an abstraction, and my form, although I didn't really have a form, is a triangle. (Sorry this is difficult to explain.) Within the triangle are separate abstractions which could be called round, and which move or bubble independently, but could be said to move collectively. I am aware of my imperfection as I look at this essence of myself.
>
> Suddenly my thinking changes; it is as if I have clicked into a different channel or flipped over into a different mode of perception. I realize, without a doubt, my perfection. ("Perfection" isn't the right word; it is more of a sense of peace, utter calm, and tranquility.) The interior, round parts stop "bubbling" and calmness pervades me, everything is smooth without distinction.

In this dream, the conceptual and linguistic give way to a more direct imagery translating to a bodily felt sense of peace and tranquility. The abstract imagery leaves the dreamer connected to the essence of experience that lies beyond the narrative basis. If we consider that epiphanies can capture the opposites of existence itself, the dream expresses such opposites through simple but potent imagery. At first there is a sense of bubbling and movement but then she adds: "my thinking suddenly changes, it is as if I clicked into a different channel . . . and I realize without a doubt, my perfection." The dream presents a series of abstract transformations that convey a strong felt-sense: "calmness pervades me." The somatic overtone of the last statement is revealing: "everything is smooth and without distinction." Not only does visual-kinesthetic synesthesia convey felt meaning, but it can be the experiential basis for impactful realizations. The resulting experience in this "different mode of perception" is a felt experience of non-duality ("without distinction") where calm and peacefulness emanate. The medium of insight in this dream is not intellectual. Rather, by having the experience, one comes to know what "perfection" feels like. This echoes Hunt's description (1989a) of synesthesia as the basis of symbolic felt meaning: "It is only when geometric mandala designs . . . are experienced as fused with tactile kinesthetic patterns that they embody and convey a deep sense of felt meaning" (191).

EMOTION, FEELING, AND DREAM CARRYOVER

We began the chapter by describing how dreams and waking experiences feed reciprocally and iteratively on each other. Vivid experiences, stress, or trauma find their way into our dream life. For instance, Blagrove, Farmer, and Williams (2004) found a correlation between low sense of well-being and the likelihood of experiencing unpleasant dreams. For his part, Schredl (2003a) found that people suffering waking stress were more likely to experience negative dreams. His study showed that the state of the participants (waking experience) is a more relevant indicator of the potential for negative dreaming than trait factors (personality). Studies on positive emotions and personality show a similar correlative trend between waking and dreaming emotions and feeling tone. Positive personality characteristics and positive waking experience correlate with dreamers' tendency to experience positive emotions in dreams (Gilchrist et al., 2007). "The concerns people express in their dreams are the concerns that they have in waking life. What they dream about is also what they think about or do when they are awake" (Hall, 1953, cited in Domhoff, 1996: 153).

SUMMARY

In this chapter, we attempted to draw out some of the most important phenomenological features of dreaming experiences:

- Predominance of embodied visual imagery, often with a recognizable central image.
- Strong correlation between visual imagery and feeling.
- Prevalence of movement within dreams.
- Presence of a narrative—simple but open-ended structure capable of bringing together the multidimensional aspects of experiences: self, others, landscape of action, emotions, and scripts—mainly organized according to a loose temporal sequence.

• Incidence of bizarre elements relative to an organizing script.

• Complementary organizing frameworks oscillating between linguistic/verbal and felt sense/imagery.

• Strong interpersonal and social presence.

• High resolution consciousness leading to believability.

• Variable degree of volition and metacognition depending on the type of dream.

• Possibility of strong carryover of feelings and imagery into waking.

• Clear feeling of the experience as distinct from waking state of consciousness.

These phenomenological features show us that dreams in many ways are not unlike waking consciousness in the wide range of experiences that they afford. From a subjective perspective, dreams are above all occasions of experience just as powerful and sometimes more so than waking experiences. Whether or not we understand them, these dream experiences give a sense of *what it is like* to go through them.

Dreams feel real because they are energized by emotions that are continuous with our waking emotional life. Dreams' feeling tone at awakening is of particular importance, reflecting a sense of resolution within the dream story or often the lack of it. Waking experience influences dreams; dreams can also leave behind perceptual and emotional impressions that can last for long periods. In the following chapter, we look in depth at both normative and impactful dreams and discuss how dreams may bring important triggers of self-knowing.

CHAPTER SIX

Types of Dreams

Toward an Ecology of Dreaming

Dreams offer a stunningly wide range of variations and possibilities, and this variety forms a kind of ecology of dreaming. Within an integral approach to dreams, a broad and inclusive phenomenology is required for a comprehensive and respectful inquiry into the role of dreams in the lives of people. It is impossible to ascribe dreams to a single function when we realize that there are so many kinds of dreams. Interest in the lived experience of dreams has impelled researchers to capture their varied landscape: their prevalence, their reoccurrence, their many motifs, their impact, or the degree of lucidity that dreamers exhibit. Some dreams—extraordinary dreams—stand out for a different reason, they call forth a different layer of experience, often still unexplained but nevertheless compelling (Krippner & Friedman, 2010). We believe that no dreams should be excluded from our consideration because their structure or content do not match current theories; rather the theory needs to expand to encompass them. While some types of dreams are not easily amenable to controlled research, their occurrence is widespread enough that they demand proper attention. In this chapter, we review key research illuminating the sheer variety of dreams.

NORMATIVE DREAMS: INDIVIDUAL AND LARGE SAMPLES

Each dream may be uniquely creative, but what patterns can we discern if we gather dreams together and look at naturally occurring clusters? Do prevalent themes fall within identifiable categories? Trying to answer these questions, Schwartz (2004)—a researcher and a visual artist—collected 1,770 of her own dreams over a fifteen-month period (averaging four dreams a night). She asked herself how she could study this large series of dreams without the burden of hand-coding them (such as with the content analysis of Hall & Van de Castle, 1966). She came up with a computerized lexical analysis that first mapped words from dream reports to create clusters of correspondence. Using this method, she found that her dreams fell into five main clusters:

> Cluster 1 (335 reports): Current affective/academic environment (verbal)
>
> Cluster 2 (350 reports): Current artistic environment (visual)
>
> Cluster 3 (271 reports): Social events, people, and family
>
> Cluster 4 (467 reports): Locomotion, outdoors
>
> Cluster 5 (290 reports): Fear, physical danger (Schwartz 2004: 20)

She then compared her own sets of dreams with the normative sample of a thousand dreams from one hundred men and one hundred women college students who were part of the 1966 Hall and Van de Castle content analysis study (Schwartz, 2004). Doing a similar lexical analysis on the Hall and Van de Castle sample allowed Schwartz to compare how these dreams coalesced in thematic space, mapped out by the repeated presence of key words. She found that dream clustering of the words was closely consistent with the semantic pattern of the five clusters she had found when studying her own dreams (see figure 10). For Schwartz, these five clusters reveal word patterns in dream reports that correspond to distinctive dimensions in thinking or within one's emotional landscape. Her research highlights striking similarities between an extensive dream series from a single individual and that of a large group (figure 10). Apart from a few interesting differences (clusters 3 and 4 in the Hall and Van de Castle sample), the dream reports from male and female students are also very similar.

Schwartz draws two main conclusions from her work. First, dreams that focus on linguistic themes (cluster 1) seem very distinct from dreams with more action, body-related clusters (clusters 2, 3, and 4). Second, emotionally salient elements of waking life (clusters 1, 2, and 3) that are found in dream reports are distinct from more "primordial" patterns connected to the presence of fear and the issue of threat encountered in dreams (cluster 5). It is as if there exist two main sets of emotional concerns, where the first set deals with more idiosyncratic (individual) emotional expressions and the second deals with a more evolutionary (universal) pattern based on the fear response. The latter includes the dreamers' response to aggressive imagery.

Cluster	**Schwartz**	**Hall and Van de Castle**
1	Current affective/ work environment (verbal)	Working environments and reference to verbal activities, reasoning and time references
2	Current artistic environment (visual)	Activity words (e.g., related to flying or war for the males and references to shopping and colors for the females).
3	Social events, people & family	Sexual and social themes, indoor spaces.
4	Locomotion, outdoors	Sport or physical activities (e.g., baseball for the males, swimming for the females)
5	Fear, physical danger	Body motion (e.g., run, drive, escape, fall, etc.), connected with the presence of vehicles, violence, and fear-related words.

FIGURE 10. LEXICAL CATEGORIES IN HALL AND VAN DE CASTLE COMPARED TO SCHWARTZ SAMPLES.

Schwartz's research provides evidence for the fine-grain distinction made earlier by Hunt (1989) between two main different organizing frameworks of dreaming. Her hypothesis that distinct mental processes contribute to certain dream experience suggests that "dreaming is not a unitary phenomenon" (28). In particular, a clear dissociation between verbal activities (corresponding to Hunt's linguistic/propositional) and motor activities (corresponding to Hunt's visual-spatial category) emerged in her analysis.[1] Some dreams tend more toward the thinking/verbal pole of experience while others express more directly the feeling pole. Nevertheless, if we take Schwartz's own sets of dreams as an example, we can see that an individual dream life spans a wide spectrum of experience.

PREVALENT DREAM THEMES

Prevalent dreams are those that most people have had at least once within their lifetime. Researchers have been interested in knowing not only about the dreams of individuals but also about whether dreamers within cultural or national groups share significant dream themes. Surprisingly, certain themes appear to be stable across cultures. Large German (Schredl et al., 2004), Canadian (Nielsen et al., 2003), and Chinese (Yu, 2008) samples have been queried about their most prevalent dreams, with the following themes topping the list:

- Being chased or pursued
- School, teachers, and studying
- Falling
- Arriving too late (e.g., missing a train, a boat, or a plane)
- Failing an examination
- Trying again and again to do something
- Sexual experiences
- Flying through the air

Because these studies show a surprisingly high degree of consistency regarding prevalent themes across nationalities and cultures, it naturally raises the question whether these prevalent themes could be considered "universal." While it may be too soon to assert that they are (more research should include a larger set of cultural groups), there is now solid evidence that these typical dreams transcend cultural borders. Such a high degree of similarity across cultures is an indication that dreams are not a random product of the mind. Furthermore, these dreams can provide an evolutionary window on common patterns of experience for our species. It is interesting to note that only two deal with cognitive themes (school, teachers, and studying; failing an examination) whereas the other eight show a prevalence of body-based or somatic imagery: falling, flying, sexual experiences, and so forth.

These studies demonstrate the normative prevalence found among large groups of dreamers. They do not show the frequently reappearing dreams of any individual dreamers. Therefore, the *prevalence* of themes across cultures is not necessarily a reflection of the *frequency* of a particular dream theme within one's life. While prevalent dreams can be important evolutionary markers, in the lives of individuals, they may not necessarily be the most important or the most significant dreams. We review these next.

IMPACTFUL DREAMS

From a subjective standpoint, not all experiences have the same value. Dreams are no exceptions. Some dreams are clearly more important and significant than others not only by virtue of the central image that they convey (Hartmann, 2008), but also by the impact they have on our lives. Kuiken and his team have dedicated years of research to describing what makes dreams impactful. In a series of studies (Busink & Kuiken, 1996; Kuiken & Sikora, 1993), they asked dreamers to report impactful dreams that met some criteria such as:

- After my dreams, I became sensitive to aspects of reality I usually ignore.
- My dream influenced my mood after I awoke.

• After my dream, I felt like contacting a person I dreamed about, visiting a place I dreamed about, or doing something that I dreamed about.

Using numerical analysis the researchers found important clusters or groupings of experience and identify four relevant categories of impactful dreams: anxiety dreams, existential dreams, alienation dreams, and transcendent dreams.

Anxiety Dreams

Anxiety dreams are negative dreams, commonly known as nightmares. They constellate around the emotion of fear or apprehension, usually for one's own safety or that of another. The dreamer tries to avoid harm or to save others, but often does not succeed. Activities in anxiety dreams follow two opposite trends. Either the dreams contain forms of paralysis or an inability to move properly, or the dreams involve strong activity, such as running or swimming. In either case, the dreamer is usually very vigilant, attuned to threats or clues that could be interpreted as threats. Avoidance of harm in dreams appears to follow the deeply ingrained automatic habits.

In these dreams, individuals are fully immersed in the landscape of action and usually do not pause to think about the strangeness of their undertaking. Dream imagery often goes through transformation in ways that intensify fear and apprehension. The endings for these kinds of dreams are usually very intense, often leading to sudden awakening. The residual feeling of lingering anxiety is very real. With practice, some individuals learn to achieve a degree of self-reflection that allows them to question the source of fear and anxiety.[2] If the dreaming self can recognize that no harm will result from facing an apparently aggressive dream character who, for example, was chasing the dreamer. What at first seemed to be a fearful face-off can result in a healing encounter.

Existential Dreams

Existential dreams are characterized by the experience of agonizing distress. Distress can be related to emotions such as grief, discouragement, guilt, anger, and confusion. In these types of agitated dreams, the emotion is often very intense. Distress, for example, can be embedded in a narrative of separation and loss, or connected by the appearance of a deceased person, such as in the following dream example. Existential dreams often portray vivid bodily sensations and sensory experience. Reports of these dreams contain moments of self-awareness that are often unsettling, where dreamers often feel that they become aware of themselves as if from the "outside." The dream endings feel very real to the dreamers, leaving behind a strong emotional impact.

An example of an existential dream is the following:

Lost in the River

> I am driving a pick-up truck with an older friend of mine, a rather famous person who has recently died. In the dream we drive next to a river. I help my friend step down from the truck. He leaves for a while, I think probably to relieve himself. I go looking for him, but can't find him. I start to panic, thinking that maybe he has fallen into the river and drowned. I start to look for him frantically, but to no avail. I woke up with an extreme sense of guilt, feeling that his disappearance was my fault.

Alienation Dreams

Although close to existential dreams in terms of negative affect, alienation dreams are missing the signature affect of guilt and fear. Instead, in alienation dreams, dreamers sometimes give expression to their frustration through anger. Alienation dreams also often contain themes of separation and rejection, whereby the dreamer experienced a lack of interpersonal inefficacy; as one dreamer reported, "I experience a pathetic sense of failure."

Transcendent Dreams

In contrast with the other three types of dreams, transcendent dreams are, at the core, positive dreams, containing feelings of joy, delight, and awe. Transcendent dreams are not defined, however, by the intensity of the positive feelings expressed. The emotional tone here overrides the intensity. In those dreams, the dreamer succeeds at what he or she is doing, attaining goals and finding good fortune (Bulkeley, 2008). The dreamer may even report magical or supernatural abilities, such as flying, being able to breathe underwater, or performing other extraordinary feats. Movements are usually graceful and effectual, actions are well balanced, and the dreamer feels powerful and lively, as if he or she could do anything. The bodily sensations are uplifting, evoking feelings of warmth, or the sense of flow and effortlessness. In some dreams, dreamers will report encounters with a phenomenon of light. There is a sense of flow that mitigates self-awareness; it is as if the dreamer is utterly content in the state he or she finds himself or herself in (the "Perfection" dream discussed in chapter 5 provides a clear example). The dream endings within transcendent dreams, although not necessarily intense, often leave the dreamer in a state of calm quiet, and there is a noted absence of negative feelings.

It is noteworthy that three of the four impactful types of dreams dwell on rather negative emotions, and that only transcendent dreams are associated with positive feelings and imagery. It is as though we spend more time trying to work things out in impactful dreams (such as anxiety, agony, or fear) than we do experiencing the fruits of our accomplishments. As a result, all four types of impactful dreams have different effects on the dreamer's waking thoughts and feelings. The tendency is for:

- *anxiety* dreams to result in a heightened sense of vigilance (e.g., apprehension about dangers such those elicited by the nightmares);

- *existential and alienation* dreams to result in dreamers noticing feelings that they were previously reluctant to acknowledge (e.g., distress related to loss; a sense of meaninglessness);

- *transcendent* dreams lead dreamers to consider previously ignored spiritual possibilities (e.g., a feeling of self-renewal or an ineffable sense of peace, love, or awe). These dreams' impact may include forms of ecstatic spiritual release, connected to a deep sense of spaciousness or timelessness wherein life suffuses all things and the separation between self and world is attenuated or seems to disappear altogether.

From Kuiken's research, we learn that many types of dreams can leave an impact. The memory trace is not only the dream image, but very often a lingering body sensation, feeling tone, or emotion. At times, the impact is like being poked to become aware of an aspect of self in need of attention. Existential dreams and alienation dreams in particular lead dreamers to ask questions about their own life, addressing matters of ultimate concern, including spiritual conviction (or lack of), life's meaning (or a sense of emptiness), and life's value (or insignificance) (Kuiken, 1995). "The form of this questioning is colored by the intense distress, especially the disturbing sadness, that emerges toward the end of existential dreams" (Hartmann & Zimberoff, 2008: 42). For this reason, existential dreams in particular are followed by increased self-perceptual depth (Kuiken et al., 2006). "Like art, impactful dreams gesture toward, without capturing, something 'more'; they move the dreamer, with enlivened feeling, toward understanding" (Kuiken et al., 2006: 276).

EXTRAORDINARY DREAMS

The complexity of the dreaming self, and the tendency of dreams to expand our sense of self, occurs through the anomalous experiences that dreams bring. Krippner, Bogzaran, and de Carvalho (2002) call these *extraordinary dreams* and identified fourteen types: creative, lucid, out-of-body, pregnancy, healing, dreams within dreams, collective, telepathic, clairvoyant, precognitive, past life, initiation, spiritual, and visitation dreams. They also show the cultural standing that these dreams traditionally have had; working with extraordinary dreams is often an integral aspect of traditional cultures. For example the Mapuche Indians of Chile use clairvoyant dreams as communication between the dreamer and others. In ancient Greece, people made elaborate pilgrimages to Asclepius' temples to perform rituals and prayers in search of healing in their dreams. As more attention is given to these dreams in contemporary literature, this helps change our perception of them as being merely anomalous. Such dreams invite us to inquire deeper about the very nature of individuals. We discuss here a few of these extraordinary dreams, especially those that are linked to the multidimensionality of being.

Out-of-Body Experiences (OBEs) in dreams challenge the scientific paradigmatic assumption linking the sense of self to the physical body. Firsthand reports of OBEs show that people have a clear sense of witnessing reality as if outside the body. OBEs in dreams indicate the complexity of the dreaming self and invite inquiry to its dimensionality. Studies have shown that instances of OBE occur in sleep paralysis, when ill, lucid dreaming, or when napping (Blackmore, 1984; Green, 1968; Levitan & LaBerge, 1991). Researchers have begun to identify the brain area associated with the out-of-body feeling: stimulation of the posterior part of the superior temporal gyrus on the right side, in a patient in whom electrodes had been implanted to suppress tinnitus, produces OBE (De Ridder et al., 2007; Ehrsson, 2007). In some cases these experiences can be disorienting and/or overwhelm the waking self (Krippner et al., 2002).[3] From a phenomenological perspective, OBE shakes the materialist foundation of consciousness: what allows the dreaming body/self to observe a scene as if "from above"? Within ancient cultures (e.g., Egypt) and many Indigenous cultures (e.g., Zuni in Southwestern United States, Quiché Maya in Central America, Sambia tribe in Papua New Guinea), soul travel is a commonly held view of the dream process. Within earth-based religions, the dimensionality of the self in dreaming and its capabilities are well recorded (Krippner & Friedman, 2010; Tedlock, 1987; Moss, 2009).

Creative dreams foreground the self's innovative capacities to construct new personal narratives, engage relationships resourcefully, solve problems, and access new ideas. Perhaps creative dreams are some of the best examples of how dreaming displays its complexity and the spectrum of possibilities that open up when we pay attention to them. Several authors have discussed various historical examples and more contemporary ways in which dreams have been used creatively, for example Bogzaran (1983); Garfield (1976); Tonay (1995); Barrett (2001); Baylor & Deslauriers (1986); Krippner & Dillard (1988).

Creativity is not only a general characteristic of the dreaming mind; the problem-solving function of dreams links dreams to a more encompassing purposefulness. The dreaming mind's attention to and reworking of current concerns is not merely passive incorporation but an active and even inventive process, bringing new reframes and solutions to known problems or concerns.

Lucid Dreaming. Individuals who experience an intensification of their awareness within their dreams may start questioning their actions in the dream and eventually become lucid. First an internal dialogue emerges as a sign of heightened self-reflection within the dream. This metacognitive consciousness is the precursor of dream lucidity. Dream lucidity is characterized by the dreamer's cognizance of his or her own state while the dream experience is unfolding. This intensification of awareness is often accompanied by increased vividness and better memory of the dream experience upon awakening.

The lucid state can lead to a heightened sense of choice, with the dreamer taking charge and exploring possible avenues of doing or being within the dream. Lucid dreamers often report a more active sense of agency in shaping the storyline of the dream as it is unfolding. Full dream cognizance can bring about greater capacity for self-modulation and the opportunity to change one's attitude, feelings, or emotions. It can also alter the degree of attention that one brings to any action or image in the dreamscape. Lucid dreaming then becomes the terrain for exploration and conscious experimentation.

Lucid dream researchers and practitioners have been able to explore lucid dreaming as a laboratory for self-inquiry and explore the nature of various experiences in dreams. Paul Tholey (1990), a sport psychologist, experimented with the transformation of the dream body for the purpose of athletic enhancement. George Gillespie (1987) explored the self in relation to the experience of light. Bogzaran (1991a) examined the impact of incubation on the dreamer's choices and the influence of core religious belief on lucid dream experiences. LaBerge (1980, 1990) focused on the scientific testing of physiological changes and similarities in waking and dreaming. LaBerge (1990) also suggests a number of induction methods for preparing the dreamer in waking states by using memory-enhancing tools. In most induction methods, whether Western or Eastern, the waking self undergoes a training to learn to enhance memory and the skill of metacognition, either through various meditative practices or the use of biofeedback devices.

Perhaps lucid dreaming is one of the most accessible states of consciousness during sleep where inquiry into the phenomena of dreaming can take place. The practice of lucid dreaming allows enhancement of consciousness in waking life, thus influencing the self and its transformative capabilities (Wangyal, 1998).

DREAMS AS SPIRITUAL EXPERIENCE

Of the previously explored dream categories, transcendent, extraordinary, and some lucid dreams have greatly impressed dreamers that they have regarded them as a form of *spiritual experience*. Research in the history of dreaming shows that spiritual dreams have been an integral aspect of many cultures (Bulkeley, 1995, 2011; Krippner et al., 2002; Tedlock, 1987, 2005; Moss, 2009; Van de Castle, 1994).

In our research, we utilized a self-defined criterion, whereby spiritual dreams were those that the dreamer identified as such (Deslauriers & Bogzaran, 1994). One of the most compelling reasons that dreams have such a close link to spirituality is the fact that dreams arise spontaneously, without willful effort on the part of the dreamer. It is as if our consciousness becomes the receptacle of privileged material, without planning or premeditation. In deliberately incubated experience, dreams spontaneously and unexpectedly arise, the imagery providing creative elaboration of the dreamers' prior beliefs and conceptualizations. For example, Bogzaran (1991a) invited dreamers to incubate experiences of the Divine in their lucid dreams. She found that the lucid dream experience of the Divine reflected the dreamers' concept of the Divine. Those with a personalized view of the Divine were more likely to dream about a personalized encounter, and the converse for those with nonpersonalized views about the Divine. Nevertheless the majority of these dreams were impactful.[4]

Spiritual dreams often seem to include a feeling of intensification. For Hunt (1989), intensification is a core process that applies to many domains and can translate into a wide range of dream imagery—both negative and positive. He describes the link between spiritual dreams and various forms of intensification. Numinous or big dreams, he says, form around intensification of a felt sense of presence; in some lucid dreams, there is an intensification of awareness; in other dreams, powerful synaesthetic experiences such as light or "energetic" phenomena become the focus of intensification; or an inner sense of deep calm and perfection may be intensified, as in the dream "Perfection" in chapter 5.

By contrast, intensification of negative feelings also can lead to experiences of dream numinosity, such as when anxiety leads to nightmarish imagery. In the following passage, Harry Hunt recounts his own childhood dream experiences of a numinous felt sense, though in his case, adverse and negatively charged, yet leading to a paradoxical realization:

> When I was a kid I had very bad night terrors . . . [I] remember negative numinosities. They were infinite; they were vast and total, malevolent and evil, and they were very powerful. They were certainly the most powerful things I had ever known. . . . If I could have experiences of that magnitude that were so awful, other people could have experiences of that magnitude that were integrating and constructive. It made sense to me—that these experiences would play an incredible role in people's feeling that life was worth living. They had a crucial function in that sense. (Hunt & Belicki, 1989: n.p.)

Within certain extraordinary dreams, the multidimensionality of dreams itself becomes an important feature. Bogzaran proposed six categories for transformative spiritual experiences leading to what she calls *hyperspace lucidity*:

- Recognizable images.
- Metamorphosis, duality, archetypal images, personalized deity.

- Geometric and abstract forms.
- Experience of light.
- Unrecognizable images and events.
- Multidimensional space.

This last category itself contains four subcategories a) transformation of the dream body; b) nonlinear time; c) positive experience; d) space of nonduality/Universal Mind (Bogzaran, 1996: 44).

Similar dimensions of *hyperspace lucidity* (Bogzaran, 1996, 2003) have been described by Aurobindo as timeless and spaceless awareness connecting with self-knowledge. In Aurobindo's developmental/evolutionary framework, these experiences are linked to the manifestation of a "Supermind," which is also seen as the source to a number of transrational processes[5] (Chaudhuri, 1965; Combs, 2009).

Within dream studies, the subjective quadrant may be the most suitable to probe the vertical depth of dream experience: from frightening ego dissolution in dreams to transcendent experiences described by dreamers who explore the frontiers of the lucid mind (see also Tandan, 2009, 2011; Waggoner, 2009; and Womack, 2003, 2009).

SUMMARY

The multiplicity of dreaming experience expresses itself in the variety of dreams that we encounter, either as individuals or as part of larger collectivity. In this chapter we looked at two main poles of dreaming phenomenology: normative and prevalent dreaming on the one hand, and impactful or extraordinary dreaming on the other. An integral view must span the entire spectrum of dream experience if it is to be inclusive. Just as environmental ecology is diverse, dreams reveal patterns of the ecology of our mind.

Large samples of individual experiences disclose patterns that most of us have experienced: flying and falling dreams, examination dreams, "missing the boat" dreams, and so forth. These universal patterns are like well-known geographical formations, specific places in the psychic map that we all visit at one point or another during our life.

For its part, research on impactful dreams discloses entire regions. These are like distinct emotional ecosystems where the embodied visual and felt sense imagery clusters around certain emotions: anxiety in nightmares; agony in existential dreams; the sense of relational ineffectiveness in alienation dreams; and that of spiritual renewal or liberation in transcendent dreams.

Extraordinary and spiritual dreams are like hidden treasures in the landscape of dreams. Their nature demands that we pay attention to them, and they often prompt us to take transformative actions in our lives. These dreams may disclose aspects of experience that are no always intelligible at first. The arc of understanding may stretch over a long period of time as we revisit these dreams periodically.

Deepening the knowledge of these diverse psychic regions can help dreamers and professionals alike face the varied ecology of dreaming. The next chapter looks at the different ways that people have creatively used to explore these multifaceted landscapes.

CHAPTER SEVEN

Dreams and Self-Inquiry

To experience a dream does not automatically guarantee understanding. Dreams may well originate from the innermost self, but they often present a creative challenge to our reflective mind. Therein lies the ubiquitous question: "What does this dream mean?" This remains the most frequently asked question by dreamers all over the world. From a theoretical standpoint, this predicament calls forth an even more basic question: Do dreams convey information or meaning? While the previous chapters addressed the phenomenology of the dream experience and types of dream experiences, this chapter addresses some of the methods and strategies for exploration of dream meaning from a first-person perspective.

We can compare dreaming to the multiple roles that trees play in our life. Trees take part in the carbon cycle as they capture CO_2 and use it for their own growth. As carbon-sequesters, trees also play an important life-sustaining role for the biosphere. The same is true for dreams. The landscape of dreams, the majority of which are never remembered, are like the rainforests of the world, important for our general health by participating in the creation of new memories. Clear-cut the forest and the carbon that has been stored there is released, with potentially harmful effects. Clear-cut dreaming from our lives, as is done experimentally in REM-deprivation studies, and the human organism is quickly thrown out of emotional and physiological balance. Remembered dreams, on the other hand, are like well-harvested and well-used timber. Their variety gives rise to multiple and creative uses. They provide raw materials for building our interior habitat; they can be used to create an artful container, or be assembled into vessels that carry us toward the horizon of self-discovery. Thus, when dreams cross the threshold of our awareness (the remembered ones), they are poised to play an even greater role in our lives.

Dreaming is fastened to the multidimensional facets of our psychic life. While the waking self may be perplexed by the unique qualities of dreams, it remains firmly at the center of the meaning-making process. This process is complex, influenced by the core assumptions the dreamer holds about dreams. Self-inquiry is often oriented by the theoretical framework one consciously or implicitly embraces. For instance, *depth psychology*, the umbrella term under which we locate the many schools of thought originating with psychoanalysis (Freudian, Jungian, Object Relations, Self-Psychology, etc.), asserts that dynamic unconscious processes play a central and determining role in our lives. The unconscious patterning of human conduct from early development, or in more contemporary terms *implicit memory* (Stern, 1998), shapes not only the nature of our desires and aspirations but also our sense of self, including our moods and emotional drives. It seems natural, then, that reflecting on our dreams would prompt us to question the nature of our own desires and our habitual—and at times maladaptive—patterns of behavior or emotion.

Philosopher Owen Flanagan (2000) asserts that dreams are self-expressive: "Dreams both reflect and participate in the project of self-creation" (161). Meaning-making is thus an extension of this self-creative process; shaped by the method or practice that dreamers employ (self-discovery, therapeutic exploration, dream groups, or other creative forms of inquiry), it is also influenced by the social context of dream inquiry.

Prior to anything else, it is important to consider one's waking attitudes toward one's own dream life. A simple place to begin is to adopt an attitude of openness toward dreams. Our own experiences and our interaction with students and clients have shown how paying careful attention to the multifaceted aspects of dreaming life can attune us to our emotional states. Being present to one's experience, whether waking or dreaming, is an important skill, which can eventually lead to refining discernment in how we navigate the existential nuances of our lives.

DREAMING AND INNER LIFE

A deeper look into dream phenomenology discloses a paradoxical fact: because dreams arise from our interiority, they naturally reflect our individuality, yet they do so in a way that bypasses personal volition. Dreams are both *ours*, in that they arise within our individual consciousness, and *not ours*, since they mostly arise and unfold of their own accord. They are, as Bert States writes, "involuntary poetry" (1988).

Dreams spontaneously unfold from implicit, or unconscious, processes. They partake of the realm of the unknown—their sources are hard to trace—but they are not unknowable. They present a view of being that differs from the sense of self we are accustomed to in waking life.[1] Although dreams often provide an imaginal response to waking concerns, there often remains a disjunction between the dreaming and waking states of consciousness. This is the main reason that dreams elicit different responses from individuals. Some people are challenged by their own dreams, seeing them as nonsensical or just plain difficult to understand. Others hold dreams in high regard, using them for personal guidance before making important life decisions. If dreams were openly and categorically meaningful, they would not elicit such divergent responses. Our perception of their intrinsic value will therefore have an impact on how we approach dreams.

People's relationships toward their dreams vary widely, not only between cultures, but also within culture (Matheny, 2002). Matheny interviewed California college students, and found that people's attitudes toward dreams ranged, on the one hand, from mild puzzlement to deep appreciation, and on the other hand, from innocent neglect to purposeful disregard. Women in general seem to have a more positive attitude toward dreams than men, and they have greater dream recall (Schredl et al.,

1996). In one study, Szmigielska and Holda (2007) showed that although many dreamers claim that dreams have influenced their behavior, women were more willing to admit that dreams have influenced their actions than are men (including thinking about them, interpreting, and sharing them). Research also shows that young women and young men display the most divergence in their attitude toward dreams (with women more positive), but the gap significantly narrows with age (Schredl & Piel, 2008).

APPROACHES TO DREAM INQUIRY

Reflecting on dreams can play an important role in deciphering and discerning the emotional and relational intricacies of our lives. In disclosing aspects of our innermost conflicts, including those we wish would remain hidden from view, dreams may be chipping at the edge of self-deception. In other words, *dreams may give us an opportunity to gain a more accurate sense of ourselves.*

The act of exploring dream follows the multidimensionality of the dream experience. Deslauriers (2009) identifies four main strategies of dreamwork found cross-culturally: a dream incubation strategy, a dream understanding strategy, a dream awareness strategy and finally a performative strategy. In what follows, we seek to distill the four overarching approaches and practices found within the field of dream studies.

Dream Incubation

Dream incubation is the practice of engaging the creative and healing potential of the dreaming state, first by setting an intention prior to the dream. The practice traces a long history from antiquity and is found in many cultures around the world. Forms of incubation are also described and practiced in religious systems such as Tibetan Buddhism, Sufism, and in many Indigenous spiritual practices. Dreamers who practice incubation can do so for their own benefit, for the benefit of another individual, or for a larger communal or societal intention.

In many traditional cultures, dreams are understood as a sacred space, distinct from waking, where communing with another world or reality is said to occur. From a modern perspective, this special "space" becomes associated either with the unconscious or the creative mind. Incubation is predicated on intention, as a way to prepare oneself to encounter that space with awareness. Setting an intention is a skillful way to focus the mind on a particular issue, to gather attention or "call forth" certain possibilities. Ancient rituals involved sleeping in a particular setting, such as in or around a temple or natural setting (Meier, 1989; Van de Castle, 1994; Moss, 2009) situated close to where the land was known to bestow healing. Thus, a potentiating connection was made not only with unseen spiritual agency, but also by communing with the forces known to dwell within a particular place.[2]

Contemporary studies on dream incorporation have shown that dreams do indeed integrate dreamers' current concerns (Nielsen & Powell, 1992). Phenomenological reports from our students also show that dream incubation amplifies dream life, especially when done within the context of a personal growth practice, such as psychotherapy, ceremony, or a dream group. Whether or not a dream provides an answer to the incubation focus, the intention itself establishes a central point of convergence around which dream imagery and the accompanying feelings and emotions play themselves out. In this way, incubation sets the stage for how the dreamer will attend to his or her dreams at a later time.

Dream Understanding

Metaphorical Self-Mapping and Dream Narrativization

Dreamers often face a common dilemma. Those who pay attention to their dreams know that some dreams offer a potential source of meaning, but that meaning is often unclear. Ullman (1969) was one of the first to draw attention to dream imagery not as symbols but as live metaphors. Following this core idea, Baylor and Deslauriers (1987) linked the process of dream understanding to metaphorical mapping. They show that, inasmuch as dreamers were able to pair the dream images with personal memories, sometimes amplifying them with associations embedded in cultural patterns, they felt they understood the dream.

The process of metaphorical mapping is best served by asking the dreamer where the image has relevance in his or her life. This self-inquiry implies a more fundamental process we call *narrativization*: the practice of making the dream part of the dreamer's life, such as answering the query, "why did I have this dream at this particular time in my life?" Dreams are refracted through the context of the dreamer's life around the time of the dream. The process of narrativization not only connects the dream to the present situation, but also retrospectively (by looking at the potential causes or sources of the dreams) or even prospectively, in looking forward to what is to come in the near future. Knudson (2001) has shown that people often have impactful dreams, but they fail to understand why they had that dream. The impact of the dream does not necessarily generate meaning, unless some link can be made between dreaming and waking life. We explore here some of the main ways of connection.

Modes of Dream Understanding

Multiple approaches can be of help in the process of dream understanding; those presented here categorized under self-inquiry, dyadic engagement, Dream Group Practice, dream reentry, and dream embodiment. Each set of practices is associated with particular intentions.

Self-inquiry As the name implies, self-inquiry refers to those practices that the dreamer undertakes alone. Self-inquiry presupposes some diligence, both in committing dreams to memory (e.g., through journaling) and in attempting to discover their meaning through reflection. Self-inquiry, such as Active Imagination (Jung, 1974), Focusing (Gendlin, 1986), Expressive Dream Art (Bogzaran, 1990a), Dreambody work (Mindell, 1982), Dream Indwelling (Deslauriers, 2004), and Dream Tending (Aizenstat, 2009), are mainly noninterpretative (described in more detail in chapter 13). They assist the dreamer in making sense of the dream by tracking feelings and associations in a nondirective manner. This stance shares some similarities with free association, in that it follows what naturally arises in the awareness of the dreamer. But it differs from it in that it does not rely on the interpretative framework that is the hallmark of psychoanalysis.

Self-inquiry practices rely on the organic process of allowing meaning to arise on its own, following the natural rhythms of the dreamer. These practices assume that the dreamer functions well and has the capacity to work with the material presented by the dream in a nondefensive manner. Self-inquiry does not present any intersubjective "corrective" (the presence of another to mirror our own shortcomings), and as such, it assumes that the dreamer can bear witness to his or her own psychic life. It presumes a readiness on the part of the dreamer to face the messages that the dream discloses. For that reason, self-inquiry requires a certain level of psychological maturity. These practices appear simple at first, but just as in meditation, their simplicity belies their potency. Their transformative power resides in the dreamer's capacity to be intensely engaged in the dream while retaining the ability to witness and track his or her inner process.

Dyadic engagement Dyadic work consists of sustained engagement between two people: a dreamer with another person, often in the role of psychotherapist or dream specialist. Dreams have remained a major avenue for self-exploration in depth psychology beginning with Freud and psychoanalysis, and continuing with C. G. Jung and the analytical and archetypal schools; in existential and humanist psychotherapy; and now in cognitive behavioral therapy with the work of Clara Hill (2004).

Even though popular imagination still expects the therapist to act in the role of the interpreter, there has been a shift toward the therapist being a facilitator of insight in the spirit of collaboration and exchange (Bonime, 1986; 1989). Dyadic engagement presents the advantage of working with someone with a more dispassionate perspective on the dream, who may be less prone to defensive responses to challenging imagery. Dreams that are brought in the therapy setting frequently deal with the therapy process itself: the initial dreams shared, transference and countertransference dreams, dreams that announce the end of therapy. Therapists, at the request of clients, may use one or more sessions to elucidate a single dream.

Crook Lyon and Hill (2004) attempted to know more about the clients' perspectives on working with dreams during ongoing psychotherapy. They found that those who present dreams in therapy are more likely to remember their dreams, value them, or have therapists who encourage them to talk about their dreams. The most helpful dream activities occurring in therapy were rated in descending order as follows: 1) interpreting the dream as being related to one's current waking life issues; 2) helping the dreamer come to his or her own interpretation of the dream; 3) encouraging the client to make associations with dream images; 4) the therapist telling the client what he or she thought the dream meant; 5) working with the client to develop and implement ways to make necessary life changes on the basis of what he or she learned from the dream; 6) encouraging the client to reexperience feeling in the dreams; and 7) suggesting changes the client could make on the basis of what he or she learned from the dream.

Dream Group Practice Dream Group Practice invites the dreamer to share and explore his or her dream with the support of a group. It can either involve doing self-exploration in the presence of others (Gestalt therapy dream group done in a "fish bowl" fashion) or having the group members directly take on the dream in the presence of the dreamer (e.g., Ullman's Dream Appreciation group). Being in a group brings a set of social dynamics that are absent in self or dyadic work, including issues of trust, social fairness, or the management of individual preferences. Dream Group Practice encourages particular patterns of interaction, such as self-disclosure, projection toward or from group members, and acting out the dream within the group.

Dream Group Practice became popular in the 1970s and 1980s through five main approaches: Gestalt therapy (Perls, 1992), process work (Mindell, 1982), social dreaming (Lawrence, 2005), Dream Appreciation technique (Ullman, 1996), and Projective Approach to Dreams (Taylor, 1992). The first two are psychotherapeutic techniques in which the dream is put to the service of therapeutic outcomes, whereas the last three focus on dream understanding independent of psychotherapeutic work. Although all these methods can bring about insights, these last three do not require the kind of meticulous follow-through that characterizes therapeutic intervention.

Dream Group Practices have been adopted in a variety of settings: schools, churches, prisons, and even the workplace. In the projective methods, individual group members are asked to take on another member's dream as if it were his or her own and then share their personal projections about that dream (Taylor, 1992; Ullman, 1996; Ullman & Zimmerman, 1979). Reflecting on the dream and what it could mean for each member helps widen the original dreamer's associations and insights. The dreamer is then invited to comment on the dream with the participants' input in mind, and an interactive discussion ensues. We will continue a more in-depth discussion of relational practices in the next chapter.

Dream reentry Dream reentry is the practice of reexperiencing the dream in waking life, often in a meditative or trancelike state, to facilitate an immersion in the dream content. Dream reentry involves the dreamer's active participation, reinvesting in the dream by bringing the dream back in present awareness in order to activate a level of vividness and immediacy that approaches the original dream experience. By reliving the dream in the waking state, the dreamer is able to revisit choices at any point within the dream and pursue creative and alternative avenues of plot unfolding. Dream reentry can be done as part of self-inquiry, or in dyadic or group settings. Dream reentry practices can take place in a variety of modalities, either verbal, for example, guided visualization (Kaplan-Williams, 1991; Olsen, 1999); hypnotic (Barrett, 2004); contemplative meditation (Deslauriers, 2004); or nonverbal, for example, dream reentry with drum (Bogzaran, 1991b; Moss, 1996). In Part III, dream reentry is presented in more detail as a part of Integral Dream Practice.

Dream embodiment Dream embodiment is a dream practice method that originated with Gestalt therapy, itself deriving from the earlier technique of psychodrama. The dreamer is asked to embody a dream image, to *become* it, and, when appropriate, to engage in a dialogue with it or with other aspects of the dream. This practice necessitates that the dreamer track his or her reactions in the present time while imagining the dream's continued unfolding, not merely projecting (verbally) what the character or object would hypothetically do or feel. Somatically, this practice entails cultivating presence, paying attention to the feelings, thoughts, and emotions welling up during the enactment. This form of practice can have an effect of bridging the distance between the "I" (as the primary center of experience) and the dream figures and entities.

By asking the dreamer to embody the different characters in a dream, embodiment expands perspective awareness: the "I" in play gets to feel the world from the perspective of what is being enacted. Dreamers report that they become close to dream images and get fresh insights into how their life encompasses various perspectives. Because in the dream narrative, dialectic of divergent forces is often present, it is not uncommon for the perspective of one actor to clash with that of another. In the famous Gestalt hot seat exercise, these opposing aspects enter into dialogue. The dreamer has the chance to explore how such conflict actually lives within him or her. Enacting a dream energizes the feeling tone of the dream, leading to an amplification of the emotional charge within the dream. This practice can contribute to the transformative power of the dream. We consider this an advanced practice and recommend that such enactment be done with an experienced facilitator—though we have witnessed graduate students do this work on their own with success by following clear directives.

DREAM AWARENESS STRATEGY

Both dream incubation and dream understanding, including dream reentry, offer a participatory avenue for the dreamer. Incubation is done before the dream occurs, while dream understanding takes place after the dream was dreamt. In contrast, in lucid dreaming the dreamer brings awareness to his or her state of consciousness *during* the dreaming process. This is the most direct way to engage with dreams, considering that becoming lucid in a dream putatively opens the dreamer to a richer array of choices. At first, the sense of waking within a dream is often exhilarating. Usually, at that point dream vividness increases and emotions open to modulation. In dreamers for whom this is a new experience, it is not uncommon for them to awaken shortly after becoming lucid.

Phenomenological reports show that dream lucidity is not always consistent throughout the entire duration of the dream. It resembles the sense of lucidity that we bring to waking consciousness. We may display it for a moment, only to be reabsorbed into the flow of our experience in the next moment, returning to an unreflective state where we do not question the state of consciousness we are in.

The dream awareness strategy is often seen as an advanced practice in Buddhist (Wangyal, 1998) and Indigenous contexts (Peters, 2004; Tedlock, 2004). The skills associated with the awareness strategy are often kept secret and subject only to person-to-person transmission.[3] The goals and intentions connected to the awareness strategy are also informed by philosophical or spiritual beliefs of particular spiritual traditions. In the modern West, the awareness strategy connected with the practice of lucid dreaming has borrowed heavily from non-Western traditions.

PERFORMATIVE STRATEGY: BEHAVIORAL, RITUAL, AND ARTISTIC EXPRESSION

The performative strategy, also referred to as the "enactive strategy" (Deslauriers, 2009), refers to practices that change the dream's focus from the mental/interior sphere to that of embodied actions. It includes but is not restricted to: dream enactment, ritual, the expressive arts, and other ways of expressing the dreams such as is found in the dream art movement (Bogzaran, 1991a; Mellick, 1996; Tonay 1995). It also includes the practice of taking concrete actions based on one's dream (Johnson, 1986).

An integral approach to dreams values the creative potential of both dreams and art as reciprocal and reinforcing practices. A psychological state induced in a dream may be revisited and changed via artistic expression, especially if it pertains to questions of self-representation and meaning. Because the performative strategy approaches dreams in a way that connects to art making, the psychological focus can be momentarily set aside to engage in a direct, nonlinguistic expression of imaginal forms.

Art is created for a multitude of reasons: to experiment with a particular aesthetic; to play with spontaneity; to access a degree of creative freedom that can find expression in poetry, painting, and other forms of artistic manifestation; and to represent spiritual dimensions that cannot be captured by language. Sometimes the dream image provides the first spark, the founding concept, or the liberating "ah-ha." From that point of departure, the artistic process takes on a life of its own. An initial idea from a dream can become the source of a series of paintings, an entire play, a poem, or a song.

When using creative modalities within a psychological context, the art is created, inasmuch as possible, with a nonjudgmental, noninterpretative frame of mind, setting aside one's inner critic. We learn about ourselves not only by the fruits of creation but also through the act of creating, which brings about its own awareness. The contribution to the artistic approach to an *Integral Dream Practice* will be explored in more depth in Part III.

Example of a Performative Practice: Body Mapping

Body mapping, a practice that we have been using for a number of years, consists of drawing the dream imagery on top of a body contour traced from the actual body of the dreamer. This expressive arts practice involves dream imagery with an emphasis on the felt sense, connecting the dream image to the somatic experience. Two registers of images (that of the dream and that of the body) are explored in relation to each other in visual form. This practice engages the link between body processes, including physical symptoms and body-based dream imagery. Because the linkage is not always obvious, this practice asks dreamers to track the felt sense of each image through guided reentry before they express it on paper. The final product opens new forms of aesthetic and symbolic expression that highlight energetic movement or blockage in relationship to particular somatic processes. The actual map can emphasize one aspect of the body while other areas of the map might remain blank; this often reveals insights into how we inhabit our own physical body. Thus, this dream practice can aid in bridging cognitive and somatic insights.

SUMMARY

Dreams are first and foremost occasions of experience, and dream imagery can be the source of powerful insights. Those who pay attention to their dreams learn to cherish the special kind of information they disclose. The impact and exploration of a dream can eventually translate into deeper self-knowledge. As a result, insights, creative acts, and new perspectives inspired by dreams can increase self-perceptual depth and shape the contours of our waking life.

In all these ways, dreams become an integral part of the self-creating process and have a role in the act of self-knowing and self-transformation. The subjective exploration of dream meaning is best done within an atmosphere of self-acceptance.

Numerous inquiry methods conjure up the subjective dimensions of dreaming. Four main strategies for the self-exploration methods were outlined: dream incubation, dream understanding, dream awareness, and a performative or expressive strategy. These strategies and the methods they offer can point to the depth of inner experience and help dreamers to bring together their inner life with the world as they experience it. Used judiciously, these methods can approximate the multidimensionality of subjective experience in dreaming. Insights gained with one particular experiential strategy can be integrated to another strategy, forming "thick" meaning-making threads. While this chapter outlined a model for subjective methods of dream exploration, Part III presents a detailed discussion of methodology and discusses the philosophical underpinnings of an Integral Dream Practice.

This chapter completes the exploration of the subjective "I" quadrant that we began in chapter 5. In the following two chapters we examine the intersubjective dimensions of dreaming life.

CHAPTER EIGHT

Dreams and Intersubjectivity

Neuroscience and psychology relegate dreaming to the interior realm: a state of self-generated brain activity and one of the last refuges of the untamed psyche. Dreams spontaneously display the complexities of our internal life and reveal the wide spectrum of our individuality. This depiction may well be accurate, but it is also incomplete, as it is based on a narrative that positions the interior self against the exterior world, the social and cultural circumstances within which the self is embedded. By putting attention mostly on the individual and private aspects of dreaming, one often fails to see how dreaming stems from relational and communal life. The next two chapters attempt to redress this imbalance.

INTERSUBJECTIVITY

Intersubjectivity is the dynamic field that is produced and enacted when one's "interior" self encounters another's. Just like a magnetic field, intersubjectivity (the relational space) is essentially invisible, though its effects are far reaching. A meeting between two or more persons creates a relational dynamic that shifts and moves along with the actors who participate in it. When we relate to others, we actively partake in the creation of an interpersonal field and at the same time are also influenced by it. Intersubjectivity is a vast domain of potentiality, where meaning can be constructed, exchanged, transmitted, imposed, hidden, or even denied. When two or more individuals meet, the opportunity exists for one or both to be transformed through their interaction.

A complex exchange exists between our sense of self, as experienced "from within," and the social milieu in which we are embedded. Connections are constantly developing between our being and those with whom we form "interbeing" relationships: spouses, lovers, parents, friends, enemies, acquaintances, and even strangers with whom we may have short but intense contact. The scope of the intersubjective domain further extends to work relationships, peer groups, and other affiliations, to wherever we experience the sense of "we-ness."

In his seminal writings on integral psychology, Chaudhuri (as cited in Shirazi, 2001) suggests that relational selfhood is an important basis of self-knowing and realization: through intimate contact with others, we get to know ourselves. Within interpersonal relationships, we gain knowledge of who we are through the mirror of the ones we love. For healthy adults, intimacy and close personal relationships are major avenues of self-growth.

For better or for worse, early interactions with those who nurtured us influence how we encounter the world—for instance, they shape how much we trust others and ourselves. Longitudinal research suggests that early nurturing and warmth have long-lasting positive effects on mental health well into adulthood (Maselko et al., 2010). Similarly, failures in early attunement and bonding between mother and infant result in attachment styles that are ambivalent or avoidant, also impacting our relationship patterns. These relational and attachment patterns also appear in our dreams. In what follows, we explore how dreams intersect with the world of "we-ness."

Relational issues take on an important place within an integral approach to dream formation and, by extension, to dream understanding. There exists, of course, a relational field *within* interiority as we interact with dream figures and people within the inner plane of dreams. This interior relationality closely mirrors the importance of relationships in waking life. When dreams move outside the realm of interiority and enter the relational field, as when dreams are shared with another person or a group, a whole set of phenomena occur. We discuss both aspects in turn.

THE MATRIX OF SELF-ORGANIZATION

In chapters 3 and 4, we have seen how dreams unfold as a self-creative and self-organizing process. This process of self-organization, however, is finely tuned to the milieu we inhabit. The social sphere we occupy is in constant movement, and dreams convert these complex social emotions into visual images. The fluid imagery in dreams is continuously revising perceptions of the self or of others. In an intricate manner, these changing perceptions result from our interactions with others and, in turn, dream content can sensitize and shape the contours of the relationships we have with others in waking life.

Complexity theory exhorts us to move beyond simple either/or polarities (e.g., self/other or nature/culture). The "we" that lives in me, as well as the various "I"s that form the "us," mutually form and inform each other. Hence, dreaming contains *both* personal (intrasubjective) and shared (intersubjective and relational) aspects. When viewed relationally, dreams appear to *demarcate psychological boundaries*: their existence establishes the threshold connecting inner and outer life. The pervasive social contents in dreams lead us to believe that they play an important role in metabolizing our relational experiences. For Kahn and Hobson (2005) dreams help prepare us for social encounters in our waking life. Dreaming helps us refine a Theory of Mind (that is, our ability to surmise and foresee the intentions of others), which is essential to survival in a social species such as ours. The social nature of dreaming life may help us attune to the feelings of others just as it does to our own.

The integral perspective puts a special emphasis on the developing self. As we gain maturity, we become more conscious of the formative importance of our relational experiences—the reciprocity that is intrinsically embedded in the give-and-take of intersubjectivity. When we begin to inquire into why certain patterns repeat in dreaming, this can lead us to ask similar questions about the nature of recurring relational patterns in waking life. By extension, it is not uncommon that people who work with their own dreams develop intimation of the dreamlike and fluid nature of waking relationships.

Furthermore, when we pay attention to the intersubjective nature of dreaming, we may become more aware of the following:

- Dream content is influenced by our waking relationships to others, and by our participation in cultural institutions. These are the staging ground for countless common agreements and enactments that define who we are and the common reality we share (Schweder, 1991, speaks of these in terms of intentional reality). Dreams partly reflect back to us this cultural or intentional reality.

- Learned patterns of relating to others form an implicit knowledge that is often made explicit in dreams. Therapeutic relationships that focus on dreams can be a source of awareness, helping to reveal and eventually heal ineffectual relational patterns.

- Empathy and emotional attunement are important factors that enhance the effectiveness of working with dreams, both in groups and in therapeutic dyads. Depth of disclosure varies according to the contexts of dream telling, the safety of the group, or emotional resonance of the group field.

- Sociocultural factors can either encourage or discourage people to inquire into their dreams. Shared assumptions and cultural beliefs about the role of dreams shape the manner in which we engage in dream practices. Exploring dreams, either in the therapeutic dyad or in dream groups, draws upon the cultural expectations that shape that encounter.

DESIRING, RELATING, FEELING, DREAMING

In the last few decades, understanding of intersubjectivity, with its essential therapeutic function, has gained recognition in modern schools of psychotherapy. An important difference between relational theory and traditional psychoanalysis resides in their contrasting theories of motivation. Freudian theory proposes that human beings are motivated by sexual and aggressive drives. These drives are biologically rooted and innate and, as such, are somewhat impervious to change. Within the psychoanalytic tradition of the last few decades, theoretical currents have emerged that incorporate relational issues. They posit that the primary motivation is to be in relationship with others. Viewed intersubjectively, other motivations also shift from being solely personal to being also relational. Impulses and desires are fundamental, but satisfaction is obtained mostly through or with relating to others.

Within relational psychoanalysis, early relationships with primary care givers play a crucial role in shaping one's expectations about how one's needs are met. Several working hypotheses, found in the theories of object relations (Fairbairn, 1952; Ogden, 2005), self psychology (Fosshage, 1997; Kohut, 1977), or relational psychoanalysis (Stern, 1985; Stolorow et al., 1987) describe how early relationships shape the self and form patterns of relating. These theories follow the basic premise of attachment theory that those with whom we create initial attachment bonds, beginning with parents and primary caretakers, significantly contribute to who we are.

In psychotherapy, the intersubjective space is understood in terms of the relational dimensions that shape the contours of the therapeutic encounter (Lichtenberg et al., 2002). Intersubjectivity in psychotherapy is often viewed in terms of transference or countertransference, that is, the way in which relational patterns are reenacted and how relational needs are expressed between the therapist and client. The nature of the therapeutic relationship between analyst and client is thus an important factor in the client's progress and healing.

Understood relationally, psychopathology arises when individuals attempt to recreate early relationship patterns within ongoing relationships, even when the latter have little or nothing to do with the former. This recreation of relational patterns serves to satisfy the individual's needs in a way that conforms to early patterning (Fosshage, 1997). Intersubjective therapy focuses on relational issues such as trust, control, loss, transparency, dependency, autonomy, and intimacy. A principal therapeutic goal is to "work through" these potentially distressing features within the client's emotional world, in relationship with others (Stern et al., 1998).

Viewing dreams from an intersubjective perspective, we begin to notice that dreams inform us about how we inhabit relationships. We see that *dreams mirror not only how we are as people, but also how we are in relation to the world around us*. This becomes particularly apparent when we attend to the emotional dimensions of dreams. Insights derived from exploring dreams create the possibility for personal and relational healing; in other words, they can allow us to move beyond unhealthy or restrictive attachment patterns learned early in life

In dreams, emotional issues are portrayed in vivid details. Intersubjective psychoanalysis, enactive psychology, and neuroscience seem to agree on the general role of emotions in human development. Our sense of self emerges, to some extent, out of interpersonal attunement, which occurs in part through emotional resonance with another. This attunement is a dance between self and others, each entraining the other to meet emotional needs—one's own, the other's, and those of the relationship (Lyons-Ruth et al., 1998). Correlated as it is to high activation of the limbic system, REM dreaming can be seen as the creative counterpart to this emotional attunement.

> Emotionality is a different *kind* of sensory capacity, supplementary and integrative. The limbic brain relies on information supplied by the traditional inroads of perception, but it converts these data into a higher-order experience that goes beyond a catalogue of visual, auditory or tactile qualities. The emotional whole—love's bottom line—is more than the sum of its sensory parts. . . . Emotionality lifts our experience and gives it depth, suddenly it matters what another person feels. (Lewis et al., 2000: 154–155)

The process of self-perceptual depth (Kuiken & Nielsen, 1996) takes on a deeper dimension when applied to the relational domain. In particular, the ways we inhabit our relationships in the dream can sensitize us to particular waking relational patterns. Some of our nightly dreams may leave significant cognitive and emotional imprints. Later, by attending to them with awareness, dreams acquire an enhanced life. Emotions that have surfaced spontaneously during the dream are felt *anew*, and become available for further exploration. We have the chance to *reexperience* the dream emotions, discover their waking relational context, and explore their ramifications.

> The creative process of dreaming generates the meaning that can be deployed to life and relationships in the outside world. This means that all of external relationships have a certain transference quality, that they derive meaning from what exists in our internal world. (Meltzer, 1984/2009: 46)

As part of the retelling and reliving the dream, we attune to our feelings or become reacquainted with them and the meaningfulness our emotions give to our relationship. For Meltzer, "the poetry of the dream . . . gives formal representations to the passions which are the meaning of our experience so that they may be operated upon by reason" (1984–2009: 47).

Dream exploration is a powerful means to develop a finely tuned awareness of emotional patterns. Dream awareness facilitates the observation of our own emotional life: how we allow (or disallow) certain emotions to unfold, crest, and eventually recede. In doing so, we notice their energizing effects on the self, others, and possibly relationships. We can also explore how to transform negative emotions, how to heal or abandon negative relational patterns.

DREAM SHARING AND INTERSUBJECTIVITY

One of the most common ways to explore dreams is to share them with others in private sessions or in groups. Dream sharing is a special form of self-disclosure. In her study on dream telling in American society, Mary Dombeck found that sharing dreams provides a dynamic case for social interactions and the search for meaning. Her research among psychotherapists shows that people are keenly sensitive to the contexts of dream telling. "For the therapists interviewed, having dreams was understood to be a way to know oneself and telling dreams was a way to show oneself. Beliefs about dream telling reflected beliefs about personhood and about the way people were accustomed to show themselves" (1991: 193).

Cultural norms influence intersubjective dream exploration in a variety of ways. First are the unspoken (implicit) agreements, socioculturally meditated, enabling shared communication between dreamers, or between client and therapist. Second, the viewpoints each participant holds about dreams will influence the intersubjective field that brings dreams as a focus of interaction. Third, the attitudes toward the types of experiences portrayed in dreams—interpersonal realms such as sexuality, spirituality, aggression, identity, transparency, and creativity—will play an important role in intersubjective dream exploration. Finally, culture shapes the common expectations about what is supposed to happen when a dream is shared.

There exists a commonsense notion that dreams reveal intimate aspects of our life. As a result, unspoken norms often prevail when consulting others about dreams. These dictate how, and to whom, dreams should be properly disclosed. Culture norms inform the relational context in which "real" dream sharing is done, in contrast to more superficial social interactions. Those we trust to tell our dreams not only reflect personal preferences but also cultural norms that shape what we come to expect from dream sharing. Traditional Indigenous cultures (Irwin, 1996, 2001; Tedlock, 1987), contemporary subcultures (the professional therapeutic subculture, for instance), and some familial cultures (Taub-Bynum, 1985) encourage dream sharing under certain conditions only.

When one tells a dream, multiple levels of meaning are simultaneously at play. The first realm of meaning in a verbal exchange is semantic—the translation of a dream content into spoken words. This level refers to our immediate understanding of what happened in the dream when we "get the dream right." Shared linguistic rules apply to dream telling so that the listeners immediately can grasp the dream, so that no matter how inexplicable, we can readily understand the dream story.

This level engages the same expectation about verbal sharing that applies in everyday interaction. As a result the listener can form an inner picture of the "dream-as-told." Even if they don't know what the dream may be *about,* we understand the dream as it was formulated and reported.

Insights may arise from dream sharing, however, the intersubjective space (in therapy, dream group or sharing with another individual) becomes a *place of inquiry*: if meaning is yet to be ascribed, together the dreamer with the support of the other(s) coalesce around some of the multiple possibilities of understanding offered for the dream. The dreamer and the relational *other* often are joined in an attempt, through various linguistic and nonlinguistic approaches, to locate the meaning of the dream for the dreamer (and in some cases for the others in the group as well).

Walter Bonime (1989) writes that

> constituting the base for collaboration in the clinical setting are two sets of information: the patient's and the therapist's. Through communication, empathy and memory, the two people seek *as high a correlation as possible* of their respective information and speculations about the patient's experience (including affect) and what it may reflect about his or her personality. (345, italics in original)

As a basic requirement of such collaborative and sensitive work with dreams, Bonime identifies the quality of awareness of the therapist, specifically the "most continuous possible concentrated attention" (345).

In dream groups, sharing a dream opens up the intersubjective space where others are invited to enter into the dreamer's inner realm. Since the layers of dream meaning are not transparent, they often necessitate amplification of the emotional content or feeling tone of the dream, based on particular associative elements, such as metaphorical significance. Interpretations or reflection may also be informed by psychological theories or folk knowledge. More likely, by actively engaging deeper levels of meaning, dream sharing becomes part of a co-created act of self-revelation (Deslauriers & Cordts, 1995).

QUALITIES OF INTERSUBJECTIVITY IN DREAM GROUPS

Dream sharing in groups can lead to the creation of a unique intersubjective space. Encounters with others stimulate inquiry and deeper exploration. Complex cycles of reciprocal exchange typically unfold. The dreamer's willingness to experience and to discover creates an opening for the input of others. For the *other*, such as in Ullman's Dream Appreciation group, the dream can become a screen for constructive projection offered safely to the dreamer. Many types of dream groups utilize this natural process of projection, a deliberate and agreed-upon procedure that Ullman referred as *play* (verbal communication). This projective technique gives structure to the intersubjective exploration of the dream, while allowing a measure of psychological safety for all involved. Since group members are speaking from within the perspective of their own experience, the object is not to get the dream right, but rather to explore the authentic response of various group members to the dream. As the associative material gathered by the group is respectfully offered, the dreamer is then free to respond in whatever ways feel relevant.

In deciphering meaning, the various perspectives offered collectively by the dream group express the multidimensionality of interpretation and reflection. For example, sharing a dream about losing a tooth can open a dialogue revealing such concerns as loss of a positive self-image. Since losing a tooth happens without volition, it may also bring up feelings of a lack of control. The image of the lost tooth can also be a metaphor for transition, pointing not only to the possibility of growth, but also indicating a need to face issues of decline and decay. Since tooth-falling dreams are a known *culture pattern dream* (Kilborne, 1981), it may also open a dialogue around how one's own ancestral culture views certain dreams (Deslauriers, 2011).

It is not uncommon for divergent perspectives to surface through the practice of dream sharing. The associative material can, on the surface, appear contradictory but often, even contradictory views benefit the dreamer. In Ullman's dream group (1984), after the dreamer has shared the dream and the group has completed the projective play on the dream image, the dreamer is then asked to contemplate these reflections in light of recent experience. For example, the dreamer is encouraged to share why, in his or her opinion, the dream took place at this particular time in his or her life. The dreamer offers additional personal material that helps create a context for the metaphorical suggestions made by the group. Through skillful questions and attunement, the group can help the dreamer assimilate the dream as an understandable event within his or her life. In that way, the dream group becomes the creative vehicle that supports the dreamer in moving the storying process further along. This exploration is central to how a dream group can be of benefit to the dreamer. Reciprocally, the dreamer's experience can touch others in the group in ways that often expresses the quality of group wisdom.

Sometimes a dream may bring up painful material or memories that cause the dreamer to psychologically shut down. Shutting down translates into internally turning away, closing oneself off from knowing more. Resistance and/or defensive attitudes associated with pain avoidance can prompt the dreamer to erect strong boundaries. Shutting down can infuse the intersubjective space with a sense of suffering or a pervading feeling of fear that limits self-perception. These moments call for empathic responses and careful attunement with the dreamer.

DREAMS AS AN ORGANIZING FACTOR IN GROUP INTERACTIONS

We have observed that while the dreamer is often energized by the group's projective suggestions, the group may, in addition, become a place for relational reenactment of the dream. For example, sharing a dream image such as losing a tooth may call into question vulnerabilities and insecurities of the dreamer, and the process of sharing in itself may become a source of anxiety. In the same vein, the group can become the place where these anxieties are overcome with the support of others. In moments such as these, the dream ceases being only text, and becomes an organizing principle for the group process—a strange attractor for social interactions. For example, a dreamer shares a dream about an intrusion into her physical space. Unbeknown to its members, the group gradually takes on, in the eyes of the dreamer, the role of a "perpetrator" especially if sharing momentarily threatens the safety and boundaries of the dreamer. With proper awareness, we can become attuned to the way dreams become an organizing principle of waking reality. In this way, dream groups can become a fertile ground for relational insights. With proper facilitation, a beneficial enactment of dream imagery can become a powerful source of insight.

Sharing dreams can constellate in the group the same palpable qualities as appeared in the dream; this process can be understood through the perspective of archetype as an organizing principle (Conforti, 2003). Archetypal non-interpretive praxis such as advocated by Hillman (1997) shies away from intellectual amplification of archetype. Rather it encourages the dreamer to see the world *through the eyes* of the dream: to become sensitized to the sudden qualities that emerge within the intersubjective field when a dream is shared.

The following dream of one of the authors, shared with colleagues, exemplifies how dreams can be a social conduit for communication about relational issues.

Anger Virgin

> I had a dream in which I met someone who was an *anger virgin*.
>
> It was not the appearance of this person, nor what she did in the dream, that was of importance. What really mattered was the fact that this person withheld acting on her anger in the same way that one would practice sexual abstinence. Just as a virgin would experience sexual feelings yet not act upon them, this *anger virgin* was clearly feeling upset but could not allow

herself to express her anger. In both cases, they would be considered a virgin.

Following are his reflections: I (Deslauriers) had this dream on the eve of an important meeting that I was to facilitate with colleagues. I knew that a member of our group needed to clear an interpersonal issue that had been simmering for many months. I began the meeting by sharing my dream. My colleagues knew of my interest and work with dreams, so beginning with my dream was a way to creatively speak to this tense situation. As facilitator of the group, I had been concerned all week about how our meeting would unfold, knowing that a confrontation was imminent. Although I had a suspicion that the person in question might be dealing with unresolved anger, we did not address the issue directly prior to the dream. Therefore, when shared, the dream was a gift, not only to me, but to the entire group as well. I shared it in the hope that it would help us open collectively to the implicit tension inside the group.

As it turned out, the group had to confront the unresolved issue and in the process, an angry outburst did occur. Although this anger was appropriate and properly directed, it was a departure from more polite but superficial interactions. At that moment, the dream image ceased to be mine; it became clear to all of those present that we had lost our "virginity" as a group in regard to the expression of anger. Fortunately, the outburst led to a needed, and more truthful, reconciliation. The dream, exemplifying the interpersonal dynamic at play, was not only useful for me but also, once shared with the group, it became (somewhat humorously) a clear representation of our group process.

SUMMARY

Intricately connected to our sense of self, dreaming is an experience that de facto arises within a relational and cultural context. Dreams are simultaneously an expression of the "I"—expressed in part by the dream ego—and the "we"—the social matrix of inner experience arising within us. An integral perspective on dreaming acknowledges and celebrates the relational and intersubjective factors that come into play in dream formation and dream understanding. Combined with the organismic and subjective dimensions of dreaming, the intersubjective space that characterizes relationships is one of the main essential creative sources of our dream life. It is a pervasive aspect, even if implicit, of all dream telling. The next chapter takes a closer look at how dreams speak to our relational concerns within the broader frame of culture.

CHAPTER NINE

Culture, Ecology, and Identity

CULTURE AND THE SHIFTING SELF

An integral perspective recognizes that the self is in part bounded by various forms of identity (e.g., ethnic, cultural, gender, or professional). Far from fixed, these identities are in a constant state of transformation. We have seen in the previous chapter how dreams relate to the interpersonal and relational world. In this chapter, we explore how intersubjectivity is further shaped by cultural attitudes that are enacted *within* relational life. For example, childrearing practices, which vary widely across cultures, shape how a child understands the intersubjective space that permeates a particular society.[1]

When the sense of self and cultural norms align, a proper sense of belonging develops. But what happens when there is disharmony between the two? Tensions and conflicts are likely to arise between self and others, and these can become a source of stress, or even worse, of alienation. How do dreams mediate these processes? How does our sense of belonging connect to our individual flourishing? How is the process of individuation supported within community-oriented cultures?

It is known that the concept of the self varies widely *across* cultures. Nowadays people face new challenges in their cultural identity, as the boundaries between cultures become gradually more fluid in a globally interconnected world. Perhaps a shared planetary awareness, with a corresponding expanded sense of self, is in process of being formed, but the course is not always smooth for all involved (a case given in the next chapter further illustrates this). Furthermore, evolving notions of self vary widely across generations *within* the same culture. Children's allegiance to their cultural roots may differ from that of their parents, possibly placing younger generations at odds with previous ones. When teaching abroad, as well as within the US, it is not uncommon to witness participants encountering intergenerational or intercultural conflicts.

Since views of the self differ between cultures, one should also be sensitive to the use of particular dream inquiry methods across cultures. Confusion can arise when methods are used cross-culturally. Cross-cultural dreamwork requires heightened sensitivity to particular cultural contexts in relation to dream awareness. An East-West education in dream awareness has taught us to value the cultures we are encountering: not only communicating the scientific and phenomenological approaches to dreams to those who are interested in them, but making a priority to ask participants to bring forth their cultural and ancestral perspectives as well. Ancestral and cultural viewpoints have too often been regarded dismissively as "folklore" not only in the West but everywhere where Western influence has a strong foothold. However, these views contain valuable cultural knowledge and wisdom, deserving an open and appreciative stance.

Respect for cultural diversity entails inviting participants to consider how people integrate divergent sets of cultural demands. In our work in Asia, for example, many individuals—particularly young and midlife adults—reported dreams that deal with conflicts between how they saw themselves as modern citizens of a global world and the pressures they feel to adhere to more traditional familial expectations. It is as if the participants had to cope with living in separate and sometimes incompatible worlds, each with its own view and requirements.

One participant's dream illustrates this dilemma. In the dream, she was living in her mother's house. Each room was at a different stage of being remodeled. The front room was decorated in a traditional style, and though completed, felt oppressive. As she moved deeper inside the house, the rooms became increasingly more modern in style but remained unfinished. For her, this dream expressed the sense of confusion arising when trying to merge two worlds. Such dreams often reveal a clash between culture and self, where divergent personal and cultural mythologies collide while in the process of being reshaped (Feinstein & Krippner, 1988).

Reflecting on the role of dreams that appear in the midst of societal shifts, Ewing (2003) proposes that dream narratives have the potential to *update* culture. Ewing asserts that as a result of the increasing flow of goods, ideas, and people across cultural and national borders, the development of culture and identity becomes a rather fluid and often inconsistent process.

> The idea of the individual as possessing a cohesive self—whether understood to be culturally constituted, innate, or a psychological, developmental achievement—has . . . been challenged. In its place we now see multiple identities, shifting self, and even an ever-fluid process of identification in which the individual never fully inhabits a stable identity. . . . We can look at the process of dreaming as a primary way in which individuals negotiate the experience of being caught between worlds and resynthesize self-conceptions in their new situations. (43–44)

By dialoguing with the dream image—and with others about our dreams—we cultivate the skill to take on multiple perspectives—that of self and of the culture for example—and we gain a greater awareness of the roles we enact culturally.

DREAMS AND THE HOLOGRAPHIC MIND

Many dream practices take place at the border between experiences of the self—which Jeannette Marie Mageo defines as "all aspects of being a person"—and experiences of identity. Mageo describes identity as the sense of self deriving from successive "acts of identification and dis-identification with elements of internal experience and with persons, groups, and representations in the cultural worlds" (2003: 7). Applying a postcolonial lens to dream inquiry, Mageo describes how dream imagery reflects a shifting social identity within two generations of Samoans. She shows how the traditional cultural values of one generation clash with those of the next, finding that the dreamer is often in pain when trying to reconcile conflicting demands from more than one cultural schema (for example around the idea of sexual modesty). Her description illuminates the fact that anthropological views of the self agree with enactivism and neurophysiology: identity is fluid and in perpetual transformation.

For Mageo, dreams are a special kind of recall, shifting between remembering and forgetting. To deal with this paradox, she proposes a holographic theory of dreaming (Mageo, 2004), suggesting that, just as an entire holograph can be duplicated from one of its parts, dream images contain within them aspects of the whole personal identity or cultural schema. The partial memories within dreams may intimate an element of a larger whole of the wider cultural matrix in which one is embedded. This in turn may trigger an attempt to reconstruct the missing part of the image. In the cases she discusses from postcolonial Samoa, the holographic schema is collective as well as individual. In order to come closer to a more complete meaning not only of the dream but also of individual actions, one needs to address "fractured" meaning systems linked to a communal past. She writes, "I am not saying that dreams are primarily about cultural meaning, certainly they are also about individual inner states, but these states vary in relation to life in a cultural world with its own peculiar history and attendant contradictions. . . . There is always a cultural dimension to personal history and to dreaming" (166). Hence, beyond the personal "daily residues" delineated by Freud, dreams may also contain cultural cues.

Mageo proposes that holographic theory completes psychoanalytic and textual approaches. Text is linked to shared meaning in the intersubjective sense, whereas psychoanalysis focuses on the dreamer's inner processes as a means to arrive at meaning. In contrast,

> [a] holographic perspective on dreams reveals how culture affects people's emotions and how these continually rebound upon culture. . . . Partial forms render fractures in a meaning system that stimulates our need to remember and reorder memory-laden images to make a new cultural meaning. (Mageo, 2004: 166–167)

Dreams are fragments that can and should be connected to larger wholes. To work with dreams is thus an attempt at recapturing the missing parts; not only at an individual level but also at a collective one. Exploration of this collective level may bring into awareness our past (the ancestral history we share with others), our present (our current cultural and ecological embeddedness), and our future (as the result of our present actions aggregating at a collective level).

DREAMS AND ANCESTRAL RECOVERY

People in contemporary Western societies often suffer from a form of fragmentation due to a lack of contact with their own ancestry. Fortunately, cultural practices are now emerging that seek to redress this sense of separation. The work of Apela (Pamela) Colorado (1988), Kimmy Johnson (2002), and Jürgen Kremer (1997, 2003) has laid important foundations in understanding the process of recovery of Indigenous mind, which calls into practice the remembrance of one's ancestral roots. Because most of our ancestors had a strong connection with place, connecting with one's ancestry often sensitizes one to a sense of place. Describing the practice of ancestral recovery, Johnson (2002) writes:

> The practice invites development and maturation of qualities of awareness, attention, and intention. . . . By remembering and reconnecting with earth-based traditions, traditions that predate the split between human and nature, this cultural practice opens the doorway to communication and communion with the world around us. (i)

The relevance of the Indigenous perspective has increased, and many today are seeking a meaningful reencounter with Indigenous knowledge, in particular through exploring their ancestry. Many Indigenous groups are reclaiming their own heritage, and parallel to this, many people whose families have emigrated from their ancestral homelands find healing in recovering their ancestral knowledge. This often requires an epistemic shift, and people often report that dreams provided guiding imagery. For example, dreams have led them to explore particular places and activities, find like-minded people through synchronous meetings, or engage in ancestral practices that often bring about healing (Krippner et al., 2002). Following the holographic metaphor of Mageo, when faced with choices on a journey to recover ancestral connections, even a fragment can point to a meaningful direction.

Within the practice of recovery of Indigenous mind, individuals are encouraged first to reflect on their own culture and, in the case of a cosmopolitan mix such as in North America, learn to situate oneself in relation to one's own ancestry. Aspects of dream life may come to the surface that might have been buried in memory—personal, familial, or even cultural. The work of Kimmy Johnson (2002) and Karen Jaenke (2001; 2006) in particular address this process of recovery through dreams.

Jaenke (2001) explains how in many traditions, relationship to ancestors "forms a central anchor for personal identity" and that this sense of self extends "into a generational awareness of connections, patterns, and stories woven into the relationship with land and cosmos." In her study, *Personal Dreamscape as Ancestral Landscape*, she explores the power of dreams to uncover deeply forgotten memory (2001). Using narrative research, she inquired into her paternal and maternal lineages, guided in part by dreams of her family ancestors, some from many generations past. After dreaming of her paternal grandmother, Jaenke writes: "By talking about ancestral dreams with family members, further connections with dream material, as well as intergenerational links between dreamers in a lineage, are revealed. . . . In this way, dreams bridge generations" (2006: 31).

The realization that one can receive an ancestral presence in dreams has a healing influence. "Discovering where breaks occurred in their family and attending to them, people mend the past while stepping into greater wholeness in the present" (Jaenke, 2006: 31). Jaenke advocates for the importance of this work to recover and inhabit a richer multigenerational perspective that reveals "the web of relationships from which the thread of one's life is spun." In Jaenke's work, the recovery of connection to one's human biological ancestors is part of a much larger process of reconnection through dreams with our deep cultural roots and our more ancient ancestors (2001).

The sense of relatedness extends from the ebb and flow of intimate relationship to the undefined and "holographic" matrix of our culture. It can extend further into the transpersonal layers of connections with those who departed but to which we are still connected through the subtle medium of dreaming. These dreams seem to engage a different register of memory. An expanded view of memory sees it as the capacity to call forth in the present moment increasingly expansive and seemingly boundless processes: 1) personal memory linked to cumulative personal experience; 2) collective memory either as a form of transitive memory (distributed within the group), cultural knowledge, or cumulative know-how; 3) ancestral memory, linked to the capacity to call forth knowledge connected to those who are separated from us by death; and 4) ecological memory. Of course, the idea of ancestral memory may be difficult for science to objectify. But anecdotal evidence, especially with visitation dreams, or dreams surrounding death, abounds, showing that dreams can be the subtle medium that mediates meaningful connection with those departed (Krippner et al., 2002; Mallon, 2005; Gratton & Séguin, 2009).

ECOLOGICAL EMBEDDEDNESS

Pressure to conform to the consumerist, techno-centric values with rising globalization has accentuated the generational gap in many traditional cultures. But parallel to this, the emerging global awareness of our interconnectedness provides impetus and scientific validation for the Indigenous perspective. The many ecological crises that we face at this time call for us to reimagine a sense of identity that may be just as primal and central than cultural identity. From a global ecological perspective, we are all participants in a large Indigenous drama that sees us as earth-bound creatures seeking to come to grips with how to live in better balance with the natural cycles of the planet. The Indigenous perspective, with its spiritual and participatory orientation to place and all its living inhabitants, has historically been at odds with the overly rational aspects of science. Fortunately, there is mounting appreciation for traditional ways of knowing—or Indigenous science (Colorado, 1988, 1996)—and its contribution to psychological and social processes; in particular those that cultivate personal and communal responsibility and awareness of our embedded relatedness (Sabini, 2002; Buzzell & Chalquist, 2009).

For example, from an Indigenous science perspective, health takes on more than individual meaning. And just as prodomic dreams may alert us to incipient or progressing disease processes, dreams may also allude to sickness and healing from the perspective of the larger being, the community, or even the ecosphere. For example, since ecological problems such as those leading to climate change are systemic, they are de facto larger than any individual can address. Any solution nevertheless requires countless individual responses to form a critical mass, to bring changes to policies, and to reverse negative trends.

If a global problem requires a group response, what is the role of dreams in this change process? Could it be that the creative potentials of dreaming that are linked to self-perceptual depth could be applied on a more collective level? If each dreamer holds a piece of the hologram, could it be that bringing our dreams together leads to some form of social-perceptual depth, a social raising of consciousness with incipient problem-solving. To that effect, Meredith Sabini and Richard Russo have adopted a social dreaming process devised by Lawrence (2005) to inquire about group response to social and ecological threats. They describe Culture Dreaming as follows:

> Culture Dreaming offers a living experience of interconnection. This deceptively simple, deceptively potent method lets participants share and explore dreams for their larger sociocultural meanings, rather than their personal. It is based on the assumption that our single

> individual dreams are particles of a larger wave function, the Dreaming, that is going on all the time. (http://dream-institute.org/culture_dreaming_calendar.htm)

In this approach, participants are invited to let dreams come to them in a meditative open space. Dreams are shared as they emerge, one dream triggering another. The dreamers then engage this original co-created dream narrative: they identify themes, issues, and concerns that may mirror those of the world at large. Dreams are viewed as a shared social resource, and for this reason, it is not necessary to dwell on the individual background or other forms of personal disclosure by the dreamers (Sabini, 2007).

From an Indigenous perspective, the whole of existence, including what in the modern world we perceived as "the environment" is conscious, aware, and partaking of the sacred matrix of life. Dreams in particular present an important modality for reconnection with the *Greater Mind* of land and place and their human and nonhuman inhabitants. The boundaries of life and sacredness fluidly move between personal self and what, by relation, is an extended self (often personalized as Great Mother). This deep knowing predates the similar insights of systems theory, and supersedes it by offering a story about our place and responsibility within this embedded universe.

Taking this inquiry seriously within her own life, Jaenke (2010) researched her own dreams that address ecological concerns over two decades. Looking back into her dream history, she traced three types of ecological dreams: earth communing, earth destruction, and earth healing. For Jaenke, earth communing dreams "reveal the necessity of recovering psychic and somatic kinship with the earth" (187). Dreams of this kind show dreamer, animals, and place as alive and sharing a deep connection. Earth destruction dreams asked her "to bear witness to elemental destruction through the earth-body connection"; whereas earth healing dreams "show the human-earth relationship is healed through balancing opposites found in the psyche and in nature" (187).

If we expand the "holographic" metaphor of Mageo beyond the cultural matrix, we can understand how these dreams can begin to address our rightful place and responsibilities within the larger biological matrix, the one from which all cultures arose. Within the integral perspective, paying attention to dreams is a way of reconnecting and participating with the Earth's rhythms.

BETWEEN CULTURES: DREAMS AND DIVERSITY

Accounts of dreaming vary widely across cultures, and many provide alternatives to the predominantly subjective or mechanistic orientation toward dreams found in the modern West (Tedlock, 1987). Non-Western cultures emphasize the confluence of the social sphere with that of the self, and include favorable attitudes toward the ontological reality of the dreaming experience. In many traditional societies and cultural subgroups, the imaginal and dreaming world is not seen as a form of unreality but rather as a perfectly real world of autonomous forms and images (Krippner et al., 2002; Bosnak, 2007; Tedlock, 2004).[2]

> Phenomenologically oriented ethnographers have observed that in many non-Western societies, dreaming and waking reality are not fully segmented or compartmentalized worlds but are rather overlapped experiences. . . . Dream experiences are never confused with waking experiences since the kind of persons in dreams are not the same kinds of persons with whom the individual is most concerned in ordinary waking life. (Tedlock, 1987: 5)

In our courses we ask students to reflect on the core assumptions they hold about dreams and their origins. Often, students will speak about a particular person in their family whose interest and positive attitude toward dreaming influenced them. We also ask them to pay attention to how dreams and dreaming are portrayed in popular culture (films, plays, novels, or other cultural artifacts) and to inquire into the meanings and values that are embedded therein. The question arises in intercultural work as to how cultural groups can learn from one another, and how we can appreciate the contributions of other groups without falling in the trap of cultural appropriation. Mindfulness is invited when borrowing piecemeal concepts or practice from other cultures, so as to critically engage issues of potential appropriation. We are also mindful that cultures are fluid processes and cultural sensitivity does not mean cultural crystallization. Tremendous amounts of creativity are expressed at the boundaries of cultures: bricolage, hybridity, fusion are all forms of creative amalgam that fertilize the ground of emerging approaches.[3]

Knowing that cultural approaches to dreams differ, diverge, and even contradict each other, how can we be together in a global world that is increasingly becoming like a big village? Diversity necessitates awareness of inclusiveness and the skill necessary to appropriately relate to and celebrate differences. In that respect, every dreamer needs to pay attention to how their own views may keep other people or other groups at bay.

Is diversity expressed and valued within professional associations that focus on dreams, such as IASD (International Association for the Study of Dreams), or within what has been called the *dream movement*? Anthony Shafton (1995a) asked the question, particularly focusing on the absence of African Americans in the American or international dream movement. Shafton reflected critically and dialogically with black and white professionals and scholars about the reasons that may be at the root of a lack of diversity. After pointing to the culturalist views of Fromm and the neoculturalism of Ullman, which deal with the fallout of race inequities in the sphere of mental health, Shafton made the following pointed remarks:

> [Despite his democratic intentions] Ullman analyzes the majority of dreams, not for social (much less racial) but for personal psychological content. In this respect he exemplifies what I was told by various professionals is a difference in how blacks and whites typically think—a difference which renders much dreamwork unattractive to Blacks. As it was put by Taub-Bynum (1984), a family therapist, Whites tend to view life and interpret dreams in "intrapsychic" terms, Blacks in terms of social milieu and spiritual reality, or "field."(Shafton, 1995a, n.p.)

This remark could be expanded to include other cultural or ethnic groups who, alongside African Americans, may espouse a more integral view that dreams speak to larger dynamics including but not limited to those of an intrapsychic character.

Bridging the racial divide, Shafton himself went on to write a book on the "African American way with dreams" (2002). He interviewed 116 African Americans, trying to gather a cross-section of the population. A larger number of participants were engaged in the arts where "there is plentiful evidence of the place of dreams in African American life" (3), especially in fiction. He found a wide diversity of views, even possibly more than among whites, due to the fact that there is a lot of attention given to dreams in the black community. Among African Americans, dreams are very much embedded in one's life, and connected to religious experience, and the importance of paying attention to and sharing dreams with the community in mind is highly valued.[4] He describes the prevalence of ancestors' dreams, the importance of predictive dreams as well as déjà-vu dreams. He also notes the openness to dreamlike experiences in the waking state that distinguishes black Americans from white Americans, and the importance of dreamlike altered states of consciousness such as visions, voices, and presences. Finally he addresses dreams about race, which are more likely to be part of the African American experience and "open a window onto the private experience of race in America" (8).

As an outsider to black culture, Shafton has created a body of work that is admirable for its disclosure of valuable culture-specific knowledge, drawing out the distinctive aspects of African American ways toward dreaming. His work also highlights the importance of preserving cultural specificity and brings deeper cultural support in its wake. Not only does it encourage appreciation of cultural differences, it also sensitizes us to hidden cultural biases, making us better prepared to respond to them.

SUMMARY

From an integral perspective, the phenomenon of dreams extends beyond the intrapsychic realm to include relational and cultural aspects, double aspects of intersubjectivity.

Dreams are social events, in continuity with waking life. Waking consciousness is finely tuned to relationships, and is in essence relational consciousness. In this chapter, we have attempted to situate the place of cultural approaches to dreaming, which by definition are as diverse as cultures themselves. For this reason, our attempt was not to repeat the numerous existent ethnographies, but rather to point out why cultural inquiry and cultural context truly matters in an integral model.

While culture informs perception through language and habits of meaning-making, we are also active participants within our culture. Our actions, especially those that enact our views of dreaming, shape and propagate particular cultural ideas and practices. The metaphor of the hologram, as suggested by Mageo, is particularly relevant. Culture and the self are in holographic relationship to one another, and dreaming presents small pieces leading one to inquire about the whole. An integral approach encourages the exploration of the interface between dream and culture, opening up a host of attending issues including: multiple and shifting identities, individuation, alienation, harmony, cultural dissociation, and eventually cultural recovery.

This chapter closes our exploration of the lower left quadrant, the "we" quadrant. In the next chapter, we explore the lower right quadrant, taking a more objective view of social systems and the different roles of dreams in different forms of societies.

CHAPTER TEN

Turning to Larger Patterns

Dreams, Society, and the Environment

Sleep appears to be a time when we are absent to the world, or in the most radical state of disconnection with the outer environment. But does society cease to exist (so to speak) when we enter sleep and dreaming? Having drawn attention to dreams at the boundary of self and others, we now turn our gaze toward social systems and the environment. We explore how dreams are responsive to our social surroundings. Given that sleep and dream exist at the edge where the self and larger systems meet, what social role have dreams played across time and throughout cultures? For example, how does dreaming interface with issues such as social identity, power, and legitimation? Do dreams respond to our political and environmental concerns?

Integral theory holds that the inner world and outer environment coemerge and comingle in a process of reciprocal interplay. Personal goals interface with the cultural values embedded in the groups we belong to, finding their expression within particular social forms. Individual needs are fulfilled with the support of (or sometimes in opposition to) a particular cultural matrix and social system. Of the four quadrants, the social aspect of dreaming and dream practices has received the least attention within dream studies.

As social creatures, we are continually trying to find better ways to achieve or maintain a sense of personal and collective well-being amid a changing world. In our ongoing quest for well-being, dreams can give us cues about our degree of adjustment to the social world, or conversely, our alienation from it. Furthermore, as with all aspects of human functioning, social groups have historically extended judgments and assessments of dreams, either positively or negatively. Such judgments either enhance or reduce their perceived value for all individuals inside the group. In this respect, it may be revealing to study the shifts of the perceived value of dreaming over time within a given group.

Although social structures transform relatively slowly, the pace of social changes has accelerated over the past century (Russell, 1998). Many groups and cultures are facing changes unprecedented in their history. As traditional modes of livelihood and language disappear, many cultural groups are at the brink of extinction. Anthropological writings about dreams refer to the fact that Indigenous people notice a shift in their dream life as a result of encroaching modernity. The perception that *dreams have left us* or *people don't dream anymore* expresses the loss of the essence of a particular way of life (Pandya, 2004). When we know scientifically that healthy individuals dream every night, statements about the loss of dreams may seem incomprehensible. Yet they call us to take a deeper look at how social structures and historical movements are connected to dreaming. Could it be that the perceived "disappearance" of dreaming is emblematic of shifting societal forms and the cultural values they embody?

By contrasting people's views of dreams throughout time and across various cultures, we gain insights into the social and cultural nature of dreaming. What patterns emerge when we place dream life *within* the larger arc of cultural transformation that occurs when social forms evolve and change? Drafting a sociocultural history of dreaming asks us to reimagine the role and social significance historically ascribed to dreams. Doing so is tricky, however, and we need to remind ourselves that all historical narratives are inevitably imprinted by the inquirer's own situation. There is no time period outside of history where total objectivity is possible. We always look from somewhere and as a result, cultural bias inevitably colors the views we take of the past.

The cultural richness that dreaming expressed within different societies has been described by authors such as Bourguignon (1954), Bulkeley (2001), David and Stroumsa (1999), Krippner and Thompson (1996), Irwin (1996), Tedlock (1987), Von Grunebaum and Caillois (1966), as well as many others. We will not repeat them. Instead we refer to a compelling ethnographic case study to illustrate the link between dreams and social forms, giving us a view of how a larger pattern may be at play. In this case, we focus on the alteration in dreaming that occurs as patterns of relating to places and people change when social systems transform.

TOWARD AN ECOLOGICAL ANTHROPOLOGY OF SLEEP

It may be surprising to know that sleep, like other natural human needs, is shaped by cultural and societal demands. Reviewing a vast body of anthropological literature, Worthman and Melby (2002) analyzed factors that affect sleep in a number of societies living on several continents and having varying modes of subsistence: foragers (hunting and gathering), pastoralists (tending livestock, often migratory), horticulturalists (subsistence farming), agriculturalists (larger scale organized farming). The authors followed the general premise that one's traditional relationship to the environment is tied to one's livelihood. Both of these in turn affect the way individuals engage with sleep. For instance, the sleep behaviors of foragers are different in many respects from those of agriculturalists because foragers don't have permanent dwellings and are often on the move.

Worthman and Melby's survey demonstrates that humans sleep under remarkably diverse circumstances. Their studies examine the diversity of practices and the presence of sleeping implements; for instance, they note that beds, bedding, and blankets in a tropical climate tend to attract mites and parasitic organisms—known vectors of illness, which makes their upkeep onerous. They also study the use and impact of open fire for warmth and comfort, and the nearness of predators and the presence of other animals, as well as the presence of nighttime pests. They describe cultural variations in different people's sleeping arrangements (often along age and gender lines), and the relative fluidity between sleep and waking states. They look at labor demands that affect sleep and the prevalence of social activity during the night, including festivities and rituals. They survey beliefs about sleep and socialization behaviors affecting sleep over one's lifetime. The variations they report among all these factors are vast and impressive. For example, reviewing social status based on age, class, or social standing, or on gender, they write:

> Status influences most dimensions of the micro- and macroecology of sleep, including workload, activity patterns, sleeping companions, and sleeping conditions. Women, for instance, almost universally sleep with infants and often with children, while men and boys are more likely to sleep in exposed or risky conditions. Poor or socially marginal individuals frequently sleep in more crowded, disrupted, and insecure situations, whereas the powerful or affluent generally repose in less populated and more controlled conditions. (92)

Their study offers some interesting generalizations: in modern Western societies sleep is seen as something that is done in one's personal space. It is expected that the sleeper will retreat to a special room where one sleeps either alone or with a mate (or sometimes a pet). The surroundings are well controlled in terms of noise level, lighting, and temperature.[1] Sleep is done in a physically secure environment with little social or physical contact. All this gives rise to a stable physical environment—a mild form of sensory deprivation. These parameters of sleep are fairly fixed, and it is not surprising that sleep laboratory environments and modern hotels try to replicate those conditions.

In many non-Western societies, sleep is often a more communal affair. Living quarters can be in a noisy and open space, especially where it houses multiple generations, each with their specific sleep needs. In rural, pastoral, or forest areas, one often sleeps with the presence of animals. Often there is a need for open fire for warmth and comfort. The necessity of tending the fire then leads to more fluid boundaries between sleep and waking.

Non-Western sleep is thus less uniform in social or physical terms, and in how it unfolds in time. Many variations of sleeping patterns exist, depending on the particular needs and ecology of people's livelihood. People with a nomadic lifestyle or foragers have encampments that are continually changing. This mitigates the accumulation of sleeping paraphernalia. In contrast with contemporary Western sleep practices, the actual material setting, either outside or in an open-air and mobile dwelling, is much less bounded. This sleeping environment is more vulnerable and may not provide the same sense of physical security as a bedroom. If one's sense of security is not tied to an enclosed and secure room, it tends to be more dependent on the close proximity of others for mutual protection. For these reasons, non-Western sleep patterns tend to be a more sensorially dynamic and social.

Many variations also exist in terms of the architecture of sleep connected with different sociocultural arrangements. Western societies tend to view sleep as monophasic: the ideal night is a single period of uninterrupted sleep. Other societies break sleep into various phases throughout the day and night. Naps are not unusual, and nightly sleep is often divided into two or more shorter periods.

One can usually track the change from agrarian to industrial society by changes in attitudes toward napping and by the establishment of various work shifts around necessary labor. Countries like China are now undergoing this type of change in the social attempt to reframe the afternoon nap as undesirable behavior, whereas previously it had been seen not only as a positive social habit but a right (the right to rest being written in the Communist constitution; see Li, 2003). The new view, however, is that a market economy cannot run properly if everyone takes off part of the workday to sleep. This seems to demonstrate that while such a practice makes sense at a local level, in a globally interconnected economy, the social costs are too great. Daytime sleep tends to disappear even from previously polyphasic cultures.[2]

What Worthman and Melby term *Western sleep*—the normative unbroken sleep consolidated in a consecutive seven to eight hours—turns out to be a modern cultural invention and is still not the norm in siesta cultures such as those found in some Mediterranean countries. Their analysis echoes the work of historian Roger Ekirch (2005), who looks at historical evidence of earlier sleep patterns in both Europe and America. He has shown that before the Industrial Revolution, and before extensive use of artificial lighting, people were known to sleep in two segments: an evening segment from 9:00 p.m. to midnight (first sleep) and a second round from 2:00 a.m. to dawn (second sleep). The intervening time was set for duties that could not be postponed. Ekirch believes that interrupted sleep is not necessarily a form of sleep disorder. It could be a natural pattern that is still active, though often understood as pathology when it breaks through our modern and artificially lit lifestyle (see also Warren, 2007).

This brief comparative inquiry into the social-environmental pattern of sleep has set the stage for a similar discussion on the shifting role of dreaming related to social organization. In the following case study, we explore how dreaming is a key aspect of group living within societies that require a high level of relational attunement for their survival.

CHANGING DREAMS AMONG THE ANDAMAN ONGEES

During the nineteenth and twentieth centuries, many Indigenous cultural groups witnessed drastic alterations in their way of life, sometimes over the span of a single generation. The following case study is drawn from Vishvajit Pandya (2004), who followed the Ongee society from the Andaman Islands (in the Indian Ocean) during the last two decades of the twentieth century. Pandya has witnessed the changes that took place as modern settlements replaced traditional sleeping sites among the Ongees. Prior to the end of the last century, the Ongees were a hunter-gatherer culture.[3] Pandya's ethnographical work describes both the Ongees' traditional understanding of dreaming and the change it is undergoing as the group's culture changes.

The Ongees' traditional dreaming culture is unique, as it emphasizes the sense of smell (in some special embodied form) rather than the usual predominance of visual imagery:

> The Ongees believe that each individual living body is made up of two distinct parts. The first part, *mateeah,* is the external body that is visible and concrete. . . . The second part, *enteeah,* is the internal body . . . that is invisible and abstract, directing the activities and feelings of the external body. As the Ongees move around in real conscious life and see sources of smell, the individual human body also leaves behind traces of body smells in different locations. *Enteeah,* the intrinsic form of the body that is detachable, goes out of the *mateeah* when an individual is asleep and collects all the smells left behind by retracing actual bodily movement. . . . Dreaming is conceived to be a process of body-internal movement around the entire island to collect the smells scattered by the individual and to smell things that the Ongees evidently did not notice the first time around. This process of collecting "smells, fragments or bits" is known as *dane korale,* a spider making its web, also a term for dreaming. . . . While smell is collected, images of various places, making up the culture's construct of space, are transferred as remembered images and smells to the sleeping individual. (143)

Individuals have their own dreams, but their interpretation, or the understanding of this recollection activity around smells, is a communal activity where the dream of one is connected to that of others.

> Because all individuals share the forest campsite and activities, it becomes possible to connect the smells and places from dreams and to construct the interpretation of a dream. Each individual dream is like a spider web, but in the process of collective interpretation small webs get interconnected to form a large spider web. (Pandya 2004: 143)

Pandya did his initial ethnographic work in 1983. During that stay, he slept at the forest campsites, witnessing sessions of discussions and singing as the Ongees went to sleep. These sessions drew together individuals who in daytime would not interact because of the fairly rigid line of demarcation that maintains distance between different age and gender subgroups. These fluid discussions weaved night dreams with day dreams, wishes and visions, as well as the nightly dreams of the Ongee spirit mediums. Pandya quotes a *torale* (spirit medium) describing his role: "I am maker of a dream like a very large spider's web from which nothing escapes. It is a web that is unlike other webs. It spreads across the horizon and thus the *torale* is able to see, smell, move and say more" (139).

As a result of the sharing session, a common interpretation is reached that influences the next day's activities, including the hunt. Thus, dreams and dream sharing serve to integrate the individuals into a coherent group, in constantly shifting ways. As Pandya notes, "The completeness of society and the individual within it involves not separating the world as it is smelled and seen while sleeping but unifying it with the world that can be smelled, seen and acted upon while awake" (144). Individuals in such tightly bounded groups rely on sharing each other's dreams to become aware of each other's feelings and perceptions and to establish a common purpose.

During a return visit in 1993, Pandya observed that the conditions of living had changed drastically: life in the circular campground within the forest had been replaced by habitation in small private houses near the plantation, where many Ongees now worked as hired hands on a shift schedule. Payments for labor were made in food rations, and fewer Ongees relied on hunting and gathering for sustenance. In addition, an increasing number of outsiders inhabited the area, and the forest was being cleared for lumber.

Pandya recorded how the Ongees described the changes:

> For us sleeping in the settlement generates only incomplete webs as sleep is broken by the [managers]. We fail to see what the body internal wants to show us in the forest so we continue to live in the settlement. Sometimes

> [other tribe members] come to sleep with us, especially on occasion when they want to remember what it is to be able to make a web! Individuals who always stay in the settlement have lost the power to get up on their own and make a large spider web based on what the different internal bodies see in the forest. People in the settlement have no large spider web! . . . For us sleeping and dreaming has changed. We dream differently since we live differently in a different space. And experiences are different. (147–148)

Pandya notes that the Andaman Ongees are in the midst of a fundamental change similar to that of other Indigenous groups who are forced by economic conditions, globalization, and changing social structures into different ways of life. The Ongees not only dream about that change, but also communicate about it: "They say that the *dane korale* (spider web, dream) is constantly changing because the spider keeps weaving it again and again" (149). They are in the process of creating new forms of social attunement in which objects of concern are changing. Pandya's ethnographic description gives clear evidence of societal disruption in collective dreaming and the process of dream displacement brought about by changes in societal forms: from hunting-gathering to market economies, and where natural rhythms are replaced by rationalized shift work and more individualized modes of sustenance.

THE LONG VIEW: DREAMS AND SOCIETAL TRANSFORMATION

While Pandya's work show us social changes that happens within the frame of a single generation, we try here to reimagine the longer arc of history with regard to dreaming (for lack of space, we mainly address what is regarded as the West). We draw on the ways dreams have been portrayed in historical texts and making inferences between dreaming and social organization. The history of ideas is mainly studied through diachronic studies: how ideas evolve across time and eras. This is well suited for inquiries spanning long periods of time. For the study of dreams, looking within sacred texts can be particularly useful. A complementary approach is to carefully study anthropological reports that remind us, however imperfectly, how Indigenous understandings of dreams, such as that of the Ongees, are reported.

Harry Hunt (1989) is one of the few theorists to address how the views of dreams change over time. Charting several loosely drawn historical periods, he sought to reclaim, and possibly explain, the multiplicity of dreams. According to Hunt, diverse forms of dreams described in historical and anthropological literature evidence a quality that is often lost or at least not observed in laboratory dreams. Normative laboratory studies often do not reflect the rich diversity of dream forms, and in particular, often do not witness the less frequent but more important or significant dreams: archetypal dreams, nightmares, lucid dreams, prophetic and telepathic or precognitive dreams, visitation dreams, and somatic/medical dreams. Hunt recognizes that within the anthropological and historical literature, these types of dreams are regarded by many societies to be the most prized. On the other hand, he observes that modern scientific literature seems to put an emphasis on the mnemonic or associative replay of daily experiences as enacted in dreams. As shown in previous chapters, dreams are increasingly understood in relationship to how they help the individual consolidate personal memory or maintain a healthy sense of self.

Hunt's methodology consists of locating dream types within the historical and classical literature and the anthropological literature. Hunt draws his typology partly from accounts of tribal dreaming by anthropologists Robert Dentan (1987) and Barbara Tedlock (1987) and from that, extrapolates to the more distant periods of Indigenous life. He also consulted the dream literature of the nineteenth century and that of the present. Here are four kinds of dreams that he highlights:

1. Personal dreams, based on "remembering" or "things you think about during the day" or "wishes of the soul."
2. Medical-somatic dreams, relevant to the shamanistic diagnosis of physical illness and/or what is often referred to as "spiritual loss" or soul loss.

3. Prophetic dreams that present omens or premonitions that may come true. Telling the dream to one's immediate group can negate dream omens; keeping silent preserves the omen's effectiveness.
4. Archetypal-spiritual dreams, which are vivid and subjectively powerful "big dreams" based on visitations by gods or spirits, encounters with one's guardian spirit, or travel of the soul to the supernatural underworld or heavens.

In each historical era and throughout phases of cultural change, Hunt (1989) finds a "shift in relative importance across a common spectrum of dream typologies" (90) described previously. He intimates that the shift has been away from archetypal, prophetic dreams in Indigenous and classical civilization (e.g., ancient Greece) and toward medical-somatic and personal-mnemic dreams in modern and postmodern societies. "But despite these shifts," he says, "in the contrasting ontological assumptions of these cultures, there is evidence that the same forms of dream experience continue to occur" (90). We understand this to mean that general patterns of dream experience seem correlated with certain sociocultural modes, even as each group differs on how to consider the essential nature of dreaming and the self (or the soul, the term that has often been used historically) (Krippner & Thompson, 1996).

Hunt' tracks pivotal shifts from the time when societal forms encouraged ways of living that supported group attunement to those that foster more individualistic concerns. Hunt's schema places the dreams of Indigenous societies in close attunement with multidimensional realities (dream sources, for instance, that include ancestors, gods/goddesses, and/or animal spirits), where contact with these nontangible realms is highly prized and even sought after. Whereas all four types of dreams are probably found in all societies, in close-knit groups where survival depends on group attunement rather than individualistic pursuit, dreaming may tap into many forms, including the experience of shared dreaming, such as we have seen among the Ongees and other Indigenous cultures.

For Hunt, one of the major forms of dreams among Indigenous people is future-oriented or prophetic dreaming. He notes, however, that in close-knit groups, these dreams more specifically entail a *performative* or *world-creating* aspect that attends to how these dreams come to pass. Thus, these dreams do not anticipate or foretell the future as much as help to bring it about. Since such dreams may influence the behavior of the group, whether to tell the dream or not is often a major decision. Societies in which dreams are given a central role in group affairs are described as *dream centered* (84). This social form of dreaming and sharing could reflect a deeper attunement with place—the spiritual legacy of the group and land to which one life's is intimately tied. Clan affiliations bring a sense of responsibility in the individual for the greater harmony of the group. As we have seen in the case of the Ongees, these close relationships can make dreams a privileged means for social attunement. However, if the basic societal fabric is torn, it is understandable that dreaming may "cease," sometimes suddenly. It is not so much that one stops dreaming in a biological sense as that the group matrix ceases to provide the focal reference for the communal "coming to know" process (Peat, 1994).

When individuals cease to feel the need to share dreams for the continued existence of their world, and where their actions no longer rely on a dream's message or purpose for their meaning, dreams risk losing their usefulness. It may take time for a new social matrix that once again includes the valued role of dreaming to take shape. Within pockets of the contemporary culture where dreams have found new value (for example, in the therapeutic community), the social impact of dreaming has been the focus of few dream practitioners, in particular Lawrence (2005) and Ullman (1996).

FROM GROUP MIND TO INDIVIDUALIZED MIND

From the archaic to the classical period, Greek society saw the reigning cults and dominant religious beliefs lose aspects of their pre-archaic mystical character. This was probably tied as well to various social changes. A new vision, distinguished by a desire for a more structured religion, replaced more ancient beliefs. For example, Apollo, the Greek god of light and sobriety, gains ascendance and authority over dark Gaia and the wild Dionysus. Along with that change, two important trends appear: naturalism and rationalism, signifying the birth of philosophy, thereby spurring the development of increasingly sophisticated theories to explain the natural world.

Wax (1999) believes that in earlier societies where group members imbued symbols with a concrete reality, members were able to read the significance of a dream without specialist assistance. Later, in more complex societies, where one finds increased stratification of social groups, dreams ceased to be readily and universally understood. The rise of urbanization in classical societies, and in particular within the Mediterranean culture, has led to dreams becoming the object of individual attention rather than group concern.

Plato mentions multiple origins of dreaming, from Divine source to the physical and emotional states of the dreamer.[4] Aristotle determined that dreams come from within the self. Hunt shows that within classical texts, dreams still continue to be understood in their mantic or prophetic sense, but over time the interpretation changes to become a reflection of the individual dreamer's future rather than a message for society as a whole. Furthermore, with the rise of the Asclepian cult,[5] dreams were cultivated for their power to bring healing to the supplicant. The language of dreams increasingly became the province of specialists who could interpret them for a particular supplicant (Meier, 1989).

With the process of urbanization, a ruling class takes power, and simultaneously, according to Wax, the role of "objective" dream interpretation also becomes established. "Within an urbanized community of common language, ritual, and symbolism, the systems of interpretation could become codified and public" (Wax, 1999: 421). The foremost example of codified procedures for the interpretation of dreams is in the authoritative book by Artemidorus Daldianus (second century BCE), which was translated widely and became a basis for many similar books in the Islamic world offering systems of dream explication (Lamoreaux, 2002).

FREUD AND THE ADVENT OF MODERN DREAMING

Changes from mythically based societies to those founded on the principle of modern rationality have been associated with a strong accent on the privatization of dreams. In Freud's

Interpretation of Dreams (1900), the spiritual and even somatic sources of dreaming are replaced by a psychological source, understood in terms of the neurological knowledge of the time however embryonic it was if we compare it to current knowledge. Not surprisingly, little mention is made of the social or cultural matrix of dreams, although many textbooks are fond of noting that psychoanalysis was born at the heyday of the Victorian era, with very restrictive social mores.

Through Freud's gaze, dreams become symptoms of psychic conflicts. Orthodox psychoanalysis established the basis of the dreaming process in the individual's developmental history and embedded its meaning in individual behavior. Freud did address sociocultural issues in other writings, however. In *Civilization and Its Discontents* (Freud, 1930), he delineated the oppositional dynamic that set the "instinctual" self against a "repressive" societal system. He proposed a vision of civilized human beings as perpetually unhappy, biologically instinctual creatures, who, through self-knowledge combined with creative sublimation, were capable of alleviating, but never eliminating, the alienating pressures of communal life. In Freud's view, the price an individual paid to become a member of a modern society was the repression or sublimation of their sexual and aggressive tendencies into socially sanctioned and productive activities. With this interpretation, a new narrative emerges: dreams become a final refuge for the instinctual self—revealing, despite censorship, our "deeper" instinctual nature that has no other avenue to fully express itself. In Freud's narrative, societal attunement emerges out of a conflict between self and others, taking the form of an introjection of moralistic rules and the development of a guilt complex: the superego.

Philosopher Ian Johnston (1999) wonders why Freud is "so determined to play down the social component of human life—to stress animal instincts rather than social needs" (n.p.). By regarding the dynamics of the individual psyche as more fundamental than the dynamics of group interaction, Freud misses the other side of the social exchange: the group's contribution to meeting individual needs. Positive psychology paints a different picture of sociality, emphasizing social needs as opposed to social repression (Seligman & Csíkszentmihályi, 2000). People whose lives are organized by healthy ties to meaningful social groups seem to be happier and more fulfilled than those whose lives are more isolated.

MULTIPLE ARBITERS OF MEANING

With the advent of modernity, dreams have gradually become seen as internalized, the subject of mentalization. For some, dreaming is even approached as "an erratic process of the nervous system of a monad, detached from social interaction" (Wax, 1999: 427). As would be expected, the current scientific narrative often objectifies dream experiences, attempting to strip them from any mysterious remains by labeling them "sleep mentation" (Antrobus, 1991) and associating them with emotional information processing. We need to juxtapose this view with the fact that while dream images may become increasingly emblematic of an individual's feelings, these may also be portraying increasing alienation from that of others.

It comes as no surprise, then, that throughout most of the twentieth century, dream interpretation in the West was the province of depth psychology, and that within the therapeutic dyad the analyst was the main arbiter of meaning. The emergence of the human potential movement in the last quarter of the century saw a proliferation of group practices that reduced the importance of the analyst as primary or sole interpreter. One should not think that the narrative of self-empowerment that emerged in the seventies did so uniquely by chance. In her 1972 best seller *Dream Power*, Faraday strongly criticized the hierarchical power imbalance between client and analyst-interpreter that supposedly robbed the dreamer of his or her own reflection in the dream's meaning. The self-empowerment narrative eventually places the dreamer as the main and final authority on his or her dream meaning. In the new ethos, the group and the therapist are seen as facilitators of a process of meaning-making that increasingly becomes the dreamer's responsibility. For Montague Ullman (1996), the role of facilitator in a dream group is one among peers, a far cry from the professional distance that characterizes the psychoanalytic exchange.

In the early 1980s, for the first time and in a truly postmodern fashion, the establishment of the Association for the Study of Dreams presented an opportunity for a "rainbow coalition" of scientists, scholars, therapists, cultural practitioners, artists, and the general public to come together around a mutual interest in dreams. In its multidisciplinarity, this group of dream explorers is accurately reflecting the multidimensionality of dreaming.

In the postmodern era, ethnic or national cultures are becoming less and less strictly defined and bounded. A global culture has allowed individuals to experience more freedom—outside of culturally bounded interpretative schemas—to allow other views, beliefs, and behaviors to influence them. In this context, the individual self is understood as the principal meaning making agent. That dreams are viewed as having a problem-solving function can be seen as an extension of the individual's creative agency: the self becomes a general problem solver within an ever-changing society.

Postmodernity shows that the stories people tell about themselves follow the personal and cultural assumptions they are working through. Postmodern thought deemphasizes and criticizes universal meaning-making schemas. It questions the validity of grand or universal theories applicable to all groups or individuals. It considers any meta-story as suspect for possibly masking an unspoken agenda of a dominant group to assert control over others, even those who have dreams at the center of their identity narratives.

DREAMS AND IDENTITY NARRATIVES

Even in the context of an increasing individualization of dreams, certain identity narratives have relied on dreams as a source of legitimacy for the group. Historically, dreams have provided the basis for religious, social, or political legitimacy. They also have been used in certain groups in the construction of ethnic identity. Edgar (2002) has looked at the dynamic interplay between dreaming, culture, and social identity. He draws upon current events to show how historically or religiously important dreams still exert political influence, as they have over long periods of time. Edgar cites two examples to show the role certain dreams play in the maintenance of nationalistic identity. The first dream, recorded in the Bible, is of Jacob's ladder in Bethel where "he 'heard' God give the land on which he lay to him and his descendants, promising this territory in perpetuity" (80). The second dream is that of Prince Lazar before the Serbian defeat at Kosovo, which is a central element in the collective memory and political legitimization of the Serbian state. Edgar suggests that "for many people the springs of personal, historical and religious identity are founded, at least to some extent, on reported and recorded dreams." For Edgar, these dreams participate in a cultural process akin to myth-making: images in the mind (dreams) become an aspect of the central mythos of a group, transmitted over generations. Edgar further critically notes that "a reported dream has a potentially special role in such 'mythhood' because it is an unverifiable, ontologically based narrative and numinous" (Edgar, 2002: 84).

When critical inquiry reaches the shores of dreams, it asks us to question universal assumptions about dreams and dreaming, for example, in relation to gender or social identity. A clear instance has been to question the "straight view" of anima and animus in Jungian theory and its relevance to those of other sexual orientations. For example, a form of "queering" of Jung's theory of sexual opposites has been proposed by McKenzie (2006). She writes: "A revision of Jungian gender theory that embraces all genders and sexualities is needed not only to inform our clinical work but also to allow us to bring Jungian thought to contemporary gender theory and to cultural struggles such as gay marriage" (401). In its critique of universal truth, postmodern thought has rekindled the contextual nature of dreams, and given a rationale for how to reflect about localized identity in the context of a globalized world.

DREAMS IN AN EVOLUTIONARY SOCIAL CONTEXT

The rise of modernity has seen the self increasingly form an internalized locus. Religion, once the intersubjective container of group experience, became increasingly confined to the singular subjective space. Modern spirituality becomes an internal phenomenon where each individual, in a relative state of cosmic alienation, chooses how best to engage with greater existential questions. This chapter traces a similar trajectory from group to singular experience in regard to dreams.

We can situate the integral approach as one movement that constellates within the postmodern era. The integral approach views dreams as emerging from a mesh of all four quadrants: no single quadrant's narrative is the master of all. Each dreamer is asked to read one's dreams from one's own context. Perhaps we are at the dawn of an integral era, where the multiple ways of being with dreams are again given their due, including community-based processes, individually based processes, and organic biological-based processes, each seen in their complex interaction and interdependency.

In this milieu, transparency and self-awareness become important criteria of growth. We assent to the fact that dreams can direct our attention to the multiple threads of knowledge about both self and culture. This includes both the manners in which culture and social forms can encourage or discourage dream inquiry, but also the way that dreams can inform us about generational fractures and cultural alienation, social issues[6] (including conformity to identity narratives), and even ecological degradation. Perhaps new dream practices (in groups and in private) may emerge that decenter the self as the final arbiter of the dreaming meaning.

A focus on evolutionary dynamics would place the complexity of the self within the various co-constitutive loci of self-formation: family; groups of affiliation (e.g., gender identity; sexual orientation; national, religious, ethnic, class, or even trauma-related identity), and institutions of all kinds that shape our life. Body and brain may be integrated subsystems that reflect the dynamics of self-organizing development, but society is seen as the *epigenetic* environment that can entrain the brain in one direction or another.

> Every perception [can be] considered to be an act of creation and every memory an act of imagination. The individualistic flavor and the extraordinary richness of selective repertoires suggest that, in each brain, epigenetic elements play major and unpredictable roles. . . . Genetic and developmental factors interact to yield systems of remarkable complexity capable of an equally remarkable degree of freedom. The constraints placed on this freedom . . . do not seem as impressive as the unending ability of . . . the brain to confront novelty, to generalize upon it and to adapt in unforeseen fashion. (Edelman, 1987: 329)

It has been argued that the major developmental shift within humanity has not been biological but cultural (Dawkins, 1976). As unpredictable and open-ended as they are, dreams fulfill an important role in imagining our place in the world, as simultaneously an individual and social self. Dreams reflect our personal developmental journey while presenting us with enigmatic, partial, and difficult visions of the dilemmas that tie self and society together in their evolutionary dance; dreams reflect the traces of alienation and fragmentation as well as recovery and remembrance of our state of interdependence.

Part III

Integral Dream Practice

Philosophy and Application

Overview

Part II situated the dream experience in relation to various aspects of human engagement—according to biology, self, relationships, and the larger ecological and social-cultural contexts. We explored the links to past memory and current concerns as well as the social and cultural origins of dream practices and their historical trajectories. Looking at the dream experience in itself, we saw that by nature dreams are creative: they are a collage of experience, imagery, and emotion linked together within a narrative frame, although at times, extraordinary dreams break from this frame.

We believe that *dreaming is the art of the mind.* Part III unfolds this foundational aspect of dreaming in practice. As unique creations, dreams can be appreciated as pieces of art perfect in their own right. At the same time, clinical and personal experience, as well as research, have demonstrated that dreams can have the potential to be deeply informative and transformative psychologically, emotionally, and spiritually.[1]

In Part III we explore some of the fundamental questions about dreams: Do dreams have meaning? If meaning is to be unfolded, how should we do so? How do methods for interpreting the meaning of dreams differ from each other? Is it possible to simply be with a dream or have an awareness of the presence of a dream without interpreting it? How can interpretive and non-interpretive approaches coalesce to form a more integral practice? And finally, even when we come to some interpretation, how do we fully integrate the insights in waking life?

To our knowledge, no single method is able to address the full variety of dreams that we experience throughout our lifetime. Perhaps that is the reason there are an abundance of "how to" books on understanding dreams. Therefore, instead of plainly suggesting techniques, we engage the issue of meaning at a philosophical level by looking at the various assumptions behind dream interpretation.

This exploration sets the stage for a detailed description of *Integral Dream Practice* itself. Integral Dream Practice is a structure of carefully interrelated methods developed by the authors that allows for a new experience of the dream and possibly the fuller integration of a dream into the dreamer's life. After describing Integral Dream Practice philosophy and the stages of the method, we illustrate it with a single but extensive example. We try to convey that to integrate a dream into one's life takes time, and to do so in a deep way, one needs to develop certain qualities of awareness and engage in creative practices that organically unfold the process of insight.

NOTE TO THE READER

Part III contains a general description of methods; it is not intended as a didactic and detailed explanation of how these methods are applied. The information presented in these chapters is provided to describe the philosophical foundations and the general components of an integrative approach, not as instructions or training on how to do the practices.

CHAPTER ELEVEN

Toward an Integral Dream Practice

> I leave theory aside as much as possible when analyzing dreams—not entirely, of course, for we always need some theory to make things intelligible. It is on the basis of theory, for instance, that I expect dreams to have a meaning.
>
> —C. G. Jung, *Dreams*

What we now call Integral Dream Practice (IDP) has grown out of the wealth of experience we have developed through teaching about dreams and through working with individuals for more than twenty-five years. Integral Dream Practice is an approach to dream awareness that encourages multiple ways of knowing, engaging the multifaceted self with the intention of gaining insights to both dreaming and waking life. Beginning with the view that we are multidimensional beings, this practice fosters a way of being with dreams that incorporates creative, somatic, and contemplative practices. A person engaging in Integral Dream Practice is guided to unfold a co-creative relationship among many aspects of their creative self through a series of methods we have developed over time. The overall purpose of Integral Dream Practice is to explore the dream holistically and be present to its creative potential.

The terms *dream work, dream working,* or *dream worker,* popularized by Jungian analyst Robert Johnson in his book *Inner Work* in 1986, have gained currency among practitioners in the field of dream studies, although not everyone in the field subscribes to this terminology. Johnson suggests that consciousness evolves through our work with the psyche. The word *work* brings to mind ideas of effort and labor in order to achieve a purpose or result. When we adjoin the word *working* with dreams, it presupposes that dreams need to be worked on or that it takes effort to benefit from them. Although it is *work* to look within, we would like to suggest a different way of addressing the subject. Could it be that dreams need greater appreciation, and an attitude of deep listening?

Our view of *working* with dreams evolved into what we call *dream awareness* (or existentially, *being-with-dreams*). Especially during the initial phase of the practice, we encourage dreamers to become *aware* of their dreams by suggesting that they pay attention to the impressions left by a dream and by inviting them to reenter the dream with intentionality. This simple invitation into dream awareness can lead to developing a deeper relationship with one's inner life. We also encourage the dreamer to allow the dream to unfold; that is, the clarity and insights from a dream develop or expand over time as the dreamer participates with this practice. For this reason, dream awareness is a crucial first step in dream education. *Dream awareness begins with the understanding that every dream is an experience that is, by nature, intrinsically creative.* Even though we try to refrain from the phrase *dream work,* in certain discussions we might refer to this common expression in the sense of *inner work.*

THE CREATIVE AND EXPERIMENTAL ROOTS OF INTEGRAL DREAM PRACTICE

The holistic stance of Integral Dream Practice implies a flexible approach to being with dreams. The integral view might appear laborious and time consuming, but paradoxically, by slowing the process, a deeper sense of connection with the self arises. A planted seed does not turn into a fruit tree overnight. Once the tree is well established, fruit will be abundant. When awareness skills are learned, it is much faster and easier to be fully present to a dream.

Integral Dream Practice not only draws from psychological knowledge but also incorporates other creative approaches to address our whole being. This combination was developed and integrated from the authors' training in many areas and to which they added creative practices and methodological refinements. Bogzaran (1983) developed a series of creative methods of working with dreams using various psychological and creative tools to explore one dream from different perspectives. In her experimental psychology seminar on sleep and dreams (1984), her students became co-experimenters who tested these methods and evaluated their impact and effectiveness in facilitating insights. Based on the students' feedback, Bogzaran created a systematic model of dream awareness. A single dream is explored repeatedly through varieties of psychological and artistic modalities, such as automatic writing, expressive arts (painting, sculpture, mask making, and so on), somatic awareness and dream groups. This work further evolved (1986) by introducing sonic entrainment (in particular the sound of a monotonous drum beat, also known as shamanic drumming) as a tool for dream reentry. In 1988, she developed Dream Creations, collaborating with the late performer Jessica Allen to include Allen's approach to Dream Theater. This integrative approach was presented at the fifth convention of the Association for the Study of Dreams.[1]

Trained with Ullman in the 1980s, Deslauriers worked with dream groups, used dream body maps, and worked with experimental theater. His research on narrative, emotion, and metaphor led him to co-develop a five-step "Dream Understanding Exercise" and a research tool, the "Dream Understanding Questionnaire," to evaluate it (Baylor & Deslauriers, 1986; 1987).

In the 1990s, the authors combined their modalities of working with dreams to create a larger perspective leading to the model of Integral Dreaming. Bogzaran developed the model by introducing elements of qualitative research such as phenomenological and creative hermeneutics, and Deslauriers contributed a cognitive-experiential aspect in script and emotional analysis (Bogzaran & Deslauriers, 1989).

Integral Dream Practice is an innovative practice that can be used in many settings where there is a focus on transformative inquiry.[2] Our work has evolved within the educational context of teaching graduate-level university courses, public workshops, and retreats and grows out of considerable time spent reflecting on the tenets of a general dream psychology adapted to the educational setting. This has meant unfolding the integral approach to dreams over the twelve- to fifteen-week period of an academic course. The resulting pedagogy became an important signature of our work and inquiry. It is known that complex or *big* dreams can unfold over an extended period of time.[3] Yet we have created an intensive version of this mode of being with dreams that works well in a retreat setting. The model and the philosophy of interdisciplinary dream practice have been shown to be life transforming for many individuals in classroom and group trainings (Bogzaran & Fowler, 2006, 2007). With its strong emphasis on the facilitation and discovery of the dreamers' personal inquiry and experience, Integral Dream Practice can be adapted to different cultural contexts.

INTEGRAL DREAMING AS AN AWARENESS PRACTICE

Because dreams are multidimensional, the method of approaching dreams needs to be multidimensional as well. The methodology within Integral Dream Practice attempts to address the dreamer's whole being through an awareness process, with the intention of the dreamer becoming a more conscious human being. This work is consonant with that of several other colleagues whose writings support dream awareness as an important avenue in assisting human transformation including Aizenstat (2009); Bosnak (2007); Garfield (1988, 1991); Gordon (2007); Hillman (1979); Mahrer (1989); and Tedlock (2005).

The goal of most dream understanding methods is to help the dreamer bridge inner life with outer existence. Integral Dream Practice (IDP) is no exception, as it encourages dreamers to understand their inner life as a raw creative force. With practice, the dreamer's attention is given to dreams that leave deeper impressions due to their emotional, visual, auditory, or kinesthetic impact. Beyond the immediate focus on dreams, we consider IDP to be a form of awareness practice, much like contemplative meditation.

The Integral Dream Practice serves the dreamer in four ways:

1. Connects the dreamer to the multidimensionality of her or his inner life.
2. Reunites the dreamer with his or her creative wholeness.
3. Facilitates transformation at the personal level, and has the potential of bringing insight to collective issues as well.
4. Can be an occasion for personal or spiritual growth.

Multiplicity of One's Inner Life

From the cellular level in our bodies to the depths of our psyche, our inner life is interwoven with layers of beliefs, emotions, and ideas that shape the complex texture of life experiences. In Part II we showed how dream experiences are essential to physiological and psychological balance. Dream awareness is one way of accessing the landscape of the inner worlds: What is the nature of the dreaming mind? What is the topography of this special state of consciousness? How do we inhabit our dreaming mind? Integrative approaches invite individuals, during waking hours, to engage the entire spectrum of experience with lucid attention; during sleeping hours, they prompt dreamers to appropriately question habitual patterns they have discovered through their waking awareness that no longer serve them.

The methods included in Integral Dream Practice can help dreamers access their creative potential and establish a fertile ground for a possibly transformative experience. More specifically, the practice creates a space for the awareness of the body (kinesthetic), the heart (emotional and relational), and the mind (cognitive), enhancing one's relationship to one's creativity. Each of these aspects of the self can unfold its own intelligence, leading toward an experiential understanding of *whole self*.

Creativity

Dreams have always been a source of creative inspiration, insight, and self-awareness and are an accessible source of creative flow. Cultivating and remembering dreams make the dreamer aware of new aspects of the creative mind. The awareness of dreams enhances creative insight and facilitates creative wholeness. To acknowledge and become aware of the creative self can be an inspiring experience but an unsettling one, too. The creative self challenges habitual ways of seeing and introduces new ways of knowing. Dream awareness can transform the self and the world by the integrating of the creative self into daily life.

Transformation

Dreams can facilitate transformative healing by engaging dimensions of our being that may have been wounded, repressed, or left underdeveloped. The psychological literature on dreams, beginning with Freud and Jung and continuing to the present, has shown that dream awareness is a powerful tool and vehicle to engage with one's personal and psychological concerns. Numerous methods of working with dreams have been shown to help with self-growth and personal insights.

Spiritual Growth

Dream awareness reconnects the dreamer to the mystery of the mind. Such awareness opens the dreamer to the vast dimension of what Jung called the Self. Dreams call for the integration of higher aspirations, insights, and spiritual intuitions into our life-world. These dimensions of experience can open doors to extraordinary inner phenomena often referred to as transpersonal, transcendent, or mystical. Perhaps these experiences, as rare as they are, can be very impactful. They form a part of the natural maturational process: special moments when we catch a glimpse of more subtle or complex aspects of the mind or of nature. These experiences may include connecting with possible selves or no self, energy streaming through the body, experiences of the void, or that of hyperspace. While there is a place for the exploration of these phenomena within Integral Dream Practice, the focus is primarily on their integration. IDP does not privilege one form of maturity over others, as the development of each individual is unique.

THE ARC OF INTEGRAL DREAM PRACTICE

The arc of Integral Dream Practice generally unfolds in two stages. First is an extended didactic session where scientific, theoretical, and historical grounding of the integral model is provided, such as was presented in Part II of this book; the second is the experiential part of IDP, which engages the following two phases:

- *Reflexive Emergence*: This phase is introspective and non-interpretive in essence. Dreamers unfold the phenomenology of dreaming—through experiential and creative methods involving dream-reentry, creative expressions, and automatic writing, culminating in a poetic synthesis.
- *Reflective Integration*: This phase provides the occasion to look back at the dreams and the reflexive emergence through a more analytic stance. Among the reflective methods are script analysis, personal mythology, and somatic and psychological inquiry.

Because a large part of the focus of Integral Dream Practice rests on the unfolding of creative dream awareness, an open attitude toward dreams needs to be cultivated in order to encounter the full range of IDP's potential. Both of these phases and the practices associated with them will be explained in detail in chapters 14 and 15.

In the next two chapters, we discuss two complementary hermeneutic perspectives. The integral way of exploring dreams demands inclusive practices that draw upon both non-interpretative (reflexive emergence) and interpretive (reflective integration) approaches to dreams. Integral Dream Practice however goes beyond these two approaches, unfolding a *hermeneutic of creation*. To be with a dream within IDP is to inquire into the nature of the creative self. This innovative hermeneutic stance is participatory: meaning is enacted inside the process of discovery. We lay down the foundations of our philosophy of practice in chapter 14 and we illustrate with an extensive example in the final chapter.

From the perspective of methodology, Integral Dream Practice mixes practices that are both ancient and modern. IDP can be learned and used by people trained in a variety of fields, and it can be adapted to group or individual work.[4] As a theory of practice, Integral Dream Practice can benefit dream practitioners from different backgrounds and training who can incorporate aspects most relevant and meaningful to them, blending these with their own expertise.

CHAPTER TWELVE

Hermeneutic of Dream Interpretation

> Every interpretation is a hypothesis, an attempt to read an unknown text. An obscure dream, taken in isolation, can hardly ever be interpreted with any certainty.
>
> —C. G. Jung, *Dreams*

By their sheer creativity, dreams generate astonishment, puzzlement, and at times dismay. Seeking meaning in them is a natural response. But doing so raises countless enigmas about their source, their direction, and whether dreams indeed contain information. The wide variety of approaches used to tease meaning from dreams only adds to the perplexity. Where does one begin?

This chapter explores the methods of approaching dreams interpretatively and the assumptions attach to them. For example, an implicit habit is to view dreams as text, the so-called unopened letters that must be properly read. Meaning-making becomes a deciphering task by probing the text of the dream or the dreamer's reactions to it. The study of understanding, called *hermeneutics,* tells us that each time we engage in the reading of a text, we do so from a given perspective and we project into the text our *presuppositions* (pre-understandings).[1] The traditional approach of seeing dreams as a text to be analyzed epitomizes what we call a *hermeneutic of interpretation*.[2] However, other approaches, equally effective, follow a non-interpretive path that puts an emphasis on the dream as an embodied experience.

To extract the contrast between interpretive and non-interpretative approaches, we have chosen two well-known stories found in the dream literature. In this chapter we examine the biblical story of Daniel, the famous dream interpreter; in the following chapter, we explore a teaching story by the Taoist philosopher Chuang Tzu. These historical stories are often cited to convey the staying power of dreams in ancient times. Looking at these stories creatively, we asked ourselves: Could it be that they act as formative myths about dream interpretation? Could they shed light on what dream understanding is supposed to be, even by questioning the very nature of the interpretative act? For us, they serve as a point of departure from which to extrapolate the philosophical and practical issues inherent in both interpretation and non-interpretation. Furthermore, by engaging with these two stories from their respective origins, we are building a bridge between Eastern and Western systems of thought and ways of approaching dreams.

THE STORY OF DANIEL

Daniel was an Israelite in exile in Babylon who had been enculturated in the rules and ways of the conqueror's court. In this story, he saved his life and that of others by correctly retelling and then interpreting the dream of Nebuchadnezzar II, king of Babylon (c. 605–562 BC). The king had a troubling nightmare "wherewith his spirit was troubled, and his sleep brake from him"[3] (KJV, Daniel 2:1). The king called upon magicians, astrologers, and wise ones not only to interpret his dream, but first he asked them to tell him (or rediscover) what the dream was! The king said: "The thing is gone from me: if ye will not make known unto me the dream, with the interpretation thereof, ye shall be cut in pieces, and your houses shall be made dunghill" (KJV, Daniel 2:5). Whoever succeeded in revealing the dream and its interpretation would receive rewards and honors; whoever failed faced doom and death.

The first point to note is that the story begins with a forgotten dream, what today is attributed either to a function of the physiology of dreaming or to an act of repression. The astute request of the king shows that he could only give his trust to whoever showed the extraordinary capacity to reveal someone else's dream. This requirement undoubtedly sets the bar very high. The wise ones responded that, except for the gods, no one could possibly show the king what his dream was. This angered the king, and he ordered all wise men of Babylon to be killed, including Daniel and his brothers.

From the point of view of "expectations toward dream experts," the story contains significant assumptions; not least of which is that seeking meaning and finding methods of dream interpretation are of vital importance—a matter of either a *correct* interpretation or death! Although, of course, a modern approach to dreaming would not pose a death threat to a dream expert if the dream were not rightly interpreted, the story dramatizes the difficult task faced by all interpreters. The horizons of dream meaning are vast, and a valid interpretation offered properly can indeed create a transformative cascade. The opposite is also true: a misinterpretation of a dream feels *dead*. Furthermore, interpretative missteps can lead to loss of regard for the interpreter (another form of death). Similarly, a kind of negative transference can creep in if interpretation is offered too sharply, is wrongly imposed, or is given too soon. Incidentally, the story shows that even a person in power can be powerless in front of a dream. But it also begs the question: How far can one's responsibility toward one's inner life be passed on to others, even those who make the art of interpretation their trade?

Aware of the king's threat, Daniel took on the task to divine (incubate) the king's dream and interpret it. To do so, he employed three key approaches: first, he called on the support of his three brothers; second, he called on the help of a higher power; and third, he looked to his own dreams to find an answer. Although the story emphasizes that only the God of the chosen people could provide the right answer, it also tells us that some answers about dreams are found in the dream state itself.[4]

Daniel's story is intriguing in the hidden assumptions it exposes about the qualifications of dream interpreters. Not only must the dream interpreter be a powerful and correct meaning-maker, but she or he must also be in touch with a larger cosmic vision (embodied here in a personalized God), acting on strong faith and seemingly displaying psychic power! Perhaps it is no coincidence that many contemporary researchers and psychologists who work with dreams also have interests in parapsychology, religious studies, and altered states of consciousness and have shared their own experience of so-called anomalous dreams.

Jung posthumously revealed in *Memories, Dreams, Reflections* (1965) and in *The Red Book* (2009) the depth of his spiritual experiences and the synchronicities that he could not expose during his early career, for fear of being ostracized (put to death professionally). Within the field of dream studies, countless authors either explicitly or implicitly discuss parapsychological aspects of dreaming (Krippner, 1985, 1990; Persinger & Krippner, 1989; Russo, 1987; Ullman & Krippner, 1973; Van de Castle, 1977). Dreams and parapsychological events remain controversial among researchers, and some have made attempts to put their skepticism to the test (Domhoff, 2000). If we look at the story of Daniel from an intersubjective stance, the theme of "dreaming for the other" opens up an important consideration. Perhaps dream interpretation does not require parapsychological gifts or skills, but it does necessitate a form of deep attunement, which nowadays is enacted in a collaborative manner between the dreamer and the therapist. Such attunement may play out differently in an Indigenous context between a dream specialist and a dreamer. Dreaming for others is practiced among many cultures, which have developed techniques for that purpose. This practice is subject to many cultural inflections, but at its core, the dreamer sets an intention before going to sleep, calling for assistance from a spiritual ally, a higher power, a god or ancestor, or more abstractly from a spiritual force. Within the modern mentality, the dream source may be understood in terms of problem-solving intelligence operating implicitly (or unconsciously).

Dream incubation was a widely used practice known throughout the Mediterranean basin (Meier, 1989). For the ancients, it would seem natural, then, that one would put dreaming to use in an intentional manner. As the story goes, Daniel has a revelatory dream in which the "secret was revealed unto him." Here the story thus makes us aware of the fluidity of the dreaming mind and its connection to insight.[5] (In chapter 4 we show how scientific research corroborates this connection.)

Daniel eventually brings his answers to the king, assigning the responsibility of his vision on his God. "No wise man, enchanter, magician or diviner can explain to the king the mystery he has asked about, but there is a God in heaven who reveals mysteries. He has shown King Nebuchadnezzar what will happen in days to come. Your dream and the visions that passed through your mind as you lay on your bed are these" (Daniel 2:27–28). This passage raises the question of the origins of dreams: Where do dreams, inspiration, insight, creativity, and imagination come from? Do their origins belong exclusively to the human source, the dreamer, or do they arise from something greater than individual consciousness? As difficult as it is to answer these questions, we believe that inquiry into dreams should consider them seriously.

Upon receiving the answer to his prayers in a dream, Daniel praises God: "Blessed be the name of God for ever and ever for wisdom and might are his. . . . He revealeth the deep and secret things, he knoweth what is in the darkness, and the light dwelleth with him" (Daniel 2:20, 22). While these capacities may have divine origins, their manifestation demands human participation to be in touch with what is in the dark recess of the psyche, and to bring light to it. The book of Daniel shows that he was the brave one who risked presenting an interpretation where all others failed, and helps the king to remember his forgotten or repressed dream. In that sense, it bears some similarity to therapeutic encounters in which the therapist assists the client to remember and reclaim discarded parts of him- or herself.

The story ends with the king being pleased and bowing to Daniel, who gathers many rewards but also attracts jealousy (which leads him to the famous encounter with the lions!). The main point of the dream was to sensitize the king to the fact that part of one's destiny escapes human agency, being in the hands of God or more simply of fate. If the dream discloses the archetypal idea that God has a plan for us, individually and collectively, and that everyone's "kingdom" will gradually come to an end, it is not clear how the king heard the dream, as a potential harbinger of either his own demise or that of his kingdom.[6]

The story of Daniel hints at the capacity for a dream to access some *higher* or, at the very least, some other source of knowing. Daniel's name itself may be an additional narrative pointer, as names sometimes give clues to the virtue portrayed by a protagonist. In this case, the virtue is discernment since in Hebrew *dan* conveys the gift of discernment or good judgment, and *iy'el* or *el* means "of or from God." Symbolically, the story intimates some crucial points about the role of wise discernment in relation to dreams. First, discernment should be applied *to* dreams in how we regard or address them. Second, and more controversial, it is possible to derive the gift of discernment *from* dreams. In other words, dreams themselves can help in the process of discernment by presenting new perspectives, images, and experiences. Of course, the two intersect especially when we attempt to discern from our dreams what it is they are offering, for example, when one tries to decipher rightful action from their understanding (Frey, 2007).

The Daniel story instructs us about the assumptions around dream interpretation and the role of the interpreter. It also invites us to consider the creative interplay between the waking and dreaming mind, and the virtue that we must bring to it. Finally, the story also addresses the potential limits of understanding and the expectations of the dreamer. We turn to the latter before we address more contemporary approaches to interpretation.

DREAMERS' EXPECTATIONS

A common reaction attends a dream "expert" or "specialist" when she or he reveals their profession to a stranger: first a puzzled stare, followed by a brief silence pursued by an immediate remark such as, "That is very interesting, let me tell you this very strange dream I had." The stranger often proceeds to share a dream without asking whether the "dream expert" wants to hear the dream or not! It is as if the stranger had kept this treasure bottled up for a long time and was waiting for the right person to have its mystery revealed. After telling the dream, the dreamer often offers a pregnant pause and then asks, sometimes demandingly, "Well, what do you think this dream means?"

The first general assumption for someone who has never worked with his/her dreams is that the dream expert has the key to the dream's meaning. The expert is the knower and the dreamer is a passive agent to whom the dream has happened. The dream becomes a puzzle to be solved, and often the dreamer is looking for a quick answer to what appears as a bizarre riddle. These expectations contribute to a diminished view of dreaming. The expert is positioned in a role of a stage magician who is given an egg (the dream) and then is supposed to wrap it in a richly colored cloth (the expert knowledge), and a flying dove will appear within seconds (the interpretation). The need for quick answers has spawned dream symbols dictionaries or other shortcuts to dream meaning. These approaches can bring momentary gratification, but in the long run they always leave serious dreamers asking for something deeper. On the other hand, contextualizing the dream, placing and integrating the meaning of a dream into waking life, may take a longer time. Could we perhaps reexamine our habitual tendency, upon receiving a dream to want to do something with it, to impose an interpretation on it?

The assumption that dreams are meant to be interpreted is common. Many approaches now teach the dreamer not to jump onto interpretation, but to approach dreams as an open inquiry. What do the dream images metaphorically stand for? How do the dream's emotions and narrative connect to the life events of the dreamer? We spoke in chapters 5 and 6 about how meaning-making is linked to a process of storying (what we called *narrativization*): when dream understanding matches the waking-life narrative around current, past, or future concerns, often the dreamer feels a deeper sense of satisfaction. Working with dreams from multiple perspectives is like painting a detail of a larger canvas: the bigger view might not reveal itself immediately. The dreamer needs to be sensitized that his or her first insights are often the beginning brushstrokes on a larger canvas of discovery.

Within the integrative model, we keep an open mind by examining and learning from both interpretive and non-interpretive avenues in order to have a larger container to hold the complexities of dreaming. The following sections briefly review a few main interpretive methods.

INTERPRETIVE APPROACHES

In his seminal book, *The Interpretation of Dreams*, Freud debates the relative value and the known pitfalls of the hermeneutic of interpretation. In the chapter describing "the method of interpreting dreams," he writes:

> A dim presentiment seems to lead [us] to assume that the dream does possess a meaning, though a hidden one, that it stands as a substitute for another mode of thinking, and that it is only a matter of finding the right way to reveal this substitute for the hidden significance of the dream to be disclosed. (1999: 78)

Freud distinguishes two major methods of dream interpretation: the symbolic method and the decoding method. He describes the *symbolic* dream interpretation method as one that "takes the dream-content as a whole and seeks to replace it with a different, intelligible, and in certain respects analogous content" (Freud, 1999: 78). He summarily discards this method as unreliable and unscientific. Freud points out that this is the method used by Joseph when interpreting the Pharaoh's dream in the biblical story of Genesis.

What Freud calls the *decoding method*, by contrast, "treats the dream as a kind of secret writing in which every sign is translated by means of a fixed key into another sign whose significance is known" (Freud, 1999: 79). Freud admitted that he found the second method more amenable to rationality and more sensitive to the particularities of his patient's condition. Within the framework of psychoanalysis, he describes how each element of a dream can be systematically analyzed, with the help of the dreamer's associations, to reveal some underlying repressed or unconscious dream thoughts, the so-called latent content, which, according to the orthodox Freudian view, is connected to the wishes of the dreamer.

Current research has shown most dreams are organized around the concerns of the individual having to do with recent experiences. Within psychoanalysis, the transformation of these concerns into wishes and the attending theory of dream formation provided for Freud the *fixed key* that unlocked dream interpretation. Biological research, and the accumulating knowledge about various types of dream have exposed the way in which Freud's theory has overstated the facts.

An integral perspective would seek to distinguish from Freudian theory the valid aspects from those that became outdated through the accumulation of disconfirming knowledge. And although wish-fulfillment in the sense of life-affirming process is one of the major motivating factors in our species, we find it unfortunate that the wide range of nuanced human concerns were reduced, in orthodox psychoanalysis, to issues of repressed infant sexuality or some entropic death drive.

To its credit, the framework of contemporary psychoanalysis has vastly expanded on Freud's original insight. As a result, dream interpretation, which had been on the wane within psychoanalysis, is finding new ground of appreciation by including intersubjective factors[7] with developmental theory (Fosshage, 2002, 2007). Pared down from the meta-psychological tenets around wish fulfillment, psychic censorship, and dream work mechanisms, Freud's two main points about dream interpretation have remained quite central:

- That dreaming embodies a kind of language of its own, one that is open to interpretation. This language of dreams is now understood as hyperassociative narrative (Hartmann, 2000), an adaptive mode of thought in continuity with waking cognition, and including extensive verbal tropes (States, 1988) and visual-motor translation of feeling states (Hunt, 1989). In other words, dream language could be seen as a form of psychic "hypertext" organized around an emotionally laden syntax, that is, the concerns of the dreamer. One can begin the reading or decoding process by inquiry into any part of the dream, and once the process has begun it can become exponentially recursive or expansive.

- The work of dream understanding consists in great part of reconstructing the context of the dreamer's life in relation to the dream "hypertext."

These two ideas have been at the core of most dream understanding methods elaborated in the twentieth century. Each method asserts its innovative stance either by:

a. privileging some mode of experience over others, for example, focusing either on emotions, intellectual/symbolic aspects, somatic experience, and so on;
b. offering some original framework around psychic functioning (e.g., compensation, repression, continuity, spiritual revelation, creativity) or
c. adopting modalities of exploration over others, for example, collaborative interviewing, role taking, projective association, free association, amplification.[8]

Besides the question of whether or not dreams have intended meaning, Freud's legacy has left us to debate some important questions: Is dream formation a process of psychic disguise? Can the dreamer safely and by him or herself arrive at dream meaning by working alone? Or can the work of dream understanding only be fruitful in concert with another, such as a therapist, who is somewhat freer from the entanglement of the psychic complexes of the client?

Such interpretive inquiries ask us to consider how to approach dreams. Two contrasting hermeneutic stances provide different answers: The *hermeneutic of suspicion* and *hermeneutic of discovery*.

The *hermeneutic of suspicion* asks: should we approach dreams and the dreamer with an attitude of caution, assuming that the dream may be a disguise or the dreamer prone to defensive misperception? If this is the case, the therapist needs to attend to the ways dreamers can delude themselves by "not seeing" or "dreaming up" convenient answers, thereby impeding psychological progress.[9]

The *hermeneutic of discovery* asks: shall we approach dreams with an attitude of trust. The dream is the best possible expression of a psychic situation. The dreamer, with proper attitude, guidance, or training, can get in touch with some valid truth about some situation (his/her own or that of others) as disclosed through the dream. Such a hermeneutic of discovery emphasizes the healthy aspects of the personality.

Bert States proposes an integrative solution here, merging the common difficulty faced by both positions: "The dream cannot be interpreted as either expression, repression or anything else, without an exhaustive examination of its context in the dreamer's psychic life" (1988: 184). In that way, States joins Paul Ricoeur, who says that dreams partake of a polar life. Kearney explains, "The basic hermeneutic lesson to be gleaned from dreams, according to Ricoeur is that images can serve to mask as well as to disclose meaning. If poetry represents the positive pole of dreams, dissimulation represents its negative pole. . . . It is the double texture of dream images—the internal transgression of one meaning by another—that invites our critical interpretation" (Kearney, 2004: 48). In both the acts of dreaming and interpreting, the self's predicament is between the joy of discovery and knowing and the taboo against knowing; or between the desire for self-knowledge and the limits of self-perception through defenses. And because of the latter, sometimes working with a dream benefits by the presence of another to overcome these limitations. As Ricoeur aptly states, "[T]here are no symbols without the beginning of interpretation; where one man dreams, prophesizes, or poetizes, another rises up to interpret. Interpretation organically belongs to symbolic thought and its double meaning" (1970: 19).

The orientation of Integral Dream Practice toward interpretation is to foster discovery. However, this stance is enacted with an awareness that the dreamer does not *always* wish to see, or integrate, all that a dream may offer. In our courses, we encourage students to develop critical subjectivity to be mindful of that.

BEYOND FREUD'S HERMENEUTICS

Jung and his followers went beyond Freud's criticism about the symbolic approach to revive the value of such method, especially through the process of what is called *amplification*. For instance,

Jung's own research showed that, when probed for associations, people's train of thought almost inevitably led to personal issues, or individual complexes. Jung noticed that the associative process often stops where unconscious inhibition sets in, or else it switches into emotionally laden material (technically called *cathexis*). For Jung, it is not necessary to begin with dream images for this process to occur, although dreams remain invaluable in this regard. Word associations can be a starting point, as can nonrepresentational images, such as the Rorschach inkblots.

According to Jung, dreams are clearly more than the starting point of an informative associative process. For him, dreams are the voice of the *inner Other*. They present the psyche's best attempt at expressing what the conscious mind is missing when attempting to address an emotionally charged issue. The *inner Other* is imputed to provide a view that complements that of waking. This idea is at the core of what Jung called "compensation."[10] Jung clearly believes in the continuity between dreams and the dreamer's current situation. What Jung wishes to translate is how the dream could relate to one's experience from a wider perspective when compared to that of the waking self. Compensation is only a special case of this continuity.

Jung's contribution to psychology was to clarify the influential role of collective imagination, framed around self-organizing psychic patterns he named archetypes. He showed how archetypes are expressed in both individual life and social life. As the same (archetypal) organizing patterns apply to both private and social life, dream contents show strong parallels to cultural myths across time and cultures.

Linked to this view, Jung also made two important contributions to the praxis of dream interpretation: symbolic amplification and the technique of active imagination. These have influenced countless contemporary dream analysts. Symbolic amplification can be explained by using the metaphor of a wheel. If free association is centrifugal, a movement *away* from the dream images in the direction of the originating complex, by contrast, amplification is a centripetal movement. Each amplification of a single image could be seen as a separate spoke of a wheel. Many amplification strands link up to particular mythological motifs, within and across cultures, connect *back* to the dream image and create a fuller picture. Just as the many spokes connect the frame of a wheel to its hub (the dream image), and strengthen its functionality, so is the personality made whole by connecting back to an archetypal field. Jung demonstrated for instance, how the symbol of the mandala, found cross-culturally and in dreams, stands as an organizing pattern of wholeness. Owing to his multidisciplinary cross-cultural interests, we consider Jung one of the main predecessors of Integral Dream Practice.

As for Jung's technique of active imagination, it asks the dreamer to return, in waking, inside the dream space and to attend to the spontaneous appearance of imagery, emotions, and experiences. In active imagination, the dreamer participates in the unfolding of waking dreams by, for example, asking questions, noticing feelings, even conversing with dream characters. As we will see in the next chapter, this movement of returning to the dream plays a central part in Integral Dream Practice. However, because active imagination has become entangled with particular Jungian interpretive assumptions (e.g., *shadow*, *anima*, or even certain sets of archetypes), we shy away from using the technique per se but hearken back to its originating principle of attentive engagement and lucid relationship with the dream images.

Over their history in the twentieth century, psychoanalysis has focused increasingly more on ego-oriented (waking) content, whereas Jungian therapy, for its part, has remained more keenly centered around an emergent work of dream interpretation, following the dreamer's inner development within the process of self-discovery. Because of their success, these two views of dreaming—the psychodynamic (Freud and his successors) and analytical (Jung and his successors)—have become embedded in the general Western culture. The belief that dreams can reveal unconscious aspects of the personality is widespread (Dombeck, 1991). Paradoxically, because these views are so widely accepted, people have often lost track of their origins.

OTHER INTERPRETIVE AVENUES

Although we will not go in depth into the many other interpretive approaches that are already described in excellent work in the literature (Fosshage & Loew, 1987; Garfield, 2001; Shafton,

1995; Van de Castle, 1994), we will describe briefly some of the main practices that are core modalities of dream work—cognitive-experiential method, structural approaches, quantitative methods, and group work—as well as non-Western modes that are often either forgotten, misappropriated, or just plainly misunderstood in the Western literature on dreams.

Cognitive-Experiential Method

A widely researched dream technique, the experiential-cognitive approach synthesized by Clara Hill (2003), is now defining a new center for the use of dreams in individual therapy. It frames the work of dream interpretation as a collaborative endeavor, where the dreamer is guided to find meaning in the dream by a clear series of open-ended questions and hints. It consists of three stages: dream exploration, dream insight, and appropriate action deriving from the dream. The method can be deployed within the therapeutic hour. It has gained favor within ego-centered therapy for sensitizing the dreamer to important, if unformulated, feelings and solutions to life problems. Research has shown the technique to be highly effective, even with people with little knowledge about the dreaming process (Castonguay & Hill, 2007).

Structural Approaches to Dreams: Script Analysis and Personal Mythology

Baylor and Deslauriers (1987) take the view that the story schema is one of the best ways for the mind to express and work out issues of complexity. To enhance this avenue, they created an analytical method called *script analysis*. This method draws from hybrid sources and combines the idea of psychic balance put forth by psychosynthesis (Assagioli, 1965) with that of the story structure. The core premise of script analysis is that the dream narrative represents a series of choice points or dream enactments. As the dream progresses, the choices being made reflect the relative state of wholeness of our being (the organism). The dream is seen as an attempt at reaching *intra*subjective wholeness expressed within *inter*subjective balance in the dream.

Different *scripts* are a reflection of different degrees of balance and harmony or imbalance and conflict between all parties involved in the unfolding dream plot. Script analysis helps dreamers understand not only dream imagery but also patterns of behavior and emotions as they unfold within the dream plot. What are the choices the dreamer makes? What choices are made by other characters? How do the dream characters affect each other? What roles and goals do each of the characters have? And what is the impact of each choice for the wholeness of the entire system? Script analysis also allows the dreamer to explore different horizons of choices within the dream. For example, using script analysis, a dreamer exploring the prevalent dream theme of being chased would be invited to reflect on the following: Who is the perpetrator/chaser? What are the choices linked to fear? What prompts the dream ego to enact escape as opposed to confrontation, invitation, transformation, merging, and so on? Using this method, Deslauriers and Cordts (1995) also show how script analysis leads dreamers to reflect on their current concerns.

In a similar vein, the work of Feinstein and Krippner on personal mythology invites dreamers to link dream emotions with important life events that have played a crucial role in forming the belief system at the core of one's *personal mythology*. This work plays on the metaphor of emotions as a holographic template that coalesces past experience, current concerns, and the search for a new, more adaptive personal mythos. Dream feeling states and emotions are interpreted as reflecting the ongoing transformation of personal mythology:

> At the core of your personal myth is a motif that shapes your perceptions, guides your development, establishes your role in society, and helps you find spiritual meaning and connections. Your mythology fuels your emotions and shapes your beliefs. As you come to understand the principles by which your personal mythology operates, you will become more able to consciously participate in its development. (Feinstein & Krippner, 1988: 26)

Structural approaches deal with the various elements of experience (for example, a core dream emotion and its opposite), reflecting on their complex dialectic.

Quantitative Approaches

Within the scientific community the question of dream meaning is often discarded or found irrelevant. Dreams are mainly indexed through neurobiological traces, and the regularity of REM sleep has been used to discredit claims that dreams may arise to express unconscious wishes or desires (Hobson, 1988). However, many scientists follow a dual path, looking at both the scientific and meaning aspects of dreaming. The statistical studies made possible, for example, by the content analysis method[11] devised by Hall and Van de Castle and described in chapter 7 take a numerical approach to meaning: frequency expresses discernable patterns. This approach of scientifically coding dreams has led to many applications as well as insights about prevalent dreams and normative dreams and has possibly produced a way to access cultural and gender differences in dreaming (Domhoff, 2000).

Contrary to other interpretative approaches that look at a single dream, content analysis needs a dream series (the more the better, but a minimum of thirty dreams will begin to display patterns). Content analysis can be used to determine objectively the specific patterns that are captured along its coding schemes (relationship patterns, misfortune, emotional tone, successful problem-solving, intensity, issues with one's family, one's body, one's work, and so on). It does not call for symbolic or metaphorical interpretation (although it does not make those irrelevant), because it presupposes that patterns in dreams and waking patterns are continuous with one another. The dreamer cannot deny numerical patterns since frequencies derived from dream contents are translated as bold (or cold!) facts. Surprisingly, content analysis can lead to an honest mirroring of the dreamer's patterns. In *The Individual and His Dreams*, Hall and Nordby (1972) illustrated the fact that core concerns can be observed over an entire *lifetime*. Although the numerical methods are widely used in research, individuals only seldom use them, as most wish to work on a single dream at a given time.

Group Practice

Exploring dreams in groups has become increasingly popular, spurred by the leadership of the late Montague Ullman

(1979) on the East Coast of the United States and in Europe, and by Jeremy Taylor (1983, 1992) on the West Coast of the United States. Interpretation is arrived through a gentle and directed projective technique, where group members take the dream as if it were their own. This method, which calls for a democratic and plurivocal mode of interpretation, leaves the dreamer in charge of integrating the various suggestions that accumulate from the members' interventions. In a sense, group work reflects the postmodern situation: distrust of overarching interpretative metanarrative such as psychoanalysis or other schools (although these are likely reflected within the group responses), and giving voice to a plurality of voices and group intelligence. A cloud of associative material is formed as the group progresses. The group takes on the role of generating the associative material at a more thematic level but prompting the dreamer to respond in kind with more personal matter. This highly participatory method enables a reciprocal gifting to take place: the dreamer offers the dream to the group, and the group offers its projective association and interpretation of the dream back to the dreamer. Selecting which associations fit best, the dreamer is given the chance to resonate with many views, more than she or he could generate on her or his own. Ideally, the synergistic combination of association creates an opening for new meaning and insights. With the dream group process, the dreamer and the group members come out richer in experience: all are involved in the group learning process based on sharing multiple perspectives.

DREAM INTERPRETATION IN A LARGER CULTURAL CONTEXT

We have seen in chapters 9 and 10 that the dream experience can be subjected to many cultural interpretations. In the field of anthropology, beliefs and attitudes toward dreams are studied within the context of a particular culture. Many cultures have, by observation and experience, distinguished different types of dreams that call for different interpretation or intervention. Although certain types of dreams are meant to be interpreted, others are used for life-guiding purposes (Krippner et al., 2002). In many cultures, such as in the Tibetan culture, dreams are even used for divination. After asking their client about their wishes and hopes, some interpreters use dream incubation and their resultant dream to interpret the dreams of their clients (Zangpo, 2008). As in the biblical story of Daniel, one's own dreams are used to divine someone else's dreams. Dreaming culture ethnography has obviously widened the narrow horizon with which dreams have usually been conceived of in the modern West. Part of the postmodern movement has been to reconnect with subaltern and often discarded views of dreams, views that actually form the heritage of Indigenous dream interpretation in the West.

Meier (1989), for example, cites numerous sources from antiquities that show the use of dreams in incubation rituals for healing. The Asclepian divine medicine was a healing cure where dreamers where initiated into a *mystery*. The priests or priestesses sometimes dreamed for the sick or acted as *mystagogues* interpreting the incubants' dreams. As part of this ritual, the incubant was reborn and healed after a visit in the underworld (often a cave where the dreaming ritual occurred). Meier quotes Reitzentstein: "The initiate in the mysteries does not merely witness what the god experiences: he experiences it himself, and thus becomes the god" (in Meier, 1989: 108).

In traditional societies dreaming was often done not just for the sake of the dreamer but also in the service of the community. In written and oral tradition, a running theme is that paying attention to dreams has been vital and essential to the survival of the group. Living Indigenous traditions remind us that the horizon of dream understanding is wider than the individual self. This implies that we can dream for others, that ancestors show themselves to us in our dreams, and that ancient memory reaching beyond personal memory may be at play in dreams. Dreams may connect us with other beings with whom we share the planet: animals, places, and even other realms of intelligence beyond the visible world. This larger sphere of concern speaks to the multidimensionality of our experience.

Because much of this knowledge has been misunderstood and discarded as superstition with the emergence of modernity, it is difficult for some to even come close to understanding the depth of the visionary experience that these dream practices involve. In a sense, dreaming may be the best bridge to approach such knowledge across cultures.

The wave of interest in shamanic healing, ancient dream practices, and Indigenous knowledge in general is a testimony to a deep desire to reconnect with our ancestry. The work by writers and teachers such as Vine Deloria Jr., Lee Irwin, Apela Colorado, and Kimmy Johnson has begun to unravel the depth of this knowledge in a way that eschews exoticism or appropriation. What they relate is not uncommon in serious group practices we encounter, where dream themes start to coalesce among members of the groups, synchronicities abound and people feel that they have entered a much more alive universe of relationships. Therefore, it should be kept in mind that the work of dreams, especially when done respectfully and with mindfulness in a group, can give rise important insights reaching beyond the self.

SUMMARY

In this chapter we addressed the common assumptions about dream interpretation by discussing the biblical story of Daniel, the dream interpreter. We also explored modern and traditional interpretive ways of approaching dreams, highlighting the broader objectives of dream understanding, the expectations and roles that come with it, and the possible horizons of the interpretive act. The next chapter opens a discussion of non-interpretive approaches to dreams.

CHAPTER THIRTEEN

Epistemic Uncertainty

Non-Interpretive Approaches to Dreams

> In dream-analysis we must never forget, even for a moment, that we move on treacherous ground where nothing is certain but uncertainty.
>
> —C. G. Jung, *Dreams*

Interpreting dreams often satisfies the desire to arrive at some definitive or firm conclusions. Interpretation adds a measure of solidity to what, in essence, is a fluid process. However if we are not careful, the dream easily becomes crystallized into a *thing* or some fixed idea of what it means. In this chapter we focus on the non-interpretive way of being with dreams, which draws our attention to the enigmatic nature of dreams. Non-interpretive approaches span a wide range: seeking no meaning but being inside a process of creative action, sensing the dream through bodily awareness, or using creative expression to arrive at insight. From our integrative view, the reflective (interpretive) approach and the non-interpretive are seen as two complementary attitudes in engaging dreams.

The legendary story of the Butterfly Dream by the Chinese philosopher Chuang Tzu will serve as our starting point.[1] This is one of the best-known stories to express the paradoxical nature of reality as we experience it. It illuminates the philosophical ground of the non-interpretive approach to dreams, one that challenges the waking habits of seeking immediate interpretive results.

Chuang Tzu discusses this dream and reflects his understanding of the human condition in the text *Qi Wu Lun*[2] (chapter 2 of Chuang Tzu's complete works). The text is found within the "Inner Chapter" discussing his complex philosophical thoughts (Chuang Tzu, 1968).[3] We focus here on the paradoxes associated with dream understanding in the context of Chuang Tzu's deep philosophical perspective which, in part, "express an understanding about the limits of understanding itself, about the limits of language and thought" (Coutinho, 2010: np).

Known by his honorific name, Chuang Tzu (*Tzu* referring to master in Chinese) Chuang Chou (Chou being his given name) was born in the city of Meng in the Hunan Province in the fourth century BCE (Coutinho, 2010).[4] He had profound spiritual insights into the work of the Taoist sage Lao Tzu and his revelation on the nature of *Tao* (The Way). With literary genius, humor, and simplicity Chuang Tzu translated the abstract concept of the *Tao* into stories. His writings made accessible the teachings of Lao Tzu for daily application.

The combination of the philosophy of both Lao Tzu and Chuang Tzu gave birth to Taoist thought. Their approach challenged concretization of the Unknown by emphasizing fluidity, flexibility, and paradox. This juxtaposition is apparent in the most important book of Lao Tzu's, *Tao Te Ching* [*Dao De Jing*], in which he writes enigmatically: "When all in the world understand beauty to be beautiful, then ugliness exists. When all understand goodness to be good, then evil exists. Thus existence suggests non-existence" (Ta-Kao, 1948: 11).

Eastern philosophy has been gradually introduced to the West since the eighteenth century, in particular that of Taoism, Buddhism, and Vedanta. The propagation of Eastern philosophy in the West has accelerated in the twentieth century. It finds its way into psychology through the works of popular writers and scholars such as British philosopher Alan Watts, Japanese professor D.T. Suzuki, and Swiss psychiatrist C.G. Jung, among many others. The integration of the East-West philosophy is still cresting, and these influences continue to affect science, literature, and the arts.

In preparation for this discussion, we need to address a couple of issues. First, Chuang Tzu referred to himself by his own name, Chuang Chou (or Zhuang Zhou in Pinyin)[5] and not his honorific name.[6] Second, there are many translations of the Butterfly Dream; since we are discussing the importance of dreams rather than examining his philosophical underpinning, we chose to use a translation by Steve Coutinho since it is the closest to the original text.

Coutinho is a Chinese scholar and the author of *Zhuangzi and Early Chinese Philosophy: Vagueness, Transformation and Paradox* (2004).

> **昔者莊周夢為蝴蝶，栩栩然蝴蝶也，自喻適志與，不知周也。俄然覺，則蘧蘧然周也。不知周之夢為蝴蝶與，蝴蝶之夢為周與？周與蝴蝶則必有分矣。此之謂物化。**
>
> Translation
>
> Once, Zhuang Zhou dreamt he was a butterfly, a fluttering butterfly, doing as he pleased ("exemplifying in his own person the satisfaction of his wishes"), unaware of Zhou. He suddenly awakened, solidly, evidently Zhou. But he did not know: was it that Zhou dreamt he was a butterfly, or that the butterfly dreamt he was Zhou? Thus, between Zhou and the butterfly a differentiation had surely come about: this is what is called the transformation of things. (Coutinho, 2010)

In this story, Chuang Tzu asks us to look at the transformation of ordinary reality by displaying a fundamental attitude toward the nature of consciousness. Similar views are found across many Eastern philosophies. For example in Taoism, this attitude is promoted by the concept of accepting *change* and developing an awareness of *fluidity* in nature; in Buddhist teachings it is exemplified in the practice *non-attachment* and cultivating *open mind*; and in Vedanta it is embodied in the idea of *transcending the limitation of self-identity*. We will explore these philosophical notions in relation to Chuang Tzu's dream and then refer to them to describe our views of the non-interpretive approach toward dreams.

First we might ask, did Chuang Tzu actually have a dream of being a butterfly, or is the story an allegory to demonstrate the interconnectedness or even contradiction between dreams and waking reality? If this is an actual dream, his reflection about it does not reduce the image to symbolic meaning. Rather, he makes an *open inquiry* as to whether the dream is actually *his*—or if it belongs to another being, in this case the butterfly. With this sudden and paradoxical perspective, he shatters the assumptions of interpretation, questioning instead the "I" that dreams. In doing this, he emphasizes the *fluidity of self-identity* by approaching his dream with an *open mind.*

For those who are interested in making-meaning, there is of course a rich symbol in that this dream focuses on a butterfly and not, for example, an elephant. Could the dream have chosen the butterfly image because it is one of the best symbols for demonstrating both a happy, wandering insect and the process of self-transformation? Chuang Tzu makes no commentary on how to seek meaning from the dream. For example, he does not remark: "If a butterfly dreams it is Chuang Tzu, what does that mean for the butterfly?" or "What is the meaning of the image of a butterfly in Chuang Tzu's dream?" Instead, he focuses on ordinary appearances and how identity is not fixed but unpredictable and subject to change. In the words of C.W. Chan, Chuang Tzu implies in the Butterfly Dream that "[t]he transformation of things proves that the differences among things are not absolute" (Chan, 1996: 1). By making an inquiry into the nature of the self, and in the most simple and disarming way, he invites us to *transcend the limitations of self-identity.*

Chuang Tzu asks a larger question that takes the self out of its fixed boundaries and thrusts it into a transdimensional perspective. With both dreaming and waking experiences there is a level of "certainty": oblivion characterizes the certainty of the dream state whereas waking comes with "unmistakable" certainty. In the story these two "certainties," when joined, create uncertainty. The mind that reflects on the sheer contrast between the two—the reflective mind—is the one that raises the existential question of "Who am I really?" The self is in question and its solidity in both waking and dreaming identities. The story also implies that beyond differences, the *ground of being*, in waking and dreaming, is ultimately one or nondual.

Chuang Tzu's attitude toward the dream implies clarity of perception that goes beyond the fixity that reduces experience to appearance. This requires the dreamer to seek deeply into the assumptions that mold the perception of apparent reality. In this way Chuang Tzu also teaches *non-attachment* to identity in both dreaming and waking and encourages flexibility of the mind. Could it be that this story points to the possibility of the illusory nature of reality? In Tibetan Buddhism, as the fourteenth-century teacher Karma Lingpa states, "One must train perceiving all daytime appearances as dream-like and illusory. . . . Once you become fully able to apprehend your dreams, train in emanating and transforming your dreams" (Lama Tharchin Rinpoché, 2009).

In light of Chuang Tzu's Butterfly Dream, we can point out four major aspects of a non-interpretive way of viewing dreams:

- Open mind and clarity
- Non-attachment
- Fluidity and flexibility
- Receptivity to transformation

Within the interpretive paradigm there is a drive to attain certainty in interpreting dream imagery. In the non-interpretive approach the dream remains a living creation constantly changing and evolving into new horizons. In a non-interpretive approach, a creative and intuitive space is fostered to view dreams and their potential as openly as possible. This form of inquiry refrains from directing how the dream unfolds. Dream understanding becomes a process that is changeable when viewed from different perspectives or by taking into account how understanding changes with the passage of time.

The non-interpretive approach is an important step in Integral Dream Practice (IDP). Within the first phase of IDP, the dream is allowed to evolve and to continue while the dreamer interacts with it consciously. To properly reenter the dream in waking, the dreamer takes an open attitude to be with the unknown. To sustain the space of not knowing is a particular skill. To obtain such a skill, we draw upon ancient meditation vehicles that teach witnessing and metacognition by being open to a larger sphere of the mind.

EPISTEMIC UNCERTAINTY

Eastern philosophy often emphasizes impermanence and teaches about the nature of grasping and aversion and the suffering that such actions engender (Wallace, 1999). How do these concepts come into play in dream awareness? The non-interpretive approach invites an attitude of letting go of preconceived, fixed ideas while lifting the veil that may be covering a deeper truth about the reality of appearances. With the realization that dreams are shifting and impermanent, perhaps certain capacities can be cultivated to maintain the proper attitude toward them. We can think, for example, of letting go of the need to solidify a particular meaning. This section addresses further how to approach not knowing, or epistemic uncertainty.

Although its original use comes from mathematics, the term *epistemic uncertainty*[7] (Oberkampf, 2005) can be applied philosophically in this discussion about meaning. Epistemology (or ways of knowing), combined with uncertainty (openness to not knowing), points to a *way of knowing about not knowing*. By nurturing an attitude of openness toward possibilities, epistemic uncertainty encourages the dreamer to examine core assumptions and beliefs that often breed a sense of certainty. Through this attitude of uncertainty, one is prepared to be with the metamorphosis of dream imagery, the changing emotions and letting go of the active stance of the self. Without a particular attachment to result there is no "right" and "wrong" view, just the one that emerges spontaneously, ready to be witnessed. Perhaps one of the major lessons of Chuang Tzu's reflection on his dream is how certain he was when he was the butterfly and how unmistakable it felt to him upon waking. This teaching of uncertainty comes directly out of his being so certain that he was one or the other: either the butterfly dreaming of being Chuang Tzu or Chuang Tzu dreaming of being the butterfly. His question challenges his own assumptions and core belief about who he is and allows him to be in the place of uncertainty and ambiguity.

Within the non-interpretive approach to dreams, the dreamer is invited to acquire skill in open-mindedness and become comfortable with uncertainty in order to gain a larger view of possibilities. Value is given to spaciousness and openness, trying not to foreclose too soon; this is at the heart of creative dreaming.

Furthermore, within the non-interpretive approach there is no claim to finding an "accurate" meaning of the dream (accuracy becomes relative); however, there is encouragement to be present to the process of discovering and allowing a natural unfolding of the dream through particular non-interpretive methodology. To continue gaining support from the observation of the Taoist philosophers, we read:

> When all things come into being Tao does not reject them. It produces them without holding possession of them. It acts without depending upon them, and raises without lording it over them. When merits are accomplished it does not lay claim to them. Because it does not lay claim to them, therefore it does not lose them. (Ta-Kao, 1948: 64.)

In the non-interpretive approach, the dream specialist, or facilitator, uses carefully chosen methods to assist the dreamer to "reexperience" the dream, allowing an organic spontaneous emergence of a new experience associated with the dream. The dream specialist becomes a catalyst who guides the dreamer into a "dreamlike" atmosphere, where the original dream is held with a nonanalytical attitude. This is also the space where new dreams arise. Meaning-making becomes a gradual integrative process rather than an immediate solution to a problem. The dreamer becomes a coparticipant in exploring the dream rather than being passive in the process. Such dynamic engagement by both the specialist and the dreamer relies on trusting the organic process even in the face of the unknown, and examining presuppositions so as not to impose premature meaning. This is a core difference from the interpretive approach, where the expert is expected either to inform the dreamer of the meaning of the dream or ask pertinent questions to draw such meaning from the dreamer (e.g., Gutheil, 1951; Delaney, 1979; Kaplan-Williams, 1991; Hill, 2003).

CONTEMPORARY NON-INTERPRETIVE APPROACH

Besides our own work, there are a host of authors, practitioners, and teachers whose work is connected with a non-interpretive approach to dreams. Among them are Robert Bosnak, Eugene Gendlin, James Hillman, Jill Mellick, Stephen Aizenstat, and Ole Vedfelt. They also share a view that dreams should be approached on "their own terms." These authors and practitioners are more likely to ask dreamers to stay as close as possible to the experience of the dream, drawing attention to the dream's felt sense, aesthetic genius, and phenomenological disclosures. As in Integral Dream Practice, they explore insights as spontaneous emergence.

In his extensive overview of the methods in dream studies, Shafton interviewed many "dream methodologists" and devotes an entire section in his *Dream Reader* (1995) to the *Non-interpretation of Dreams*. He refers to Henry Beck, who remarks that the telling of a dream may be therapeutic without the dream being either understood or interpreted (377). Shafton attempts to unearth the sense of "non-interpretation," which comes to mean a form of understanding that allows the meaning to come from the dreamers. He refers to Dream Creations (Bogzaran, 1990), now expanded to IDP, as one of the methods that focus on reexperiencing the feeling and images of a dream as fully as possible, eventually leading to meaning spontaneously emerging from the dreamer. While it is difficult to convey in words the phenomenological impact of these methods, the potential for non-interpretive work to elicit insights and to access powerful emotional or somatic experiences should not be underestimated. The apparent simplicity of the work can be deceptive. It uses subtle yet powerful methods that require in-depth training and proper application.

Shafton's investigation uses the word *non-interpretation* in a very inclusive manner.[8] In his review, he includes not only the experiential component noted previously, but also methods that take dreams as the starting point for dream action, ritual, performance or deliberate change in behavior, or methods that use imaginative practice to alter the dreams or bring about imaginal transformation. Of the non-interpretive practitioners, the late James Hillman has been for more than four decades one of the most vocal advocates for approaching dreams on their own terms. He sharply criticizes the utilitarian view of dream working done for the benefit of the waking self, stating that the assumptions of the waking mind often are a hindrance in being with dreams. Hillman takes a very strong stand on the rational mind's imposition on dreams. He insists on the need to engage in a kind of reversal, to start seeing the world *through* the dream images (Hillman, 1979). This view is at the root of archetypal psychology, a neo-Jungian movement of which Hillman is one of the main proponents. His work has influenced countless others, including Robert Bosnak, who cites him as kindred spirit.

Bosnak's work draws also from phenomenologists who favor the notion of *embodiment* as a way of approaching a dream non-interpretively. For Bosnak (2007), the dream "presents a total world, so real that you are convinced you are awake" (9); a world-creating power he calls "embodied imagination," a quasi-physical environment with its own intelligence. From his point of view, a dream creates "strong responses in the body" because it takes a body to experience imagination. Paradoxically, he writes: "Phenomena, when carefully observed, exude meaningfulness without us necessarily knowing what they particularly mean" (13). In a sense, the body, like the dream, becomes a landscape through which consciousness can travel and glean meaningful insights accrued by the (re)experience of embodied states, and amplified by deep attention. Such is the work that can transform, in a dreamlike state, long-held traumatic scars or patterns organized around difficult emotional states.

Even before coalescing the methods that would eventually be called Integral Dream Practice, one of us, Bogzaran, took an integrative approach by combining existential, creative, and somatic approaches (Reichian) promoting openness to the dream's bodily impressions and creative nature. The work emphasizes *being-with* the dream through various embodied and creative modalities as a way of practicing *lucid waking*. She combines sonic entrainment[9] as a way to reexperience the dream and express the dream through nonverbal artistic modalities. This approach has been to contact the dream with no presupposed ideas and allow the dream to reveal itself; by being present to the creative process, insight naturally arises. The approach brings body awareness with the dream by way of movements and uses gesture drawings following automatic writing, where insights arise naturally for the dreamer (Bogzaran, 1991).

Psychologist Jill Mellick, in *The Natural Artistry of Dreams*, strongly advocates refraining from interpreting dreams and even challenges the narrative aspect of dreams. "Who said that all dreams are stories? And according to whose definition of story? . . . Many dreams are not stories at all but natural plays, paintings, poems" (23). Mellick creates a clear distinction between "traditional" and "innovative" ways of looking at dreams and provides a list of qualities for each, encouraging the reader to opt for the innovative way. The traditional list includes verbs such as "analyze, interpret, identify, hypothesize, and work on," while the innovative list includes "nourish, explore, associate, be with, play with" (29). Mellick's innovative category is open-ended and qualitatively oriented. The view that dreams have a creative voice and that one should let a dream be its own autonomous event without imposition runs across many non-interpretive ways of being with dreams. She writes, "We need to let dreams paint themselves, dance themselves, sculpt themselves, begin at the end and end at the beginning, spiral in on themselves, meander without climax or major turning point" (1996: 25). To do so she promotes and describes creative ways of working with and perceiving dreams.

Danish Jungian analyst Ole Vedfelt, in his book *The Dimensions of Dreams* (2002), takes a clinical approach to the multidimensionality of dreams.[10] His work resonates with the integral model. In practice, he notes, what happens in the therapy room trumps any theory when it comes to working with dreams, and even the great dream theorists "are often obliged to overstep their own bounds. . . . If we turn to the practical therapeutic situation, which is far less censored than the publicized accounts, I think there will be much agreement that the flexibility with regard to theory and method is many times greater" (2002: 336).

Vedfelt summarizes the roots of psychoanalytical work and its relationship to the modern view of dream interpretation. Using the open-ended language of the phenomenological method, he ponders the meaning of the word *interpretation*, wondering whether we use it for its known explanatory approach or for other inventive approaches to see if it is "possible to unfold what we can regard as 'enfolded' aspects of the dream. Interpretation can then be understood in a creative and artistic sense, which doesn't prevent us from subjecting an interpretation to scientific scrutiny" (344–345). As in the integral model, his inclusive view values dream understanding from different levels, perspectives, and experiences. Moreover, he expands the classical Freudian method of association to include dimensional knowing: "Associations can have varying depth and thus relate to various strata of the multilayered material that belongs to the dream. . . . An interpretation that observes the dream's emotional energy and is not merely intellectual will benefit by being able to jump from one experiential dimension to the other—this we would call a multidimensional association method" (346–347).

For Vedfelt this type of method, which we consider to be partly a non-interpretive approach, is not bound to a definitive interpretation but is guided by the dreamer and the interpreter's background and approach. Ideally, the session becomes a coparticipative event in which the dreamer and the interpreter share the responsibility as to the direction of the dream work. Vedfelt concludes, "And so to interpret becomes a creative unfolding of the dream's implicit dynamism and meaning" (352). This dynamic intersubjective exchange, then, becomes a ground for potentially touching upon different dimensions of the dream.

Clinical psychologist Stephen Aizenstat calls his approach *Dream Tending*. He considers dreams as "living images" and tries to awaken the experience of the dream by tending to their presence with deep listening (2009: 24). The principal approach of Dream Tending shares similar themes with other non-interpretive approaches as it allows the dream to slowly unfold its wisdom.

INTEGRAL DREAM PRACTICE AND THE NON-INTERPRETIVE APPROACH

Non-interpretive approaches are organic in nature, expressive and open-ended. They invite the dreamers and specialists to cultivate, refine, and recognize the subtle arising of thoughts, emotions, and somatic experience. While not grasping to any immediate meaning, the process allows the creative mind naturally to organize the emerging insights. Perhaps it is paradoxical to give structure to this type of approach; however some organization to verbalize the process is helpful for the reader.

Within the framework of *epistemic uncertainty*, the dreamer and the specialist engage the dream without having presuppositions about its meaning. When dreams are not viewed as reified text, the mind is open to explore unknown territories. Integral Dream Practice encompasses three main non-interpretive practices:

- Dream re-entry: This approach orients one's awareness to review and expand the dream in the form of a lucid (re) engagement.

- Embodied imagination, body awareness, or felt sense: This approach privileges how the dream and bodily/somatic life intersect, facilitating an exploration of the coemergence of images, emotions, and felt sense through increasing body awareness.

- Dream creations and innovation: This avenue follows dream unfolding in action or in the creative arts. These mainly nonverbal approaches are combined with the processes of translation and expression using the creative medium of art.

SUMMARY

We began the chapter by drawing the lessons from the ancient story of the Butterfly Dream of Chuang Tzu. We explored the attitude of viewing dreams from a place of uncertainty and how practitioners of the non-interpretive approach share in common an open-minded attitude toward dreams. We end the chapter by linking it to the previous one dealing with interpretive approaches. Using the Chinese philosophical terms yin (receptive) and yang (active), we can view the non-interpretive approach as yin and the interpretive as yang. They each have their own powerful force; however if one dominates over the other, there is imbalance. For example, too much yin causes sluggishness (lack of reflection) and too much yang can be destructive (controlling meaning). When non-interpretive and interpretive (or reflective) approaches are done properly, Integral Dream Practice regards them both as complementarily valuable. We combine the best of both approaches to create a dance between the two. In the next chapter we go step by step to build a theory of practice for Integral Dream Practice based on this general principle of balance and harmony between different approaches.

CHAPTER FOURTEEN

Philosophy of Practice

> Sleep-like trance opens the gate of the subliminal to us; for in sleep, as in trance, we retire behind the veil of the limited waking personality and it is behind this veil that the subliminal has its existence.
>
> —Sri Aurobindo, *The Life Divine*

In the last two chapters, we explored a continuum of approaches to dreams, ranging from interpretive to non-interpretive. In this chapter we introduce the philosophy that underlies our integrative view in approaching dreams, *Integral Dream Practice (IDP).* Integral Dream Practice uses a wide range of methods to address a single dream, first non-interpretively and then reflectively. Each method has its own depth and complexity. Common to these methods is a quality of awareness that 1) sees the dream as a living experience and 2) brings contemplative attention to all aspects of experience. Integral Dream Practice engages the dreamer in two distinct phases with the following assumptions: in the first phase, it views dreamers as creators with innate abilities to access spontaneous creation; in the second phase, it engages dreamers as self-reflective researchers who inquire into their own dream creation with an open mind. IDP follows the dream organically and encourages dreamers to reflect and unfold the dream over time.

PHILOSOPHICAL APPROACH

Our approach to dreams integrates an East-West philosophical attitude. It acknowledges the mystery of the dreaming mind with its creative potential while it also seeks reflective ways to bring insight.

Dreams are lived phenomena. Within our model of IDP, we draw upon phenomenological writings, in particular the work of Husserl (1983), Merleau-Ponty (1962), and Kidd and Kidd (1990) and apply them to foster a phenomenological attitude toward dreams. This attitude emphasizes the following:

- Dreams as an experience
- Questioning presuppositions
- Somatic awareness
- Phenomenological creativity

Dreams as an Experience

We approach dreams first as a creative experience. Even before anything is laid on the dream, the first step is to be aware of this experience, and then *to be-with* the experience. *Being-with-dreams* and exploring them allows contact with one's inner worlds. Whether such awareness is a deeper exploration into the self or a way of seeing through the illusion of the self, dreams offer a purely creative experience. The integral approach to dreams encourages a variety of methods to enable the dreamer to expand the horizon of discovery. The dreamer makes the inquiry as a process of creative exploration—reexperiencing, amplifying, and synthesizing the dream experience into waking life.

Questioning Presuppositions

Methods of working with dreams to extract or attach meaning are often introduced without questioning the presuppositions, attitudes, or core beliefs that stand behind them. Our own experience has shown us that any method can have a reductive effect when exploring dreams. Do core beliefs direct the way in which a dream is perceived? Could they limit the perception and experience of the dreamer?

We assert that examining presuppositions,[1] or assumptions, is an essential practice for both the dreamer and the educator/therapist, in particular the general assumption that dreams need to be interpreted, often by an outside agent rather than the dreamer. Habits of meaning-making have been reinforced by the stories about dream interpretation (see the story of Daniel discussed in chapter 11) and by modern psychological views. The practice of interpreting dreams also has deep roots with our ancestors and many current Indigenous cultures (Irwin, 1994; Krippner, 1987; Krippner et al., 2002; Tedlock, 1987, 2005).

Incorporating phenomenological inquiry, we examine the challenges that methods impose when approaching dreams. Many proponents of the phenomenological method, including Martin Heidegger (1962), Hans-Georg Gadamer (1975), and Henri Bergson (1912), also address the limitations of methods. In the integral approach to dreams, first an inquiry and then a revision in the attitude of the dreamer and the educator/therapist enable both to take a new perspective and to return to the *things in themselves*—the lived experience.

Within the integral view, we acknowledge the complexities of the dreaming mind and question the waking mind's superior attitude toward the dreaming phenomena. Inquiring about the relationship between waking perception and the dreaming experience is an essential step in Integral Dream Practice.

From an Eastern philosophical point of view, this space is known as the "beginner's mind" and it is perhaps best explained by Shunryu Suzuki Roshi in his well-known statement: "If your mind is empty, it is always ready for anything; it is open to everything. In the beginner's mind there are many possibilities; in the expert's mind there are few" (1970: 21).

Edmund Husserl introduced the term *bracketing* or *epoché* (suspension of judgments or prior beliefs) to gain awareness of prior attitude, to "bracket" our presuppositions so that one can *be with* the experience. Husserl explains:

> [This method is] simply in order to suspend or neutralize a certain dogmatic *attitude* toward reality, that is, in order to be able to focus more narrowly and directly on the phenomenological given—the objects just as they appear. In short, the epoché entails a change of attitude toward reality, and not an exclusion of reality. It is only through such a suspension that we will be able to approach reality in a way that will allow for a disclosure of its true sense. (Zahavi, 2003: 45)

Offering methods of reflection rather than interpreting the dream for the other can have a completely different outcome. Of course, we need to ask whether bracketing the entirety of one's presuppositions is likely when we consider dreams. It may never be achieved completely, but simply asking the question is a necessary step within an integral context.[2]

Somatic Awareness

Integral Dream Practice acknowledges that dreams are somatic events. From our point of view, addressing dreams as a whole experience, there is no strict division between body, mind, emotion, and spirit. *Dreams are fully embodied experience.* Somatic awareness is an essential aspect of Integral Dream Practice, whether approaching the dream non-interpretively or reflectively.

Inquiry into dreams and somatic awareness brings several questions: What traces does dreaming leave in our bodies and how do we awaken to these subtle impressions? Where are dream emotions located in the body? What impact do they have? Knowing that dreams have a tendency to involve negative emotions, how does the body metabolize them? How do we self-regulate or refine emotions?

In Eastern contemplative traditions, body awareness is incorporated within self-inquiry and the embodiment of deities.[3] In Indigenous cultures, rituals, dance, or other forms of expression and enactments are of central importance. In the West, the body has been negated from a spiritual perspective and is not seen as a source of knowledge as important as the rational intellect. However, within the Western psychological system, Wilhelm Reich (1976, 1979), a contemporary of Freud and Jung, revolutionized psychoanalytical practice by bringing the awareness of the body to a focus on the inner energetic movement.[4] Unlike Freud and Jung, who made dreams a central theme in their psychoanalytical practice, Reich centered on body awareness, the core of what is now called *somatic psychology*. Although he did not focus on dreams, Reich's concept of *character armoring* is of great interest when working with dreams. Regarding the factors that cause the character to assume its definite form, Reich writes:

> The character consists in a chronic change of the ego which one might describe as a *hardening*. This hardening is the actual basis for the becoming chronic of the characteristic mode of reaction; its purpose is to protect the ego from external and internal dangers. As a protective formation that has become chronic, it merits the designation "armoring," for it clearly constitutes a restriction of the psychic mobility of the personality as a whole. (Reich, 1976: 172)

Within Reichian therapy, simple breathing practice uncovers forgotten memories and unblocks the subtle energy of what Reich called "streaming" (Bean, 1971). This method also echoes the various Eastern practices in breathing, such as the Chinese practice of Chi Gong (Qigong) and the Indian method of Pranayama within yoga (Weaver, 1987).

Alexander Lowen (1975) furthered Reich's work by focusing on the body's structure and the release of body tensions, in particular releasing the armoring around the heart in order to contact what he calls the "loving core." John Pierrakos (1987) took the idea further, engaging in an East-West dialogue on body and energy. He developed *Core Energetics,* which views the body as a field of energy with the capacity not only to love but also to heal. Charlotte Selver and Charles Brooks developed Sensory Awareness to bring somatic knowledge as "experience through senses," an organic process of being fully aware of the body's intelligence. Selver named this the *re-discovery of experience* (Littlewood & Roche, 2004).

The pioneering work of Keleman (1981), Mindell (1982), Garfield (1979, 1988) and Gendlin (1985) connected body awareness to dreams. Stanley Keleman primarily focuses on somatic awareness in his psychotherapy practice and writes how dreaming mirrors the issues brought up in the sessions. "Dreaming presents us with how the somatic self is rehearsing and getting ready to appear. Dreams are the soma's interiority seeking embodiment. . . . To work somatically with a dream is to feel the characters in the dream as desires or emotions seeking to be embodied in the awake reality" (Keleman, 2010: n.p.).

Arnold Mindell, inspired by Carl Jung's views of dream symbolism and the body, popularized the term *dreambody.* Mindell aligned himself with the Eastern spiritual traditions and merged them with Western psychology to resituate the concept of the unconscious. He sees the unconscious as dreaming itself,[5] thus the dreambody is an integrated aspect of the unconscious. "The less conscious the individual, the more the unconscious or the dreambody is experienced only as a force coming from the outside inducing disturbances into life" (1982: 167).

In her visionary work *Pathway to Ecstasy* (1979), Patricia Garfield also took an Eastern view to understand her dreams and their physical relationship to body. She presents her dreams as a symbolic interpretation of her body. Later, in *Women's Bodies, Women's Dreams* (1988), she traces the life cycle of women and their bodies as experienced in their dreams.

Eugene Gendlin's approach is to *let your body interpret your dreams* (1985), applying the focusing method he had previously developed. The dreamer is asked to become aware of the *felt sense* in the body as a way to find meaning in dreams.

And recently, Robert Bosnak's *Embodiment* (2007) addressed a broader issue about dreaming and the split between mind and body.

From early on, as somatic practitioners, we integrated body awareness in our approach to dreams. We have made special attempts not to divide the mind from the body. *Dream experience is a whole experience.* It is mental, somatic, psychological, creative, and physical. Integral Dream Practice uses movement, visual and poetic expressions to trace somatic experiences.[6] As dreams resurface to the physical body, it allows the awareness of subtle energetic phenomena.

Phenomenological Creativity

Rather than assuming that waking consciousness is most qualified to ponder the dream experience, we propose that the dreaming mind is creation itself. Dream experiences are a spontaneous creation of deep inner structures, both representational (narrative) and nonrepresentational. The waking consciousness—what Hillman calls "day world style of thinking"—is often linear and literal and may limit meaning, leaving aside the much larger sphere of the multidimensional world of dreaming.

Integral Dream Practice encourages the dreamer to enter the imaginal realm, to express the "psychic automatism" and only later to articulate the process by way of reflection. Vital to IDP is its emphasis on the creative process in dream awareness, allowing for a natural arising of insights and for possible meaning to be integrated as part of evolving consciousness. The core assumption in this method is that the dreaming mind is of the same nature as the creative mind and that, through dream creation, the dreaming mind is cultivated in waking. In this process the dream is seen as a creation and the dreamer as an artist. If we perceive dreams as a complete creation of our mind, then engaging with dreams means to become in-touch-with and experience our creative self. Within the IDP there are many opportunities to engage in what we call "creative expressions." Some of these expressions will be discussed in the next chapter.

NON-WESTERN PHENOMENOLOGICAL TRADITIONS

Integral Dream Practice, in its methodology, is deeply connected to Indigenous wisdom traditions. In particular, the use of meditation, body awareness methods, and the use of various instruments (e.g., shamanic/rhythmic drumming) for the practice of dream reentry.[7]

Integral Dream Practice draws upon a mild alteration of consciousness, that is, eliciting a kind of dreamlike state in order to reconnect with dreams. This has its root in non-Western approaches of being with dreams. Across various cultures, our ancestors created rituals to open themselves to different types of dreams and to aspects of the dreaming/creative mind. We consider Indigenous approaches as having elements that are both traditional and contemporary. They are traditional in that they express oral knowledge that is passed down through stories, practices, and ritual enactment (personal or collective) and that keeps alive the values linked to cultural perspectives, beliefs, and attitudes. They are contemporary because these practices are kept alive through time, often in the face of extreme adversity.[8]

With the reemergence of the wisdom traditions and nature-based philosophy, we find indications that, although aspects of the modern era have been beneficial for the evolution of human existence, other aspects have been detrimental to the human soul and our spiritual well-being. The growing interest in holistic thinking—integrating mind, body, and spirit—is bringing a quality essential for the survival of the human species. Integral Dream Practice seeks to heal the split between mind and body, to come back to a natural place in better harmony with nature; dreaming is seen as a powerful imaginal vehicle for healing, inspiration, guidance, initiation, and spiritual growth.

We have stated that somatic awareness is key to IDP. Working with dreams through body awareness is not a new concept. The arbitrary separation of body and mind is irrelevant to earth-based spiritual traditions. Engaging the body as a way of accessing dream awareness has been an integral practice within the shamanic traditions (Tedlock, 2005).[9]

PHENOMENOLOGY AS A RESEARCH PRACTICE APPLIED TO DREAMS

Integral Dream Practice draws from the qualitative and phenomenological research method in the humanities and from the Eastern philosophical attitude. Within phenomenology, inspiration is taken from the Experiential Method advocated by James Kidd and Sunnie Kidd (1990). Focusing on the philosophical and theoretical models of Henri Bergson, Maurice Merleau-Ponty, William James, and Pierre Thévenaz, Kidd and Kidd developed an inquiry method to explore metaphysical inquiry through phenomenology called the *Experiential Method*. They state, "It is in experience that the irreducible nature of personal meaning is disclosed and can be described" (Kidd & Kidd, 1990: 1). The method calls upon two distinct functions of consciousness, *reflexive* and *reflective*. "The primordial function of consciousness is the reflexive rather than reflective. The reflexive is immediate, an intensification of consciousness. The reflective is mediate, a recuperating consciousness. The reflexive is a centripetal movement, a constituting power more original than intentionality. The reflective is a centrifugal movement" (1990: 9).

The reflexive function of consciousness relates to a wide range of concepts, such as intuition, creativity, Aurobindo's "illumined mind," and other similar metaphysical concepts. Kidd and Kidd make a parallel between what Thévenaz calls reflexive in the philosophy of intuition in Bergson, emphasizing the primordiality of the intuitive. "By intuition is meant a kind of intellectual sympathy by which one places oneself within an object in order to coincide with what is unique in it and consequently inexpressible" (Bergson, 1942: 7).

In his comparative analysis of Bergson's view of intuition with Aurobindo's model of Supermind, Maitra (1968) gives an in-depth analysis of the differences between the subtle levels of Aurobindo's model of consciousness and Bergson's definition of intuition. Maitra clarifies that "By intuition he [Bergson] means a direct approach to reality, as opposed to the round-about way of approaching it with the help of the intellect" (69). This direct approach is the key to the reflexive aspect of consciousness.

The model of Integral Dream Practice works when the facilitator is attuned to the intuitive ways of knowing and the dreamer open to the reflexive function of consciousness. From the Indian philosophy of Aurobindo, the concept of Integral Yoga also confirms our Integral Dream Practice. The self-expression is a natural engagement with the first phase of IDP. Integral Dream Practice takes a philosophical view that dreams arise out of the reflexive function of consciousness, and thus need to be approached first with methods that support the phenomena on their own terms.

We have seen in Part II that some dream experiences can be more ordinary while others can be quite extraordinary. Dream experiences can range from simple day-residue dreams to impactful and life-transforming dreams. Any single method of inquiry would be inadequate to face the enigma of dreams. For that reason our model attempts to match in practice the complexity of the dreaming itself. It combines the horizontality of diverse methods with the verticality of the reflexive and reflective functions of consciousness. Together they give a holistic *Integral Experience*[10] (see also the example in chapter 16).

In application and practice, we draw a parallel between the *reflexive* function of consciousness and the *non-interpretive* approaches to dreams, and conversely, between the *reflective* function and *interpretive* approaches. We consider that meaning naturally unfolds from a spacious engagement with the experience of the dream itself. The ensuing reflective or interpretive phase connects these spontaneously emerging insights into meaning by fostering the integration of dream experiences into the particular of the dreamer's waking life.

Perhaps the concept of *hsin* in Chinese philosophical terms is the most appropriate holistic and integrative term for embodying the concept of Integral Dream Practice. *Hsin*, heart and mind, addresses the problem of dualism—of separating intuition and intellect. Our overarching philosophical container for the model of Integral Dream Practice, then, contains both reflexive and reflective methods, wherein the reflexive draws upon intuitive knowing and the reflective engages the intellect.

Within Integral Dream Practice there are five movements for unfolding the dream, each with practices particular to its movement.[11] In the next chapter we will discuss in detail the two phases: Reflexive Emergence and Reflective Integration, and the five movements they contain, and further discuss the philosophy of IDP and how the practices are applied.

CHAPTER FIFTEEN

Hermeneutic of Creation

The Five Movements of Integral Dream Practice

> It is imperative that we should not pare down the meaning of the dream to fit some narrow doctrine.
>
> —C. G. Jung, *Dreams*

To engage in Integral Dream Practice is to unfold a deep inquiry into the nature of the creative self. Dreams are an open potential that may be expanded through a meaning-making process. In the lineage of Chuang Tzu, we embrace the creative tension between knowing and not knowing when exploring dreams, so as to allow new possibilities to emerge.

The underlying arch of IDP involves the integral vision of connecting spirit, mind, body, creativity, and community. Although it is customary to discuss or engage each of these areas separately by compartmentalizing mind, body, and spirit, this action often defeats the purpose of holism. Thus our focus in the Integral Dream Practice is to address the awareness of these aspects without separating them conceptually. We introduce methods that foreground some of these aspects in turn but always connected to the whole. For example, to be with dreams and the body we do not isolate creativity. To use creativity we do not isolate body, mind, spirit, and so on.

We maintain that the "irrational" nature of the dreaming mind contains its own logic within the context of the creative mind. From the Integral Dream Practice model, the facilitator/specialist, through various creative, contemplative, and existential methods, allows the dreamer to explore the dimensions of a single dream to expand its depth. This is what we call *a Hermeneutic of Creation*.

Integral Dream Practice consists of two main phases: *reflexive emergence* and *reflective integration.* Each contains distinct creative activities to engage, interact with, and unfold the dream. Each of these two phases is self-contained and can be explored independently of the other, although greater benefit can be achieved if both are used. In this chapter we describe these two phases, the five movements they contain, and guiding principles and pragmatic methods attached to them. Figure 11 presents visually the sequence of the two phases and the five movements of Integral Dream Practice.

		IDP Movements	**Process**	**Practices**
PHASE I	Reflexive Emergence	1)Dream re-entry	Allowing spontaneous appearance; non-interpretive, auto-poetic	Re-entry methods: e.g., sonic entrainment, dream indwelling, active imagination
		2)Creative Expressions	Participating in creative acts.	Expressive dream art: e.g., body map, dream theater and other creative acts
		3)Poetic Synthesis	Returning to text	Poetic articulation
PHASE II	Reflective Integration	4)Reflective Analysis	Connecting dreams to waking life, metaphorical mapping, auto-noetic reflection	Reflective methods: e.g., somatic awareness narrative script analysis personal mythology and others
		5)Integrative Acts	Identify transformative action. Self-perceptual depth. Connection between self and society	Lucid waking practices

FIGURE 11. THE TWO PHASES AND FIVE MOVEMENTS OF IDP.

PHASE I: REFLEXIVE EMERGENCE

The first phase of Integral Dream Practice, Reflexive Emergence, follows the organic, nonanalytical process of being-with the dream. Drawing from the work of Thévenaz, for whom the intuitive function of consciousness is primordial and *reflexive*, Kidd and Kidd (1990: 9) note that "the reflexive is immediate, an intensification of consciousness." In the context of dream awareness, we define the *reflexive* function as *turning toward the dream by allowing the spontaneous emergence of the dream experience to occur in a contemplative or altered state of consciousness without attempting to achieve active interpretation.* This aspect of IDP acknowledges the mind as a source of creative inspiration: dreams and dream awareness are a product of this creative consciousness.

MOVEMENT 1: DREAM REENTRY

To approach dreams, first we actively return to the experience of dreams' original source: the dreaming mind. This reentry and reexperiencing the dream is like walking into a field where there is a transparent and fluid gateway between conscious and the unconscious (or where implicit processes become explicit as part of the practice). The reentry allows the dreamer to explore the dream consciously. Returning back to the dream consciously creates an experience akin to lucid dreaming, where the dreamer becomes a witness and at the same time a participant in the creative expressions of the dream. The dream reentry thus becomes a *royal road to lucidity* or a *royal road to consciousness.* At times, during this process, dreamers may access what is known in many ancient traditions as the nondual mind.[1]

To be mindful of dreaming experiences and to be willing to experience the dreams and the depth of the inner world in dreamlike states is an essential part of the Integral Dream Practice. Therefore, the first step in the practice is *to meet the dream in its own environment by accessing the dreaming mind in waking through the method of dream reentry and hypnagogic practice.*

The practice of lucidity is a form of mindfulness practice, and dreamers in this movement learn to cultivate the ability to witness their own thoughts, feelings, and actions without judgment. IDP views the importance of *cultivation of presence* as an essential step toward bridging dreaming life and waking life. It incorporates self-reflectiveness, promoted by several contemplative traditions, as a skill of witnessing the wilderness of the mind. In IDP, contemplative skills allow one to observe changes in experiences, however subtle, through engaging in creative, reflective, and integrative acts.

Freud viewed the unconscious as the repository of repressed material, desires, and thoughts. Jung for his part viewed dreams through the eye of compensation and as an archetypal display framing the individuation process. *Within Integral Dreaming, we view dreams as a co-creative process.* As we discussed in Part II, dreaming and waking are in many ways continuous. The splitting off of the imaginal realms of dreaming from the rational (but still creative) waking mind is a fairly new and modern development. However, a healthy relationship and dialogue between the two can be maintained with awareness. This fluid connection between the dreaming mind and the waking mind is valued in several Indigenous cultures, including among the Australian Aborigine, Balinese, several African and Brazilian Indigenous traditions, and most Native American cultures (Tedlock, 1987; Krippner et al., 2002).

The reentry into the *dreaming mind* is an entrance into the magnificence of the creative mind, where the dreamer becomes a mindful observer and/or an active participant within the dream. Dream reentry allows waking awareness and dream awareness to fuse momentarily: a dreamer can have the experience of being lucidly present inside one's own dream. Within this environment choices can be explored. More important, the dreamer has the opportunity to be mindful of the depth, the emotional texture, and the overall multidimensional architecture of the dream.

Methods of Dream Reentry

There exist many ways of reexperiencing dreams. We note here six principal methods for dream re-entry, some of them developed and taught by the authors. These methods are used to reconnect with dreams or to embody them in various forms. Each of these takes the dreamer back to a dreamlike space. In some methods the dreamer is more receptive while in others she or he is more active. The six methods of dream reentry are:

1. Hypnagogic dream reentry, lucidity practice at the onset of sleep.
2. Dream reentry with hypnotherapy, guided visualization, or active imagination.
3. Dream reentry with shamanic drum or other entrainment devices.
4. Dream reentry through the body with movement and sound.
5. Dream reentry through contemplative practices, e.g., meditation, Dream Indwelling.
6. Hypnopompic dream reentry through mindfulness practices.

Although the modalities of reentry vary from one method to another, they share the induction of a creative state of engagement, with an attenuation of cognitive analytical process. Dream reentry is invoked either by a meditative state of consciousness, deep relaxation (mild hypnotic state), or a dreamlike altered state of consciousness brought about by sonic driving (such as shamanic drumming) or other forms of entrainment. Following the idea of a state-specific science (Tart, 1969), dream reentry provides the opportunity to come as close as possible to a dreamlike state in order to inquire and explore it.

As an illustration, we discuss more in-depth the third method: dream reentry with shamanic drum. The use of sonic entrainment with rhythmic drumming has been used cross-culturally to induce an altered state of consciousness. Its effects have been observed for thousands of years in rituals and ceremonies and as a way to bring the community together. The effect of shamanic drumming on the brain and its capacity to induce a dreamlike state has also been documented scientifically (Maxfield, 1990). These shamanic practices are proven methods that have been tested in both traditional and modern settings. Contemporary methods of induction of altered states have also included hypnotherapy and biofeedback, which teach clients how to produce an open and receptive state of consciousness. Jung himself proposed the practice of active imagination as a mode of reentry, where the dreamer is invited to enter into dialogue with different dream characters.[2]

We have been using a number of dream reentry methods for this phase of IDP: *Shamanic Lucid Dreaming* was developed by Bogzaran (1986)[3] and *Dream Indwelling*, a contemplative form of reentry was developed by Deslauriers (2001).[4]

Movement 2: Creative Expressions

The dreaming mind is one of the many expressions of the creative mind. Dreaming, by its nature and structure, is creative. Conversely, engaging with the creative process in waking accesses a state of mind similar to the dreaming mind. Integral Dream Practice promotes creativity as an essential tool to be in touch with the dream. The view is that dreams are a complete creation of our mind and dream creation is the natural nonverbal approach to the dream.

From an artistic point of view, dreams can be seen as personal and transpersonal experiences, shaped by emotions, with the multidimensional impressions left by dream characters, settings, objects, and interactions. Artists are individuals who have the capacity to access original ideas and are able to leave a lasting impression of their creative mind.[5] They can synthesize ideas to create anew and then capture these ideas and insights or experiences with their craft. Similarly, those who are aware of their dreams are in touch with their original dream creations. Through practice and skill they can transform these unique imprints into a tangible expression. Let's imagine that dreams are a time-based multimedia interactive art installation. This dream exhibition space has tremendous possibilities that reach beyond the confines of waking reality. This surreal space of the dream "installation" is like immersive contemporary art works in which the individual is invited to interact with their content. The art/dream is not frozen in time. As long as the dreamer keeps the inquiry alive, dreams are evolving creations. There are no limitations but those imposed by the dreamer. Briefly stated, *dreams are a continuous space of creation*. The creative nature of the mind is ever flowing with originality; it opens the way to making new connections and exploring new combinations.

During the second movement of IDP, Creative Expression, dreamers are invited to engage with this space of creation through various modalities of expressive arts. This engagement serves as a bridge between the reflexive reconnection with the dream and the creative functions of consciousness. In this movement, insights about the dream might arise spontaneously without a particular effort or deliberate search for meaning. Using multimodal creative approaches, expressive art promotes nonverbal ways of expressing one's emotions, ideas, and concepts, to access nonanalytically aspects of the self (Bogzaran, 1983; McNiff, 1981; Mellick, 1996; Rogers, 1985).

Within IDP, Creative Expressions expands on previous practices (*Expressive Dream Art*) designed by one of the authors (Bogzaran, 1990), which combine dream exploration with expressive arts. The latter is based on the presupposition that the creative mind and the creative process are intimately intertwined with the dreaming mind. Exploring the dream using different art modalities is one way of being in touch with the inner worlds. Combined with dream reentry, Creative Expressions is a noninterpretive, embodied way to reexperience dreams.

The theory and practice of Expressive Dream Art states that when a dream is embodied in different modalities, insights can arise through the creative expression. In theory, as part of Expressive Dream Art, dreamers embark on four distinct phases of exploration: abstraction, chaos, integration, and reflection. Within the abstraction phase the dreamer, without trying to understand the dream, comes in touch with the feeling tone of the dream and expresses this *felt sense* through colors, sounds, movements, or short sentences or poetic expressions. Within the chaos phase, the dreamer engages, with indiscriminate expression, any of the dream images and feelings. In this automatic action, the dreamer opens to the creative process. In the integration phase, the dreamer takes the central image or impactful emotion of the dream and explores it further using a medium of his/her choice. For some, this might be drawing, for others, writing, and so on. Within this phase the dreamer often experiences several insights into the dream. In the last phase, reflection, the dreamer takes some time to look inside and outside, to find holistic ways of integrating the insights that have appeared in the other phases. Within this framework, dreams are seen as creation and the dreamer as artist. Being with a dream is to co-participate with the *dream in creation*.

The expressive arts employed in IDP include creative writing (in particular, poetry); spontaneous movement and dance; sound (with spontaneous vocalization or the use of instruments); visual modalities (collage, painting, drawing); theater (mask making, performance); sculpture (especially clay). When given more time and space to unfold their creation, our students have also experimented with new media (animation, computer-based photo-collage, video), installation (found objects, altar making), and sand tray.

Integral Dream Practice, continuing the legacy of Dream Creations (Bogzaran, 1986), adapts the central practice of sonic entrainment in the service of Expressive Dream Art. It uses the steady beat of shamanic drumming to induce an hypnagogic state and invite the dreamer to use the visual arts as a creative bridge with the dream. (An experienced practitioner needs to guide this method, see notice to the reader at the beginning of the book.) After a session with this practice, editor and journalist Anna Racicot wrote: "The sound of [the] drum had given me the impetus to explore my dream to unsuspected intensities of meaning and feeling. The other participants, I surmised from their expressions, had used these methods of non-analytical dream working with similar success. Drumming, drawing, and dreamwork were not the non sequiturs they might have seemed, but methods which, when combined, yielded an avenue into the unconscious of surprising depth" (1992: 18).

The wisdom of meeting the dream from a nonanalytical approach is perhaps a common practice within the artistic community. In his first surrealist manifesto André Breton summarizes such urges: "The imagination is perhaps on the point of reasserting itself, of reclaiming its rights. If the depths of our mind contain within it strange forces capable of augmenting those on the surface, or of waging a victorious battle against them, there is every reason to seize them—first to seize them, then, if need be, to submit them to the control of our reason" (1972: 10).

Automatic Writing

A number of creative expressions can be explored in the IDP sequence. Every creative expression is followed by automatic writing—that is, writing spontaneously without using analytical thinking. This practice is inspired by Surrealism, in particular, the philosophy and writings of Guillaume Apollinaire, who used automatic writing to create his poetry. Georges Lemaitre gives a poetic rendition of Apollinaire's automatic writings: "Their unique fragrance arouses in us a nostalgic longing because they originate in the inner most recesses of the human soul; or, according to Apollinaire, because they are impregnated with the supreme spiritual essence that permeates the whole universe." Lemaitre explains that "in order to start this magic flow of words and thoughts Guillaume Apollinaire did not have recourse to strenuous and patient effort. He simply sat at his desk and let his pen run over the paper, allowing the sentences to form freely, independently, even incoherently" (Lemaitre, 1941: 113).

First, the method of dream reentry allows the dreamer to lucidly reexperience their dreams. Then, the automatic writing following this practice encourages the dreamer to be present to a spontaneous flow of insight/creation without censoring. Automatic writing is a creative solvent for the linear arrangement of rational thinking, opening dreamers to the surprises of their inner wildness.

Historically, it is presumed that automatic writing is heir to Freud's free association method. Viewed within the prism of IDP, we consider the latter as Freud's own form of creative expression. Freud instructed dreamers to automatically express their thoughts and feelings and encouraged the verbal chains of words to freely flow from the narrative of the dream. Breton incorporated Freud's free associative process into automatic writing to create a dreamlike literature. Breton's contribution was to promote and allow writers to play with the state "in-between" the dreaming and waking states. Surrealist writing is fluid, irrational, creative, and mind-shifting. Scrambling words from their linearity, we come close to dreams. Spontaneous writing allows the waking mind to verbally meet the dreaming mind. The assemblage of words might at first seem nonsensical: strange, unexpected, and sometimes bizarre or even repetitive. It is an organic process that can lead to surprising creative outcomes. For the surrealists, automatism connects the individual to the vitality of a creative source with a spiritual center as its magnet (Lemaitre, 1941).

In IDP, automatic writing is an essential aspect of the entire process of reflexive emergence. Case studies showed that doing automatic writing immediately after dream reentry with a shamanic drum offered insights to the dream for the dreamer (Bogzaran, 1991). In IDP, we devote didactic time to educate dreamers about the mechanism of automatic writing and the generation of spontaneous poetic expression. The next movement, *Poetic Synthesis,* builds on the successive automatic writing that is done throughout.

Movement 3: Poetic Synthesis

The phase of Reflexive Emergence finds closure with the practice of Poetic Synthesis. Poetic Synthesis is a creative form of conducting phenomenological inquiry. Developed by Bogzaran in her doctoral dissertation as a minimalist way of addressing complex spiritual and creative phenomena, the process of *Poetic Synthesis condenses the wildness of automatism into simple phrases of lyrical insights* (Bogzaran, 1996).

With the assumption that if conditions are right we all can be poets, the process of Poetic Synthesis brings rich and complex information into simple phrases that can illumine the dream. This practice, of course, is for the benefit of the dreamer, but if it is done in groups, the poetic insights that are shared with others can bring about group cohesion and a tangible expression of group wisdom. If published, these pieces can also benefit the greater community.

Poetic Synthesis contains three segments: 1) *Returning to texts* and rereading the dream and all automatic writings, 2) creating a *collage of experiential expressions*[6] or a cluster of themes and 3) completing a *poetic articulation.*

Returning to Texts

The method of Poetic Synthesis relies on intuitive knowing, with which dreamers return back to the dream and the automatic texts. They are invited to underline *what stands out* for them. Within the automatic writing there might be irrational yet highly poetic phrases. Those seemingly nonsensical words are often the connectors to some unfiltered and original insight. The choice of words and arising themes builds an internal movement and becomes the beginning of an integrative experience. This internal movement can be a series of sudden insights or fragments of memories fostering new creative illumination or the emergence of meaning. This moment of contact between the nonanalytical approaches and the rising of analytical thinking engages the dreamer in a poetic space, still without deliberately attributing meaning.

Collage of Experiential Expressions or Theme Cluster

A first clustering of the themes that emerge out of the writings determines the words or phrases that are chosen for a final Poetic Synthesis. Instead of amplifying the themes, the words and phrases are put together in the form of a collage, rearranged, and condensed into a poetic form. As the clustering is taking place, choosing phrases that naturally have more resonance with the dreamer leads to development of a poetic process. In this phase of Poetic Synthesis the dreamer is encouraged to keep an open mind to the imaginal. At this juncture the dreamer has the choice to allow the flow of creativity to completely lead the creation of a synthesis, rather than controlling the process into a known outcome. Silvano Arieti, a pioneer in the field of creativity research, discusses a creative person and how important it is for the individual to allow a contact to the primary process. He writes: "This accessibility to the primary process may require a state of passivity similar to that of dreaming; but the passivity cannot involve the artist's whole psyche. On the contrary, it contrasts with the increased alertness on the part of the psyche that deals with the secondary process and presides over the artistic synthesis. Thus in the act of aesthetic creation, a complicated mental mechanism takes place that combines greater than usual passivity and greater than usual activity" (1976: 185).

Poetic Articulation

By choosing a dream to explore consciously, an intention is set to begin an inquiry. The dreamer becomes the researcher of his/her own inner world. As the process deepens, the dreamer/researcher take on a unifying momentum.

A final process of unification allows the reordering of the remaining words and sentences, culminating in a heartfelt poetic articulation. This articulation might not be rational, but it remains aligned with the poetic nature of dreams. Within this process, the dream and the dreamer become intertwined in a kind of "epistemic bond." *The epistemic bond is an engagement with the dream where the dreamer no longer can separate him- or herself from the flow of inner realizations.* The autonoetic aspect of the dreams becomes manifest and a sense of *inner-knowing* may arise. It is not uncommon that this inner knowing continues to unfold through time. This process has often been seen as akin to the alchemical process of self-transformation. Through this engagement, unexpected archetypal experiences naturally follow.

Poetic Synthesis is another act of creation in which the dreamer becomes the poet of his or her own inner primary process and the witness of new discoveries. "Spontaneity is an expression of the universal life that runs through everything and everybody" (Onslow Ford, 1978: 52). Sustaining this creative spontaneity and allowing the poetic space to flow is a skill that is gained over time, and gains in power as the seed for innovation and new creations. In the modern era the self has become disconnected from its vital dreaming and creative nature. The meeting of creative self and the act of creation is a form of reclamation. In discussing philosophy and biology and the role of dreams, Gordon Globus comments, "The world that we always already find ourselves thrown in continually settles out of a spontaneous eruption. . . . Dreaming provides the wedge that opens our perilous postmodern human condition in which world and self as primary realities are lost" (1995: 130, 133).

The first phase of IDP, Reflexive Emergence, culminates with Poetic Synthesis. Yet the process continues implicitly as insights continually arise with new experiences. A *Hermeneutic of Creation* has been put into motion, which does not end with the session of dream exploration. Often the dream that is the subject of such attention takes on a central organizing role in a person's life, where subsequent life occurrences are seen through the prism of the dream and the creative insights it produced.

A more formal process of reflection on the psychological meaning of the dream is the focus of the next phase of IDP.

PHASE II: REFLECTIVE INTEGRATION

Many levels of knowing occur during the first phase of Reflexive Emergence, and this first phase can be self-contained. The dream can be perfectly engaged at the level of reexperience and creative expression. In this case, the dream can remain an enigma from the point of view of dream interpretation, in the formal sense of the term. The second phase of IDP moves toward a multidimensional meaning-making process and builds on more cognitive and reflective aspects of consciousness. In this phase we invite the dreamer to go further with the dreams if they choose to.

If the first phase fostered receptivity and allowed the dreaming mind to reveal itself to the dreamer, in the second phase the dreamer more actively engages dream understanding. The nature of this engagement is modulated by the psychological commitment on the part of the dreamer.

Movement 4: Reflective Analysis

Reflective Analysis is the most common and central to many current dream practices. In this phase, the *reflective function of consciousness re-turns toward meaning through phenomenological and cognitive modalities.* Through reflective modalities such as script analysis, the exploration of personal mythology, or somatic awareness, the dreamer works with and reflects upon the dream in relation to his/her personal life. The dreamer can choose to reflect on the *whatness* of the dream (the particular content such as the central image) and *howness* (particular feelings or felt senses). Although this process is more analytical, it still values the organic emergence of personal meaning as part of analysis in contrast to ready-made answers.

Without objectifying experience, the reflective process invites inquiry to the dreamer's behavioral or relational patterns that may appear in the dream content or structure. In this phase of IDP the dreamer works with a trained facilitator, therapist, or educator who supports the dreamer to make the connection between the dream imagery and the dreamer's waking patterns. It is important to note that if the facilitator brings a particular interpretive lens, this will color the dreamer's experience and the meaning-making process.

A common practice that we use during this stage is the exploration of personal mythology (Feinstein & Krippner, 1988). Briefly stated, in this practice the dreamer is first led to identify a central emotion, then guided to explore where in his or her life that emotion first occurred. The exploration of personal mythology is consonant with enactive psychology (see chapter 4). It seeks to explore how dreamers embody particular beliefs, behavioral patterns, and knowledge about the world and how these are bundled with the memories marking events. Once this "bundle" has been teased out, the dreamer is led back to the dream and to explore how it resonates or illuminates the dream. Because the work of personal mythology is dialectical in nature, the dreamer is then invited to explore an opposite emotion to the first and to trace an embodied bundle of memory/belief/behavior associated with that emotion, and again letting this resonate and illuminate the dream.

If the approach is working with somatic therapy, the dreamer and their insights will be focused on how the experience and the dream is living and affecting the body and how the dreamer can work through the somatic knowing to further explore the dream.

This phase of the practice can also take a more contemplative or meditative approach. Often the depth of insights and realizations that arise naturally from nonanalytical engagements has its own pace. By using meditative skills to observe the inner works of the psyche and taking time to be with insights, further meaning naturally arises. Jung says, "We have obviously been so busy with the question of what we think that we entirely forget to ask what the unconscious psyche thinks about us" (Jung, 1964: 102).

Movement 5: Integrative Act

The Integrative Act encourages dreamers, as inquirers, to ponder their reflective and creative experience and explore a culminating point of integration. It is "a re-turning toward the context of objective/normative values which guide personal choices, action and self-meaning" (Kidd & Kidd, 1990: 2). In other words, dreamers have a chance to connect insights and realizations gained through the process of exploring the dream not only to their personal life but also to a larger context. Social, interpersonal, or transpersonal ramifications can be explored here. If the first phase was the creative amalgamation or union with the dream phenomena by personal inquiry, the second phase moves toward integrative and holistic emergence. Here the dreamer is invited to make more lucid choices in waking and take a step toward a "uniting dynamic movement." Integration in this case means a possible alignment between inner experience (the dream) and an outer expression (transformative action). This aspect of the Integrative Act is best demonstrated and described through example. In the next chapter we illustrated the long-term arc of transformation and integration.

SUMMARY

The overarching process of these two phases of Integral Dream Practice forms what we call a *Hermeneutic of Creation*. A Hermeneutic of Creation asserts that being with dreams is a phenomenon in motion. We tried to capture symbolically this complex iterative process in figure 12. The Hermeneutic of Creation is an integrative, explorative, and creative way of working with dreams, with an open mind, to allow the creative, spontaneous nature of the mind to interact with the reflective cognitive aspects of the mind. This lucid integration of the autopoietic and autonoetic creates a new place of meeting with limitless creative potential and possibilities.

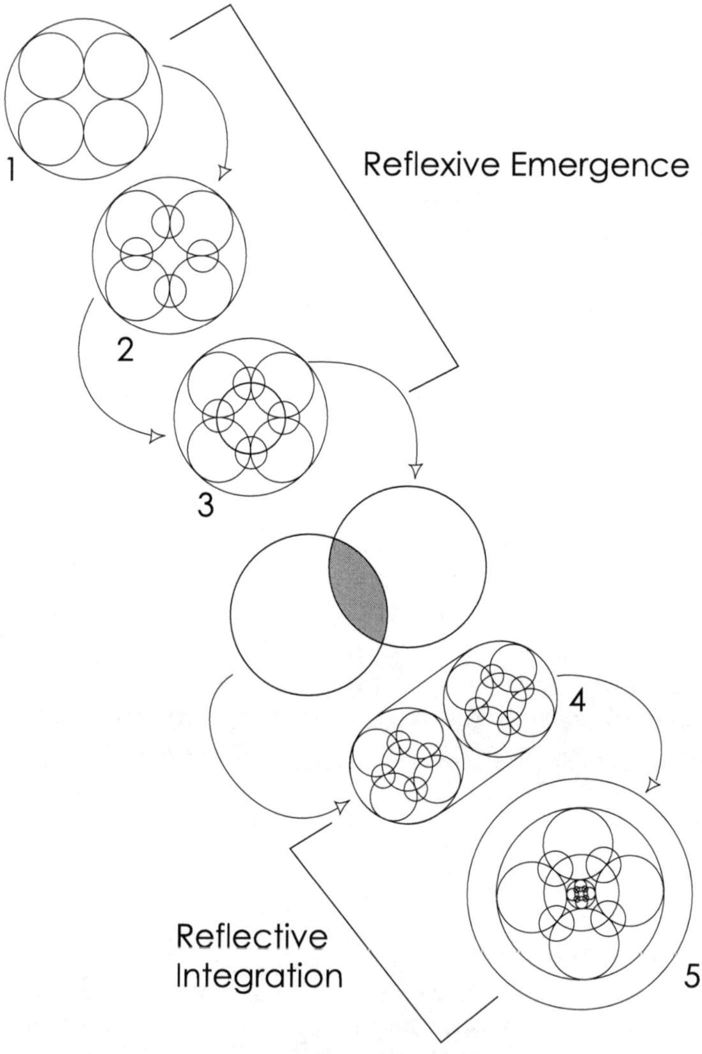

FIGURE 12. SYMBOLIC REPRESENTATION OF THE PROCESS OF IDP.

CREATIVITY AND AWARENESS UNFOLDS THE DIMENSIONALITY OF BEING

Exploring the complexity of dreams cannot be reduced to a single method. In this chapter we explored the two phases of IDP: Reflexive Emergence and Reflective Integration.

In the first phase, Reflexive Emergence foregrounds the practice of Dream Reentry and various Creative Expressions and culminates in Poetic Synthesis. First dream reentry allows the dreamer to return to the original source where the dream was created. Then a continuous creative expression/embodiment enables the dreamer to contact the flow of inner realizations without grasping or attaching to that flow, culminating in a Poetic Synthesis.

The completion of the first phase of IDP does not bring an end to the emergent process, but its reorientation. If in the first phase insights arise out of exploring the dream in creative and expressive ways, in the second phase, Reflective Integration, more verbal and cognitive practices are followed by integrative acts. In this phase, the dreamer unfolds his/her personal myth in relation to the dream and the previous insights gained from working nonanalytically with the dream. The five movements of IDP demonstrate the possibilities of being with dreams from a non-interpretive approach and from a reflective approach. The combination of both these approaches forms a *Hermeneutic of Creation*, where the dream is not so much decoded but rather engaged with creatively. In the next chapter we explore in depth the dream of a participant in order to give a preview of the possibilities embedded in some of the Integral Dream Practices.

CHAPTER SIXTEEN

Dreams in Creation

The Ursa Major Dream

This chapter describes the experience of an individual who explored her dream and the IDP method. Integral Dream Practice is built upon the assumption that the key to dream awareness, insights, and understanding is in the hands of the dreamer. As the facilitator offers the method of exploration, the dreamer is in charge of her own process. This chapter demonstrates how the dreamer engages wholeheartedly with the methods of dream reentry, creative enactments, and poetic synthesis. To activate the integration phase, we interviewed the dreamer, asking her to describe her experience in relation to her current life. We keep her own words in order to stay true to her experience, the context of the dream in her life, and her own reflections. This example illustrates the two phases of IDP: Reflexive Emergence and Reflective Integration.

Given the poetic nature of the first phase of IDP, Reflexive Emergence, we encourage the reader to engage with the writing with an open mind. For the second phase, the reader may even generate some associations to the dream, as the dream and the reflections presented by the dreamer echo deep archetypal and existential concerns. We hope that this qualitative description will be inspiring and allow the reader to poetically co-participate with the process. But first we discuss the subject of choosing a dream and give a short description of the setting in which the participant experienced Integral Dream Practice.

CHOOSING THE DREAM

Some dreams, by their impactful nature, emotional intensity, salient imagery, or recurrent insistence leave strong impressions on the psyche. Since in IDP the dream is the central event around which different dimensions of the dreamer's life are engaged, the selected dream is of significance. For a sustained period, the dream becomes an anchor for self-inquiry and reflection.

Even though a dream might be taken as an isolated experience, as a result of paying attention to it, other dream narratives resurface and current or past concerns come to the fore. *Our assumptions are that a dream is only a part of a string of related experiences and that in the process of unfolding the dream, a stream of connections will then unfold.*

How to translate a complex experience like a dream is also an issue. Text tends to reduce a dream into words, which poses a challenge. Vedfelt (2002) summarizes this challenge: "what we call the dream is a fragment taken out of context" (337). As dreams are multidimensional, recording them in writing ought to diminish some of this complex texture. Integral Dream Practice encourages different creative ways of recording dreams to facilitate bringing the dream into a living experience. In our courses on Dreams and Creativity, we encourage students to take one dream and explore it from different creative modalities such as poetry, drawing, theater, movement, computer animation, sculpture, among others.[1] Even with all these creative methodologies, part of the dream may remain elusive.[2]

URSA MAJOR DREAM: CONTEXT AND SETTING

For this book, a number of participants expressed willingness to share their dreams and describe their personal experiences of the Integral Dream Practice process. We gathered many accounts from students and from professionals who have attended our graduate courses on dreams and training workshops and retreats. In the process of writing this book, however, it became clear that it was best to use a single example in order to illustrate the breadth and depth of IDP. We have purposefully not offered many dream examples throughout the book, but we dedicate this entire chapter to one dream and its process at length. Even one chapter is not enough for exploring the dream, its context, and its impacts.

By selecting a single dream from a willing participant we move deeper into the creative and reflective process of IDP.[3] The methods within IDP can take different configurations but, as mentioned in chapters 14 and 15, it begins with a nonanalytical phase (Reflexive Emergence) and moves into a more interpretive phase (Reflective Integration). This process follows an organic movement from automatism (creative expressions) to articulation (reflective consciousness). The most important aspect of this process relies on the dreamer's willingness to 1) deeply and authentically engage with the creative enactments and 2) participate in a self-inquiry and reflective process.

The participant who offered her dream took a three-day dream intensive retreat geared toward individuals seeking professional development. The retreat, organized by the Dream Institute of Northern California, took place in Bodega Bay in northern California (July 2004) and was taught by Fariba Bogzaran. The participants were from various disciplines: psychologists, writers, poets, and university professors.[4] The private setting provided a contemplative atmosphere and helped the participants to slow down to nature's pace. The focus of interactions was with other participants only and with the natural surroundings. The specific methods and practices in IDP are particularly conducive to intensive trainings but also work well when applied systematically over a period of weeks.[5]

The Integral Dream Practice is organized around different modalities to access the multiple facets of the dream and the self. The method engages individuals and the group cognitively, experientially, creatively, somatically, poetically, and finally reflectively. The participants mainly worked on their own, under the guidance of the teacher, and they did not disclose their personal lives nor their dreams until the reflective phase. In IDP, in order to preserve the privacy of the participants and their creative autonomy, disclosure of personal material in the group is optional.

The retreat began by a lecture on the science of dreaming and the phenomenology of one night of sleep, when the participants engage factual knowledge offered by science and current research. In this first encounter, critical thinking and analytical questions about sleep and dreams are encouraged. Participants learn about types of dreams and discuss the potential functions and range of extraordinary dreams. This educational component of IDP aligns with an integral pedagogy.[6] The intellectual preamble enables the group to learn about the field of dream studies and offers the opportunity to connect with other members without disclosing personal information.

On the second day, participants were invited to engage with the Reflexive Emergence of IDP by applying nonanalytical approaches to explore a dream of their choice. This was followed by a series of Creative Acts. In the process of Reflexive Emergence,[7] participants carried on a deep *intrasubjective* engagement with their creative mind. Each practice was followed by a session of automatic writing.

The morning of the third day was devoted to *re-turning* to their creation by composing a poetic synthesis. Participants could, if they wished, share their poetic composition with the rest of the group. This was followed by a reflective sharing of insights and of the experiential highlights of the retreat. Because of the length of the retreat, the emphasis was on the first phase of IDP, Reflexive Emergence. However, instructions on Reflective Integration were offered to the dreamers so that they could work with the dream—going forward as they reengaged with their daily life. The participants were informed about the long-term nature of the IDP process and were encouraged to continue exploring and reflecting on the same dream and or the insights they had gained during the retreat.[8]

For the purpose of this book, the dreamer was interviewed three years after the retreat. She was asked to share about her experience and the impact of the IDP method, in particular her automatic writings, and some of her creative enactments.

THE DREAMER

Lynne Ehlers (the dreamer's real name is used with her permission) has kindly agreed to contribute her dream and her experience of this integrative process. Lynne holds a PhD in psychology and is a licensed clinical psychologist with a Jungian orientation. She maintains a private practice in Berkeley and San Francisco. She has been working intensively with dreams, first her own, then her clients' since the early 1970s. Her professional background blends a lifelong interest in myths, dreams, fairy tales, sand play, and other symbolic systems. As a teacher, Lynne has created courses on the archetypal symbolism of dreams and sand play. She teaches these courses as part of a series entitled *The Language of the Dream*. Her dissertation, *The Alchemical Nigredo, Albedo, Citrinitas and Rubedo: Stages of Transformation: A Case Study* (1992), explored dreams through the template of alchemy. She has contributed articles to the *Journal of Sandplay Therapy* including Kali (2000). She teaches in various universities in the San Francisco Bay Area.

We have invited Lynne to be part of this book project for several reasons. First we trusted that as a teacher and writer, she not only would be able to articulate her experience but also communicate the subtle complexities within the reflective process. We were also interested in the fact that she had developed an approach to dreams, different from IDP. For her to embark wholeheartedly on a new way of exploring dreams demonstrates her open-mindedness. This illustrates that integrative methods in exploring dreams enrich those with extensive professional experience with other approaches. We realize that many individuals might not have as much knowledge about dreams and symbolism as Lynne has to articulate the integration phase; however we chose her example to demonstrate the possibilities of this particular approach.

Lynne's willingness to be interviewed on several occasions over the course of three years offers the reader a rare perspective on how one dream can unfold over time. She mentioned in one of the interviews that she was willing "to be on hands and knees to explore the creative enactments," even though this particular type of personal engagement was not something she had done before. We also chose her dream because of its archetypal overtones. We believed that this dream, though very personal to Lynne, could be an inspirational gift to others.[9]

THE DREAM

Lynne chose to explore a dream she had had many years earlier. She did so because, for her, the dream still carried a "charge"; it had remained enigmatic and was still very present in her psyche. Given her background as a Jungian-oriented psychologist, we thought she might have worked extensively with this dream prior to the retreat. When we inquired about that, she informed us that at the time the dream occurred, she was finishing her dissertation and was very busy with her outer life. She had not explored the dream, yet the dream had remained vivid in her memory.

To give a detailed report of the entire process of Lynne's dream exploration using Integral Dream Practice methods is beyond the scope of this chapter. Rather we chose selected practices within the Reflexive Emergence phase of IDP to provide context for the second phase of IDP, Reflective Integration.

Title: *URSA MAJOR*
Date: 2/27/1995

I walk outside, look up into the inky sky and see a VERY BRIGHT STAR twinkling, pulsing, then moving around, first in a spiral inward, then in a spiral outward, then in a series of brilliant patterns, which are awesome, like fireworks in the sky. The star then travels in a wide arc across the sky and disappears into a vast mass of brown fur. I see that the fur is part of the chest of a sleeping bear. The bear—a huge brown bear—wakes up, comes alive, and reaches around in the area of its solar plexus, heart or throat. The star has lodged itself somewhere in this region, but the bear is not harmed. In fact, the bear's reaction seems more like wonderment. I am in awe witnessing this, and relieved that the bear is all right.

REFLEXIVE EMERGENCE

The reflexive step in IDP is dream reentry or reexperiencing the dream. Dream reentry offers a way of reconnecting with the dream through methods that induce a dreamlike state in waking. Because of the facilitator's particular expertise, the method used was reentry with rhythmic drumming. Using the knowledge in science of sleep and shamanic practices, Bogzaran uses rhythmic drumming to support the induction of a hypnagogic state. A variety of experiences can happen during this state but ideally, if the participants are able to sustain lucidity while in a semi-sleep, hypnagogic state, they can reenter the dream vividly. They experience what it is like to be inside the dream lucidly. This metacognitive state of consciousness is akin to lucid dreaming, a practice of sustained awareness in the dream state. Similar to meditation practices, the participants can learn to apply the right amount of attention while experiencing this particular state of consciousness. Too much laxity and one falls asleep; too much control and one ends up "thinking" about the dream more than experiencing the dream. Once the skill is learned, the dreamer can sustain the lucid state while at the same time allowing the spontaneous dream state to arise.

While listening to the sound of the drum, Lynne reentered her dream and reexperienced the dream she had several years prior. Once the drumming ended, participants engaged in automatic writing. The following is Lynne's automatic writing after her reentry experience.

> My longing heart leaps to the beat of the drum as tears leap to my eyes. I meet Garuda [mythical birth] "I know you; may I fly to the heavens with you?" I ask respectfully. "Yes, you may hop on my back." And his wings beat to the rhythm of the drum. Far, far, we flew to the starry sky . . .
>
> There I saw the star. It was my star and I became the star . . . brilliant, pulsing, pulsing to the rhythm of my breath . . . then turning, spiraling, to the left . . . a great spiral in the sky . . . then right . . . then in a swan

> dive I arc across the sky, come to a great furry vastness and shoot into it.
>
> I am inside the sleeping bear—my entry awakens it, and now inside, I become the great bear . . . huge, alive, awake. I feel my jaw and great teeth. I feel my huge body. I feel my great paws stretch and move. "Who are you?" I ask. "Who am I? I am the Great Bear—Ursa—Ursula—I am huge, I am slow . . . I am powerful. I have been asleep—you have awakened me—Who am I, asleep in the sky? Papa bear? Mama bear? Baby bear? Protective bear? Grouchy bear? Bear up—Bear down? Unbearable? Bearable? Lair of the bear? Bear in mind? Bearer of the unbearable. Bear in the heaven . . . soul bear. . . . Bear energy . . . Big, alert, silent, protective."

The reexperience of the dream combined with automatic writing allows the creative mind / dreaming mind to flow into waking consciousness.[10] Lynne's automatic writing describes what emerges without censorship. The writing becomes a spontaneous visual poetic chaos, where free association permits a flood of expression without effort or control. Its form resembles Gertrude Stein's sound poetry. Stein said she did not hear a language, she heard tones and voices and rhythms.[11]

Creative Expressions

Within IDP there are a host of creative acts used depending on the setting, the time available, and the group. The creative enactments can involve any expressive art method.[12] For the purposes of this chapter, we have chosen two of the creative enactments that Lynne participated in during the retreat: Movement and Existential Practice.

Movement

After setting the context for this creative practice with extensive instruction, participants take the dream's central image, emotion, or other aspects of the dream and imagine them inside their body. For example, if the central image is a powerful tiger, the dreamer calls upon the tiger inside and moves freely with the qualities and energy of the tiger. This form of embodiment of the dream calls upon an increased awareness of the body; it invites the participant to access somatic intuitive knowing.

An element of play is present in the movement or embodiment calling for a release of mental stagnation, ideally freeing the mind/body to reexperience the dream but this time from the perspective of the body. This process is also led by the sound of shamanic drumming. Some participants take this creative expression into a theatrical embodiment of the dream and enact with sound and movement and dance the dream experience. Others might wish to make micro-movements or hold particular postures. In this case, the participant chose to embody the dream, and the process allowed a spontaneous emergence of new insights to create a deeper connection to the dream. The objective of this practice is to bring somatic awareness to the dream experience.

The following is Lynne's automatic writing after the creative enactment movement.

> Big bear, awaken bear, bear, bear, bear, bear nose, bear mouth, bear jaw, bear teeth, bear pads, bear paws, bear claws, bear claws dig, escape, scratch, eat, open, eat, sweet honey drips, salivate Taste, sweet, delicious, more—tongue drools, licks, swallows, nose smells, tongue drools, tummy fed, hungry, funny, fed, walks, awaken, big, stops, looks, crisp, sharp—filled by pungent smells and sounds . . .
>
> I see—I hear—I taste—I sniff—pause, no hurry—no urgency—I am in my body—bear body—big bear body—slow—lumbering—deliberate—stop-paw-claw-smell-eat—big bear body is slow—deliberate—calm—unhurried—easy—EMBODIED . . . in my body, body-me-body
>
> Me-Bodied, Me-Body, Me-BOD-DEE, IN-BODY, EMBODIED.

In this practice Lynne took on the image of the bear and moved with the bear, becoming the bear, feeling the star inside of the bear. The automatic writing once again brought her attention to all those feelings not as mental events but with their full embodied felt sense. We particularly chose this creative expression to demonstrate a dream that yearned for embodiment. This reconnection was a central theme for Lynne as it repeats in her writing and in her process.

Existential Practice

One of the creative inquiries in exploring dreams concerns their existential nature and essence. In many cases, unfolding dream images and emotions can connect us to a deep core of our being. One of the best ways to experience this connection is to focus on a particular dream image or emotion and explore it in depth with a simple existential question, presented repeatedly. In this Existential Practice, we apply the question "who are you?" to a dream's image or emotion.[13] Within a retreat setting (or classroom), the participants are invited to pair with a partner such that one becomes the interviewer. The role of the interviewer is to ask the simple question "who are you?" and be present as an active listener to the answers given. Without sharing the dream narrative, the dreamer begins to answer the question as freely and creatively as possible. The dreamer finds himself or herself immersed in the many details associated with different aspects of the dream. In this practice, the question becomes the trigger for an automatic flow of consciousness, engaging the dreamer's whole being while saying: "I am . . ."

This practice encourages trust in one's creative nature while at the same time it engages deeply with the existential questioning of identity. The spontaneous answers bring new images, a poetic space, and emotional resonance to awareness. Often insights flow both through the dreamer and the interviewer.

The first answers often begin with the actual image presented in the dream, then shift to others that amplify it, and eventually move to fresh and unexpected associative material. Once the dreamer pauses and when the time is right, the question is asked again, moving even deeper into the arising current of experience. This practice could be seen as a modified form of free association, but organized around the question of deep identity. The answers often address the more mundane concerns of the waking ego first. It is likely, however, that if the dreamer allows it, these answers can touch upon profound layers of being, such as where identity touches upon the paradox of nonduality. The following is Lynne's automatic writing after the creative enactment of the Existential Practice.

Partner (P) asked "Who are you?"

Lynne (L) I am BEAR. I am big. I am heavy, ponderous, slow, hungry! I am shaggy. I am warm. I am impervious to rain and cold and wet. I am a swimmer. I am an eater of salmon and berries and sweet honey. I am fast, I am quiet. I am alert. I am a long nose, I am these teeth, I am these paws, I am these claws. I dig, I paw, I scratch, I scrape, I find honey, I salivate. I am slow, I am deep drumming. I am the drum, I am steady. I am constant, I am fast and slow. I am ponderous and light. I am big, I am large, I am heavy, I am sure, I am steady, I am calm, I am peace, I am heart, I am lungs, I am nose, I am sight, I am insight, I am instinct, I am bone, I am.

(P) Who are you?

(L) I am the honey, I am the sweetness, I am the bear, I am strong, I don't mind the pain [of bee stings], I am in love with the honey. I am honey, I am amber, I am thick, I am sweet, I am sticky, I am runny, I am delicious, I am sweet deliciousness. Delicious! Desired! Desirable in my deliciousness, I am unto myself, I need nothing more.

(P) Who are you?

(L) I am the fish eaten by the bear, I am the fish of the bear, I am the drum, I am the sound of the drum, I am steady, I am the measure of the beat, I am fast, I am slow, I am lazy, I am dragging.

(P) Who are you?

(L) I am awake. I am my eye; I see, I take in the world I am my mouth; I take in the taste of the world I am my nose; I take in the smell of the world. I am my ears; I take in the sounds of the world. I am my paws; I feel the world.

(P) Who are you?

(L) I am the bear. I am awake. I am the eye, I see the world, I see the beauty of ugly. I am the nose. I smell the world.

So far, the dreamer had written her thoughts in the privacy of her journal but now, for the first time, she discloses aspects of her dream to another. The quality of the experience may be enriched by the presence of a witness. Facing each other, with eyes open or closed, the dreamer and the witness become attuned to each other in a compassionate bond. The *intersubjective space* brings about a supportive environment for the dreamer to be heard and to be gently carried forward in her exploration.

During and after this practice, the dreamer often moves to a deeper and more contemplative space. A sense of connection develops not only toward the self, but also to a *larger collective consciousness*. The mind quiets down, and the exchange between partners becomes like a *meditative verbalization*. In later reflections, participants often speak about feelings of connection, transcendence, and oneness.

Poetic Synthesis: Returning to Texts

At the end of the creative enactments, similar to a qualitative researcher, the participants are invited to reread their dreams and all the automatic writings they have produced. Using phenomenological methods, the participants attentively and with open minds follow their *felt sense* and underline words or sentences that *stand out* according to their expressive or energetic qualities. They then string together these expressions as a creative word collage and take some time to compose a piece that carries poetic overtones, thus the name of the practice: *Poetic Synthesis*. What emerges is usually a short text from a paragraph to a page in length, evocative of the dreamer's experience, context, and history. Dreamers are then invited to read their creation to the entire group.[14] The creative introspection of the Reflexive Emergence phase ends with the poetic recitation. For those hearing it, the Poetic Synthesis might not have any meaning or it might be overflowing with meaning.

As part of an intensive retreat, the Poetic Synthesis is constructed *after* the third day; within a classroom setting, it takes place toward the end of the semester or a quarter. The process of returning to the dream and the automatic writings brings refinement to the rawness of automatic and creative expression. Poetic Synthesis gives a sense of closure and provides an occasion to integrate the creative, somatic, or existential practices done in this phase. In our experience, this form of artistic integration brings inspiration and elation to the dreamer. With a modicum of analytical input, insights into the dream continue to surface; dreamers feel empowered that these insights emerged out of their own efforts, creative enactments, and learned skills. Dreamers often comment on the singular and communal artistry that is being displayed during the recitation.

Lynne's *Poetic Synthesis*

Longing heart—a star—radiates—pulses
Spirals left—spirals right
Arcs across a starry velvet sky
—Vast cave of a sleeping bear—
And enters a shaggy vastness
Sleeper awakes!
Ponderous—pondering!
Nose sniffs—the pungent—sharp and sweet
Ears hear—the sighs of the dying—fear of flying
Eyes see blood and beauty
Paws scratch and scrape—feel icy cold and warm soft
moss
Lips drip / tongue licks—greets / bitter bears / sweet
amber honey . . .

When the Poetic Synthesis is read out loud in the group, often there is a sense of *awe* and *aha,* not so much for catching the meaning of the dream but for the sense of intuitive knowing, a felt sense that suffuses the group. The process has offered a creative and cohesive connection between the dream, the dreamers, and their essence. No interpretations are offered by the facilitator as the dreamers recount the experience. At the most, a thoughtful inquiry can be made to bridge the dream to waking life or to bring to the foreground some creative actions implied in the process.

At the end of the retreat, the participants were encouraged to share their *memories, dreams, and reflections*[15] connected with the dream and the process in a final discussion. They were encouraged to continue reflecting and unfolding the dream; to continue being with the insights that emerged out of the retreat and to pay attention to how the creative engagement with the dream connects with their lives and work. The practices found within Reflexive Emergence processes can be applied as part of a larger process of self-inquiry. How dreamers take the insights into their lives and integrate them is their choice. Some move on to explore other dreams while others continue to explore the same dream using other methods.

REFLECTIVE INTEGRATION

In order to follow up with the integration phase, we contacted Lynne three years after the retreat for an in-person interview and two years after that for a second interview by telephone. There was also an exchange of e-mails. We informed her about this book and she agreed to be interviewed to discuss whether exploring this dream in the retreat had any lasting impact upon her. In particular, she was asked about her own view of the process and her experience with the goal of eliciting stories about any observable changes that may have occurred in her life connected to this particular process. These questions brought a number of realizations that she willingly and openly shared.

Reflective Analysis

We asked Lynne questions about her experience relating to the dream in the past few years. Even after the passage of so much time, she was still visibly moved by this entire experience. She comments:

> As I reflect on the dream and the work I did on it in your retreat, its importance to me cannot be underestimated. I think this dream is one of the Big Dreams of my life,

> because years later, it continues to do its work on me, and perhaps it will for the rest of my life. The dream begins with my peering into the darkness of the heavens, where I see a shining star. Only now, in retrospect, do I see this star as my soul, shining through the darkness of unknowing, pulsing to the rhythm of my own heart. It lies in the realm of the transpersonal. But it does not stay there; it moves into the brown furry body of a living bear—into the realm of the personal. That's why this dream is so crucially important.
>
> By becoming the star, I realized that its movement—a spiral inward and a spiral outward—follows the trajectory of my life: a descent via a lengthy analysis into the very depths of my soul, followed by a movement to bring the treasures and knowledge gained in the depths out into the world. As I copied the actual dream for you, I was struck by a part I had forgotten: the "series of brilliant patterns" which the star makes as it arcs across the sky. It occurred to me that this could be my soul's continuing journey through this lifetime. At a more concrete level, the brilliant patterns might have to do with the brilliant and beautiful slide images of nature and art I use to teach my courses on the Language of the Dream. The star's dazzle also flies in the face of childhood self-doubt and beliefs about myself as insignificant and invisible. In moments when I doubt myself or get discouraged about the obstacles to bringing my teaching into the world, the vision of the star in the sky inspires me and gives me the energy and the courage to persevere.

Her knowledge of the psychological and cultural meaning of symbols helped her frame a larger narrative around the dream, as she retells the experience:

> In the dream, this star is also the agent through which the sleeping bear is awakened. Something in me that was asleep or lying dormant is awakened and brought to life. Oh! Now it dawns on me: my dream of the star entering into the body of the bear can be understood as my soul entering my body and awakening it. Working

> with the dream in the retreat was an extremely important part of this awakening. Being an intuitive, I have had very little body-awareness. Working in the body of the bear, *becoming* the bear, and "feeling into" all parts of the bear—its nose, teeth, paws and claws—increased my awareness of all of my senses and brought me into my body in a way that no dream analysis alone could. I *loved* being in the body of the bear: large, slow, lumbering, powerful. After all, a bear is so large, so fierce and so powerful it has no natural enemies, its thick coat is a protection from the elements, and a she-bear can be fierce in the protection of her young.

At this point of *reflective analysis,* personal associations connect with personal script and personal mythology. Lynne continues her reflections by connecting the dream to childhood events and how these realizations at this time in her life helped her transform her personal myth.

> I realize as I speak that the bear in my dream is a compensation for how I felt as a child: small, weak and vulnerable. To actually step into the body of the bear via IDP was to begin to transform those early feelings, and to become embodied in a way I never had before. I also loved being the honey, getting into my own deliciousness. If the star in my dream represents spirit or soul and the bear represents my body, then IDP was a beautiful way to bring Spirit into Matter, or Soul into Body. This reminds me of a beautiful watercolor by William Blake called *The Reunion of the Soul and the Body.*[16]
>
> It's ecstatic. When the deep longing of the soul for the body is realized, that is, when spirit enters matter and we become ensouled or embodied, the experience is ecstatic. I think becoming the honey and the salmon the bear eats was part of the ecstasy.

Integrative Act

How are insights from a dream integrated? What are the steps to bring its wisdom into everyday life? The dreamer follows a

Figure 13. William Blake (1813)
The Reunion of the Soul and the Body.

process of mindfully making life choices, integrating insights gained from unfolding the dream experience. This is a form of *lucid waking practice*. Lynne's authentic engagement with this dream, her reflection and willingness not only to gain insights but also to take action to transform her life, is an example of how exploring dreams for a long period of time from different modalities can have a lasting impact. She writes:

> Although I did not focus on this next portion of the dream (i.e. the point of entry of the star into the solar plexus, heart or throat of the bear) during the retreat, applying Integral Dream Practice to it has helped its meaning to continue to unfold, and has had an enormous impact on my sense of self since then.

When speaking to Lynne it became clear that, of all creative enactments explored in the retreat, Movement and embodying the dream was the most powerful practice for her.[17] She associated herself as an intuitive rather than as body centered. She spoke of having problems in the past with her posture by a chronic hunching from constriction of the solar plexus. She associated this posture with an earlier "need to please, to be nice and an inability to stand up for myself." She continues her reflection and personal associations:

> For me, the solar plexus is the locus of one's self-esteem. Because of early life traumas, my solar plexus was collapsed by constriction and fear, like a balloon without air. Working with the dream in the soul/body helped bring this area of my body to consciousness. Specifically, I applied the words of the automatic writing exercise—slow—deliberate—calm—unhurried—easy—EMBODIED—to my solar plexus. Like my movement in the body of the bear, I imagined the energy of the solar plexus as slow, deliberate, purposeful and unafraid.

Lynne was asked to describe her experience, of exploring this dream through the IDP process, and its potential integration into her life. As she describes her experience one can observe the movement of consciousness from reflective to interpretive. At the end of the second phase of IDP, moving from reflective to interpretive is a natural process as the dreamer makes an attempt to understand the process in its entirety. Lynne's particularly poignant example demonstrates how deep realizations occur with mindful intent and sustained reflection. She writes:

> In the years since, my solar plexus has become the ever-present focus of a mindfulness meditation on expansion, openness and integrity: on standing tall, standing to my truth, and living beyond the edges of my fear. For example, I have a fear of public speaking, but prior to speaking engagements, to get inside the solar plexus of the bear imaginally and to speak from its center emboldens me. In working with vulnerable clients, I also notice the she-bear's protective fierceness in me. Just as kundalini energy moves upward through the chakras [energy centers in the central channel in the spine], so embodied soul-energy moves upward. To have the soul enter the heart chakra is to begin to work, live and love closer to the heart, to genuine relatedness and joy. This, too, is a mindfulness work in progress. To have soul enter the throat chakra is to speak up, speak out and bring voice to the murmurs of the heart. And a stronger solar plexus lends strength to the entire endeavor. Through working on this dream via this process of Integral Dream Practice (IDP) I feel transformed and ever transforming.

In our last contact with Lynne, she mentioned that when she found the dream in her files, it indeed appeared that she had not worked on it at the time, but she had written one sentence next to it: "*The self has awakened, the dormant hibernating Great Bear in me. What will happen next?*" Her initial spontaneous response to the dream appears to be a precognitive realization of her later exploration and integrative process on the dream during the retreat. The unfolding meaning of "big dreams" can have a prolonged arc spanning decades. "*Even though I was in analysis at the time I have no recollection of working with this dream,*" she said. By exploring the dream in different creative and reflective modalities, she was *"able to bring the psyche into soma; that is bring the unconscious into my body then to re-experience it at a somatic level."* Lynne spoke at length about the impact of the star coming through the solar plexus as an important aspect of this dream for her. *"Ever since the retreat the energy of the dream pulsating and entering inside my body has affected my posture. To breathe in without fear is revolutionary. I feel more courage, sitting tall, walking tall, so it becomes ever present within me."* Reflecting on the dreambody process, Arnold Mindell writes: "The study of dreambody processes gives mythology a root in the flesh" (1982: 198).

IDP also encourages dream awareness to unfold at the level of community. We asked Lynne if these changes had impacted her *interpersonal relationships* and how her *new being* is in relation to her work and community. For her, the process has brought a new texture into her daily life in her relationship with everyone in her life. She comments:

> When I speak with people, I find myself increasingly aware of speaking "tall," that is, speaking my truth with integrity and without fear. Coming from a place of needing to please, rather than from a place of authority was more comfortable for me than speaking up. Speaking up is uncomfortable, but now the air gets clear. Being more honest is life changing. It takes more effort to make nice. Ultimately it is more relaxing to be true.

The passage Lynne wrote in her journal: *"The self has awakened, the dormant hibernating Great Bear in me. What will happen next?"* was actualized by taking a leap of faith and reexperiencing the dream with an open mind; fluidly engaging in the Creative Enactments; committing to mindful refection and taking charge in Integrative Acts. Nine years after her dream she awakened the dream and answered her question.

SUMMARY

The wisdom of IDP rests in its open-ended approach to dreams, without presuppositions. It invites the dreamer to embrace the dream through creative, reflective, and integrative action. Engagement with the entirety of the activities within IDP may elicit a holistic and integrative experience. The example explored in this chapter represents the experience of one individual among many who have gone through the process of Integral Dream Practice.[18] This chapter honors how one can explore a dream intensively through non-interpretative approaches with creative expressions. It also conveys how the dreamer's insights, reflection, and transformative action enabled her to integrate the dream into her waking life.

Epilogue

In this book, we have embraced the wide scope of the field of dream studies as well as focused on the details of science, phenomenology, culture, society, and ecology. We showed that dreams are *autopoietic*, that is, spontaneously and creatively self-organized. Furthermore, we proposed that developing a deep relationship to dreams unfolds their *autonoetic* potential: self-awareness and lucidity within a nested world.

Integral thinking fosters an open-minded attitude and encourages questions and dialogue about the nature of the dreaming mind across disciplines. Diving into the sea of knowledge offered by dreams not only incites awe but continually leads us to ask: How aware are we of our dreams? What is our relationship to them and how do we integrate dreaming into our life? How do we expand beyond our comfort zone to open ourselves to other ways of knowing and different ways of seeing?

While modernity has relegated dreaming to the private sphere, leading to the disappearance of some forms of collective dreaming, integral philosophy critically reimagines this confining narrative. Dreams are contingent on the complex functioning of a number of neurophysiological systems, including those linked to the sleep-wake cycle and those implicated in memory formation, self-representation, and conscious embodiment.

Dreams also play an important role at the psychological level, providing the support for learning, insight, and emotional integration. Directly mirroring our creative and purposeful being, dreams reveal a wide range of facets: cognitive, emotional, somatic, volitional, spiritual, and so on. They also disclose our constant and changing participation in relational dynamics—family, workplace, and peer groups—where the world-as-we-know-it gets revealed to us through our various enactments and identities. Moreover, because we are de facto engaged in larger social-ecological systems, dreams may help us to refocus our awareness to better understand our relationship to these wider systems, even intimating a larger cosmological identity.

Integral dreaming intimates that dreams contribute not only to self-knowing but also to self-realization. Some types of dreams have profound spiritual impact and strong transformative qualities. But an important question remains open: Can dreams give us a preview of the next phase of our evolution at all levels? If dreams do indeed play a part in our well-being, then it is crucial to understand well-being *integrally*: health and sanity are not only confined to the body and the self, but extend to our family, our community, our society, and our planet. Integral Dreaming acknowledges that dreaming is an essential aspect of who we are, in relation to larger interconnected systems both visible and invisible.

The multilayered, multidimensional, and complex nature of our own being is only one part of the complexity within which we are embedded. An Integral Dream Practice views dreams as *self in creation* and promotes co-participating in that creation. In theory and practice, it is crucial that the elements that make dreams a unique state of consciousness be valued on their own terms, especially given that the range of inquiry and creativity within the dreaming mind seems limitless. Through our creative nature and the cultivation of awareness, we have the capacity not only to make important inner changes, but also to integrate the wisdom of this knowledge to potentially contribute to a major transformative act. Arriving at the end of this long discourse, we still ask ourselves: Do dreams have meaning? Should they be subjected to interpretation or elucidation? Are they merely habits of our own creations? We have one certainty within this sea of uncertainty: that dreams are creative windows to our inner worlds and can play an important role in our awakening. There are traditions that seek to dissolve the content of dreams as habitual patterns, but even within them, one must first recognize what are habits of the mind. Dream awareness is one of many keys to view the complexities of our inner life and to bring lucidity into the integration of our whole being. Whether dreams are important messages, or illusions, we keep an open mind and embrace different views about this enigmatic experience. Our hope is that *Integral Dreaming* brings a new paradigm to the field of dream studies—one that is holistic, inclusive, and embracing—inviting all to unfold ever-new insights within the vastness of this ocean of discovery.

Notes

INTRODUCTION

1. As expounded by Haridas Chaudhuri (1965).

CHAPTER ONE. A LARGER CALLING: THE FIELD OF INTEGRAL STUDIES

1. For further readings on Hegel in relation to the topic of the mind/body problem, phenomenology, and methods, see Hegel's *Phenomenology of Spirit* (1977).

2. In Aurobindo's writings, Eastern thought referred to the integration of the three main traditional yogas of India: *karma* (service), *bakhti* (devotional), and *raja* (meditation) yoga.

CHAPTER TWO. AN INTEGRAL APPROACH TO DREAMING

1. Examples of religious symbolism that links multiplicity to wholeness include: the multipointed star found in several traditions, such as Judaism, Hinduism, and Baha'i; the cross used in Celtic and Christian traditions; the hexagram in Chinese traditions; tree of life of the Kabbala; the sacred medicine wheel used by Native American traditions; and mandalic *thangka* paintings recording Tibetan Buddhist cosmology. Such understanding can also be (re)enacted in complex

rituals offering individuals a participatory taste of a valued state, often organized around certain virtues or self-renewal.

2. "Habits of the mind, linked to temperament and the accumulation of experiences (especially traumatic ones) can generate gaps in the sense of self" (Cortright, 2007) and can be the cause of the constriction of awareness. Psychotherapy and other psychospiritual practices are often geared toward overcoming these restrictions, enabling what is now understood as the psychology of "flourishing."

3. In the previous chapter, we briefly spoke about nonduality as related to the psychospiritual meaning of *integral.*

4. The multidimensional self eventually includes an understanding by the self that negates the self as a reified reality.

5. See, for instance, Domhoff (2003); Hall (1953); Hall and Van de Castle (1966); Van de Castle (1977, 1994).

6. For example, dreams can be attended to before we go to sleep, with the practice of incubation; during their occurrence, with the practice of lucid dreaming; and after the dream, with the many practices of dream understanding and dream expression. See also chapter 7.

7. In chapter 15, we demonstrate how a dream analyst takes on different methods of working with dreams.

8. We began teaching a course on Integral Dreaming in 2002 at JFKU and applied the particular model we envisioned. We met with Wilber in Boulder, Colorado on different occasions in early 2000 and participated in his small, collegial integral seminars to gain more understanding of his synthesizing model of different disciplines and the complexity behind his thinking.

9. At conferences of the International Association for the Studies of Dreams, participants are exposed to presenters' creativity from every discipline as they communicate their findings, research, or practice of understanding dreams, enabling learning across domains. This meta-awareness allows connection *within* disciplines and thus promotes learning and integration of the material.

10. One of the shortcomings of integral and eclectic approaches is that they require widespread knowledge, with the risk of sacrificing depth of knowledge in the service of breadth. When one gathers so many ideas and puts them in dialogue, one might miss the fine points that focused expertise brings to any single aspect or quadrant.

CHAPTER THREE. THE CREATIVE BRAIN AND THE SCIENCE OF SLEEP AND DREAMS

1. A host of theoretical and evidence-based approaches to understanding the process of dreaming exists. These include the cognitive

aspects of dreaming (Foulkes, 1985, 1999; Moffitt et al., 1993); the evolutionary aspects (Revonsuo, 2000); clinical aspects and personality dimensions (Hartmann, 1999); the underlying psychophysiological processes (Braun et al., 1997; Hobson, 1994; Hobson et al., 2000); the neurological substrate (Jouvet, 1999) combined with psychoanalytical considerations (Solms, 1997, 1999); as well as connectionist (Globus, 1987, 1995; Hartmann, 1999) and neural network (Antrobus, 1991, 2000) models for understanding the dreaming brain. In this chapter, we cannot capture the fine details of all this accumulative work. We will try to focus on paradigmatic research to illustrate how dreams participate in the autopoietic (self-organization) process.

2. Sleep, in good quality and in the right amount, is an important cornerstone of physical and mental health (de Benedictis et al., 2007). Recent epidemiological research has found a sweet spot for optimal sleep length, the norm ranging between 6.5 to 7.5 hours. When sleep researcher Kripke and his team (2002) examined death rate in relation to the average nightly amount of sleep, they found that both too little or too much sleep are correlated with increased health issues. Too little sleep has been known to be detrimental to health, but longer sleep (more than eight hours) has only recently been associated with increased morbidity, surprisingly more than with having only six hours of sleep.

3. Readers interested in an in-depth specialized review should consult the three volumes edited by Barrett and McNamara (2007) on the science of dreaming.

4. Scientists, by focusing on problems that are relevant to their epistemological stance, have sometimes alienated clinicians and others for whom dreams are more than neurobiological processes. Within the field of dream studies in particular, the scientific method, despite its strengths, has been hindered in its scope by: 1) the belief among some scientists that the scientific story about dreams is the only true one (known as scientism); 2) the fact that this story attempts to reduce dreaming to its underlying mechanisms and that when we will understand these components, we will know all we need to know about dreams (reductionism). Both scientism and reductionism have conspired against science being fully integrated with other perspectives on dreams. As a result, the scientific portrayal of dreaming can have a disenchanting effect because it cannot always make sense of people's subjective dream life or the depth and potency of the dreaming experience.

5. Desynchronized EEG records show many different kinds of brain frequencies. This is thought to indicate a varying pattern of firing of brain cells, that many different areas of the brain are active, at the same time and to a varying degree. Brain activity in both REM

and vigilant wakefulness is indicated by a random desynchronized pattern. In contrast, NREM stages 3 and 4 are highly synchronized sleep, associated with low activation or the lack of conscious activation, both characteristics of deep sleep.

6. One cycle per second is also known as one hertz.

7. There are differences in how Eastern and Western thought view slow-wave sleep. Within the Western scientific and psychological systems, this stage of consciousness is often seen as paradigmatic of *un*consciousness. While the physiological importance of slow-wave sleep has been established in regard to physical health, there is little said about its psychological or spiritual value. Given the lack of dream content, it is not valued in regard to dreaming. Dreamless (deep) sleep seems to be the exemplar of *un*consciousness. However, from the Eastern Hindu and Buddhist points of view, the "dreamless sleep" is revered as a state of consciousness devoid of subjective dream content; there is still faint consciousness, which under observation may be felt as objectless consciousness. For this reason, it is considered a state of great importance (Gillespie, 2002). On the other hand, we should not assume that what, within modern science, has been identified as deep sleep (stage 3 and 4 of sleep) is identical to what in the East is translated with the same expression or as dreamless sleep. Important philosophical points are often lost in translation. Researcher Lynn Mason's (1995) study on stages 3 and 4 sleep linked Eastern meditation practice (Transcendental Meditation) with Western methods of observation and showed the presence of a witnessing awareness even in a state of "lost consciousness."

8. In neuroscience, long-term potentiation (LTP) is the long-lasting improvement in communication between two neurons that results from stimulating them simultaneously. Since neurons communicate via chemical synapses, and because memories are believed to be stored within these synapses, LTP is widely considered one of the major cellular mechanisms that underlie learning and memory.

9. An informal questionnaire to twenty participants who had been awakened four to five times each night over two nights yielded a clear pattern: none of the participants remembered being awakened more than three times.

10. This overlap between the two states of dreaming and waking makes the hypnopompic phase particularly compelling for those who are interested in developing dream cognizance or lucid dreaming.

11. Hobson's early activation-synthesis model drew many criticisms, one of the main ones being that it did not reflect the phenomenological reality of the dream experience (Deslauriers, 1990). Dreamers don't experience dreams as a slide show, with imagery bursts interpreted backward as a story. As Hobson himself later admitted, the story schema is at the core of the experience of dreaming.

12. Imaging techniques not only measure brain activity but also pinpoint more precisely the brain's structure associated with this activity. Imaging studies are fairly invasive and expensive (the number of participants in particular studies are often very few), and often demand participants be sleep deprived in order for them to sleep in an MRI machine. Thus, imaging techniques may not be as representative of normal conditions of sleep as less-intrusive polysomnographic methods.

CHAPTER FOUR. EMBODIED AND PURPOSEFUL DREAMING

1. The role of dreaming in the process of insight is paradoxical: although dreaming serves an important function, it is prone to being forgotten. In deep sleep, we don't keep any memory trace of the physical regenerative process; it is as if this function is best done outside the purview of consciousness. Could it be the same for dreaming? Could its integrative function occur just because the brain experiences REM and dreaming, without the need for a specific experience to be called back into memory? Wagner et al.'s (2004) research seems to point out that dreaming fulfills some of its functions by the very nature of its occurrence.

2. The idea of epigenetic landscape was first proposed by Waddington in the 1940s (see also Waddington, 1957). The word *epigenetic* can be used to describe many aspects (besides DNA) that influence the development of an organism. In particular, it applies to the study of how gene expression is modulated by experience and the environment. Beyond genetic propensity, how a gene is expressed will vary as a function of environmental circumstance. For example, a mother who is nurturing can influence the expression of certain genes that are part of the stress cascade in the child; research has shown that such influences may have long-term effect throughout the life of the individual (Maselko et al., 2010).

3. How one personally perceives dreams, along the continuum from useful to meaningless, may be in part related to the success one has had in deciphering meaning from them. Having an experience of dreams' meaningfulness makes it easier to assign value to them.

CHAPTER FIVE. THE SUBJECTIVE EXPERIENCE OF DREAMS

1. These three chapters represent the Upper-Left Quadrant, the "I" quadrant, dealing with subjective human consciousness in

Wilber's AQAL model. Wilber (2006) added a complexity to the quadrant model by describing two zones in each of the quadrant. In the UL quadrant these two zones represent an embodied phenomenological perspective ("my own experience") and a structural phenomenological perspective ("my experience" as seen by others). Wilber argues that we never feel moving from one developmental structure to the next (such as described by Piaget and others); however, these phenomenological structures can be perceived by others and even put to the test.

2. This is also described as somato-visual imagery by Hunt (1989).

3. Compared to the other senses, there are surprisingly few instances of olfactory and gustatory events in dreams. This is interesting in light of the fact that those proximal senses are crucial in waking life and survival (for instance: the link between scent and sexual activity, the importance of discerning the smell of smoke and fire or that of rotten food). Very few studies have looked at the sense of touch in dreams, although it is known that the sense of "pain" is often mild or absent compared to waking experience.

4. The word *narrativization* is a neologism we created to convey the sense that we understand dreams by *making* them part of our life story, by inserting them in the plot of our life. This process is different than *narration*, which is to tell the story (such as it is). We felt the need to create this word to convey the active and creative dimension of "storying" this important aspect of our life.

CHAPTER SIX. TYPES OF DREAMS: TOWARD AN ECOLOGY OF DREAMING

1. Connecting first-person description to third-person approaches, Schwartz (2004) writes: "This dissociation implies that these two kinds of activity are most likely to prevail in different dream episodes. According to this hypothesis, this dissociation suggests that brain circuits subtending the ability to manipulate language or communicate verbally may become active during sleep independently of the brain regions involved in motor behavior, and vice versa. This also corroborates the idea that the anatomical segregation of brain functions is mostly preserved during sleep . . . [and suggests] that different dream reports might involve distinct cognitive functions, which are known to be functionally segregated in the human brain" (28–29).

2. Lucid dreaming training has been studied as healing modality for frequent nightmare sufferers (Galvin, 1990; Zadra, 1996).

3. A related phenomenon and just as easily disturbing is *sleep paralysis*: dreams during which the dreamer feels immobilized, often with an ominous presence in the room. Since this kind of experience often takes place at the end of the REM cycle and waking cycle, its occurrence challenges both the dreaming and waking self at the same time. The self is often frightened unless (or until) a moment of lucidity occurs. With increased fear comes more disturbing dream imagery; meanwhile the waking self tries to solve the problem of paralysis by moving or shouting (Hurd, 2011). On one hand, the frightened dreaming self falls prey to other dream characters (the so-called famous incubus experience), who cause constraint in breathing; on the other hand, the waking self, feeling the fear, gets a glimpse that this is a dream, and tries to exit the situation. Bogzaran gives an account of how sleep paralysis can act as a threshold to lucid dreaming, with detailed instructions on how to transform the frightening emotion caused by sleep paralysis and bring increased self-reflectiveness (Krippner et al., 2002).

4. People have used different expressions to index this phenomenon, depending on their religious tradition and beliefs: God (through many religious appellations), Higher Power, the Goddess, Source, Higher Mind, the Awakened Mind, the Holy Spirit, Great Spirit, the Inner Self, the Higher Self.

5. Aurobindo also refers to the progressive development of the Supermind as having several stagelike manifestations: Higher Mind, Illumined Mind, Intuitive Mind, and Overmind (Aurobindo, 1989).

CHAPTER SEVEN. DREAMS AND SELF-INQUIRY

1. Two main theories address the nature of the reciprocal relationship between dreams and waking life. The compensatory hypothesis (Jung 1972) affirms that dreams may present information to the dreamer that brings attention to what the waking ego may not pay attention to. In contrast the continuation hypothesis (Hall & Nordby, 1972) proposes that dreams reflect directly, albeit metaphorically, the concerns of the dreamers. Empirical research has favored the latter while support for Jung's theory derives from clinical cases and some empirical evidence (Bell & Cook, 1998). We believe that there is no need to settle the score in favor of one or the other, as the dream formation may be calling forth more than one explanatory principle.

2. The original meaning of *numen*, from which we derive the term *numinous*, speaks of local indwelling spirits.

3. In some of the spiritual traditions such as Tibetan Buddhism, Sufism, Taoism, and other traditions, oral transmission of dream practices is important.

CHAPTER NINE. CULTURE, ECOLOGY, AND IDENTITY

1. Roland (1988) has documented the development of a we-self in Asian childrearing practices (such as in Japan), which places a strong emphasis on interdependence. This contrasts with modern Western childrearing practices that emphasize the value of individuality, self-reliance and self-assertion.

2. Not unlike the multifaceted view of the self that is presented by modern psychology (e.g. Freud's model of the psyche as composed of a conscious and unconscious function, split between the ego, id and super-ego; Jung's model of the personal and objective unconscious), indigenous approaches describes the human being has composed many parts. Indigenous approaches are integral in understanding the person as an amalgam of two or more *soul*-aspects. One *soul* is generally connected to the physical being, one is connected to emotion/ mental/ cognitive/ consciousness being; and one is connected to a larger spiritual sphere or a source that is shared by all but through which we participate in unique ways because of our relational connection through ancestry, or coextensive relationship to all beings.

3. The integral approach is sui generis an eclectic one but must be mindful of its own partiality even in its claim of inclusion. Truly inclusive is the "universe in itself," any representation of it will forever fall short.

4. People of diverse cultures do pay attention to their dreams, while not necessarily taking dreams as a subject of professional and academic pursuit. Such individuals have told us that they are circumspect about taking dreams a career, and only did so because they had been strongly called to do so. Bogzaran and Fowler (2007)'s study also shows that even within Western culture, those who take the study of dreams to a professional level feel an internal drive, a "call" to take make dreams central to their vocational pursuit.

CHAPTER TEN. TURNING TO LARGER PATTERNS: DREAMS, SOCIETY, AND THE ENVIRONMENT

1. Worthman and Melby (2002) note that the use of fuel sources (for the building's temperature control, light, and protection) contributes a significant ecological impact by our species, one that is likely

unnoticed. In the same ways that eating, traveling, and consuming habits have been questioned from the standpoint of sustainability, modern sleeping arrangements could be examined in terms of the ways they factor into our energetic, and possibly wasteful, footprint.

2. Under these circumstances, napping tends to become an indulgence for those who can afford it or those who need it, such children, the sick, or the elderly. On the other hand, part of the contemporary modern culture has caught up to the natural brain rhythm, and in many cases is framing the afternoon "dip" as one of the worst times to have productive meetings. A trend exists to create areas where napping could be done at work (Baxter & Kroll-Smith, 2005). Some workplaces even offer the benefit of power napping (a type of short nap, of less than twenty minutes, stopping before one enters stages of deep sleep). "Colonizing the nap at work is part of a larger trend that is reconfiguring the once bounded relationships between home and work and public and private space and time" (Baxter & Kroll-Smith, 2005: 33). But normalizing the workplace nap is far from being the norm in modern contemporary societies.

3. We take objection to the use of the term "primitive" to denote the early stage of societal arrangement, as it connotes negative and chauvinistic overtones from the perspective of the "modern" or contemporary person. We prefer the more activity-based description hunter-gatherer or agricultural-horticultural society that better describes the mode of subsistence of Indigenous human groups that in many cases elaborates a profound and keen sense of relationship with the place where they live. Their methods of Indigenous science creates a place for dreaming that stands at the center of many of the most essential activities of these groups (for example, using dream information in locating game or in identifying healing properties of plants necessary for successful healing). The kind of "communion" with nature that occurs during the dreamtime, offering dreams of the hunt or healing dreams, is coupled with a keen sense of observation and heightened intuition.

4. To this day, tensions continue to exist between different theories when viewing the source of dreams. Either they come from some known external or quasi-external sources, such as the gods, or they are seen purely as a natural phenomenon, part of the life of body/mind that can be explained without recourse to an independent influence. It is interesting to note a modern replay of this tension. In his book *Thirteen Dreams Freud Never Had*, Hobson (2005) takes on the persona of Freud and imaginatively writes as Freud would if he could have been witness to the development in brain science at the beginning of the twenty-first century. He imagines Freud correcting his own

mistakes: a Freud that now clearly sees that dreams have a purely material origin in the neurophysiology of the brain within the dream-wake cycle, and not the expression of unconscious drives.

5. The cult of Asclepius is said to have lasted a millennium (approx. 500 BCE to 500 CE) and ended with the rise of Christianity, which persecuted Asclepius's followers. Originally a pre-Greek god or daemon, he was consulted as an oracle, and became associated with the dog (symbol of the psychopomp) and the serpent (symbol of healing and rejuvenation). The son of Apollo, he was killed by Zeus for having brought back a man from death. In ancient Greece, he was revered as a powerful healer and had a widespread cult. Sanctuaries built in his honor were places of incubation, where supplicants would travel to receive dreams (epiphanies) and healing (see Meier, 1989).

6. Bulkeley (2006, 2008a) has shown, for example, how dreams relate to political affiliation in a context of the American political scene of the 1990s and 2000s.

PART III. OVERVIEW

1. See, for example, the work of Barasch (2000); Bogart (2009); Clift & Clift (1992); Fosshage & Loew (1987); Garfield (1979, 1988, 1991); Gackenbach (1989); Kelzer (1999); Krippner (1990); and Van de Castle (1994).

CHAPTER ELEVEN. TOWARD AN INTEGRAL DREAM PRACTICE

1. Bogzaran combined the scientific findings with the phenomenology of dreaming, communicating the multidimensional aspect of dreaming through multimedia theater. She invited a group of artists and performers to work together for four months to observe their dreams and choose archetypal images and dream types and to study the scientific characteristics of one night of sleep. This multimedia production, *Recreating One Night of Sleep* (1988), demonstrated how psychological process, scientific inquiry, and artistic modalities could be integrated to portray the multidimensionality of the dreaming process. The piece conveyed to the scientists and clinicians at the conference that dreams are not one-dimensional and that exploring dreams can be approached multidimensionally. Furthermore, by presenting the theory in a way that circumvented conventional verbal speech, predominant at conferences and professional communication, viewers were inspired and challenged to reconsider their assumptions and approaches about dreams (Reed, 1989).

2. For example, when teaching dreams at the university level, we emphasize all aspects of dream science, theory, philosophy, and practice, and the practice is broken down to fit the shorter time frames of a class session, but continues for a period of twelve to fifteen weeks. Within a retreat setting, the science, philosophy, and practice sequence of IDP is covered in an intensive fashion. Within a private session, selected aspects of philosophy and practice are shared as appropriate to the client's situation.

3. Bogzaran works with her own "big" dreams for long periods (extending over years), using creative means of expression to integrate the multidimensionality of the dreams. See also the case example offered in chapter 16.

4. With proper facilitation, IDP can be used with participants who have little or no experience with being-with their dreams. Conversely, we have also seen its benefits even with those who have had a long-standing relationship with their dreams.

CHAPTER TWELVE. HERMENEUTIC OF DREAM INTERPRETATION

1. See chapter 14 for presuppositions.

2. For a Gadamerian discussion of dream interpretation see, for example, Bulkeley (1994).

3. The Bible indicates that the king did not remember his dream. He not only wanted his dream interpreted but also recalled. Other scholars indicate that he knew his dream, but he was testing the interpreter to see if he was knowledgeable enough to divine both the dream and its interpretation.

4. Ricoeur (1967) addresses this issue in a more philosophical manner, showing that there is a strong connection between cosmic symbols and personal symbols. He writes: "To manifest the 'sacred' *in* the cosmos and to manifest it *in* the psyche are the same thing. . . . Cosmos and psyche are two poles of the same 'expressivity' " (12–13, italics in the original).

5. In the arc of the interpretive movement, the arrival of insight can come from many sources, most often from waking inferences; but it must be noted that at times, it can come from one's dreams. Nowadays, we might think of Daniel as standing as the therapist trying to help a client and having the experience of a "counter-transference" dream—that is, a dream of the therapist about a patient. Not unlike Daniel's story, such a dream can inform the analyst's understanding of a patient's unconscious predicament, their forgotten "dream," if we apply the story image in a psychological context.

6. The main image of the dream shows a giant figure, with a golden head, silver chest and arms, brass belly, and feet of iron and clay. Daniel interprets the image as that of the king himself (the golden head), and the fate of the kingdoms after him, which will be successively weaker (silver, brass, iron, and clay) as the giant figure is brought to ruin by a "stone that was cut out without hands." The king's dream and its interpretation speak about the past, the present, and future of the king and the fate of his kingdom. The point is made to him clearly that God is more powerful than human willpower, trumping the power wielded by a king, even at its apogee.

From a psychological perspective, we can ask what is the dreamer's relationship to insights coming from a dream? Even though the king praised Daniel after receiving the interpretation, it seems that the meaning of the dream does nothing to extinguish the king's narcissism or bring a remedy that could have prevented his eventual demise. One needs to ask, if an interpretation comes from outside, even inspired by God and given by the best interpreter, is it particularly effective? Dream interpretation is not sufficient by itself; it also requires the dreamer's response. This also begs the question: What are alternate ways to come to meaning other than from an external source? Of course, these questions presuppose that the purpose of dreams is transformation and integration into a changed future for the dreamer.

7. Lippmann (1998) has warned that even transference has become a new object of reductive interpretation, as when most dreams are viewed as reflections of the therapeutic dynamics.

8. There are different forms of amplification. Neo-Jungian archetypal amplification privileges image, emphasizing reverence toward the dream images for what they are, and in their own realm. This underlies a praxis of appreciation in contrast to a utilitarian stance seeking to use dreams for self-improvement. Dreams become the prism *through* which waking life is perceived.

9. This hermeneutic of suspicion brings to the fore ways to approach and possibly overcome the defensive (or repressive) aspects of personality. One needs to bear in mind that defense often comes about as a result of pain and trauma. Therefore, to uncover a defense is to be willing to address the pain it covers.

10. We find it unfortunate that for many, compensation has been reduced to a simple-minded heuristic of oppositional imagery. For example, if the dream affect is sad, it may be compensating for the "opposite" position, an avoidance of sadness in waking life, or a too rosy attitude. In that way, to contrast the "continuity" hypothesis with the "compensatory" hypothesis is a misrepresentation of Jung.

11. There exist many approaches to studying dream content objectively using statistical methods. The numerically aided phenomenological method devised by Don Kuiken provides a way to address impactful dreams (see chapter 6) but has not been used to analyze a single dreamer's dreams. A host of other authors have attempted to understand dream meaning using numerical methods, such as word clusters (e.g., the lexical analysis of Schwartz) or other dimensions of consciousness (e.g., degree of self-reflectiveness, see Purcell et al., 1986).

CHAPTER THIRTEEN. EPISTEMIC UNCERTAINTY: NON-INTERPRETIVE APPROACHES TO DREAMS

1. There are different spellings of the honorific name Chuang Tzu. The recent Pinyin Chinese spelling is Zhuangzi. However, in this text we are using the known romanization form: Chuang Tzu. Also Chuang Tzu's proper name, Chuang Chou, is translated Zhuang Zhou in Pinyin.

2. *Qi Wu Lun* translates as "On Making Things Equal / Smoothing Things Out."

3. "Inner Chapter," written by Chuang Tzu and translated by Burton Watson in 1968. The exact date of publication is not known but the estimated dates of Chuang Tzu's life are ca. 369–ca. 298 BC.

4. Exact date is not known, but scholars speculate he was a younger contemporary of Mencius (371–289 BC) (Lian Chew, 1993).

5. "The newer spelling system is called pinyin (meaning "phonetic"); the old system is called 'Wade-Giles,' and is named after the two 19th century British scholars who invented it. Pinyin is the system promoted by the Chinese government, and scholars have, for the most part, adopted the new conventions. New books are increasingly using pinyin instead of Wade-Giles" (Coutinho, personal correspondence, 2010).

6. This is important to clarify as in the actual dream he refers to his own name and in many publications this distinction is not made, leading some to confusion.

7. Epistemic uncertainty is defined as an uncertainty that is due to a lack of knowledge. In mathematics this applies to quantities or processes of a system or the environment. It is also referred to as subjective uncertainty to contrast it with objective uncertainty.

8. Shafton also encountered a few practitioners who claimed to refuse to impose any interpretation on a dream, but who nonetheless end up doing so. Among a few examples he offers that of Delaney's interview approach, which, though it seems non-interpretive, is directive.

9. Bogzaran uses many different sonic entrainment instruments, such as rattles, bells, and drums. She has also created rituals (Fire Medicine Circle, 1989) to elicit dreamlike altered states of consciousness to easily access the creative and the dreaming mind.

10. Vedfelt first investigates the history, theories, and research on the function of dreams, then expounds on the psychological frameworks for working with dreams coming from Freud, Jung, Adler, Boss, Perls, and others, including both innovative and non-Western approaches to dreams. He does not present a unified model or theory that makes sense of these disparate theories, although he connects them together in their diversity.

CHAPTER FOURTEEN. PHILOSOPHY OF PRACTICE

1. Langan (1987) promotes in the context of phenomenology the examination of presuppositions.

2. Questioning whether dreams are meant for interpretation (and the assumptions underlying interpretation) can be construed as part of a larger evolutionary process in particular because it fosters transparency and critical subjectivity. In his book *The Ever-Present Origin*, Gebser (1986) discusses an evolutionary model that situates an integral stage of consciousness as superseding a mental stage of consciousness that was raised to prominence during the Enlightenment period. The integral stage is characterized by the essential quality of transparency, that is, a clear knowledge of the assumptions behind one's own attitude, action, and thinking.

3. For example, within the Tibetan Buddhist and Bön traditions, certain deities are embodied through dance and rituals; in the Hindu and Balinese traditions, different manifestations of gods are embodied and ritualized (Ginn, 1990). In the Sufi tradition, the whirling dervishes embody the divine and turn to gain mystical union. Embodying the sacred is an essential aspect of cross-cultural ritual practices.

4. Reich was a visionary in the psychoanalytical circle and his work was not understood generally in his lifetime. However, much of what we call *somatic psychology* today derives from his work. An Austrian-American psychiatrist and psychoanalyst, Reich was born in 1897 in Austria and died in 1957 in prison in the United States. His interest with body awareness began with his work on sexology; in his first meeting with Freud, at the University of Vienna in 1919, he acquired literature for his topic from Freud. Freud became a major influence on his work and he soon became a guest member of the Vienna Psychoanalytic Association. He finished his medical degree in Vienna and studied neuropsychiatry. In 1922 he began his private practice and worked as a clinical assistant and deputy director at

Freud's psychoanalytic polyclinic. It was through his second wife, Elsa Lindenberg, that he was introduced to Laban Movement Analysis, which involved a system of breathing and somatic responsiveness. Reich developed a complex theory of personality in *Character Analysis* (1979) and *The Sexual Revolution* (1945).

5. See an extensive interview with Mindell by Bodian (2007).

6. Bogzaran applies the breathing and energetic principles used in the ancient practice of T'ai Chi, the somatic Reichian therapy combined with surrealist psychic automatism, to work creatively with body awareness. Deslauriers uses a body mapping method to trace the dream to create a visual representation of somatic experience.

7. Scientific observation has corroborated the effectiveness and beneficial impact of these powerful methods (see, e.g., Maxfield, 1990).

8. Cycles of appreciation and aversion from the more dominant group can be seen throughout history in the various phases of colonization and decolonization. These cycles often leave in their wake cultural scars within Indigenous groups trying to preserve and reconnect with traditional ways of knowing. It is understandable that the indiscriminate borrowing of Indigenous methods have been met with the criticism of cultural appropriation.

9. Because Indigenous knowledge was and has been orally transmitted and often not written down, we often wrongly assume the knowledge did not or does not exist. In fact, in shamanic healing, dream practices have been passed down mainly orally and through private or group trainings for thousands of years. In the prolific written tradition of Tibetan Buddhism, much of the philosophy is communicated through writing, but rituals are communicated by oral transmission and are not made available to the general public.

10. In his *Introduction to Metaphysics* (1942), Bergson concludes his philosophy of intuition with the concept of *Integral Experience*.

11. Each aspect of these five movements has gone through a process of development and refinement for a number of years, either in classroom or retreat settings or in private counseling sessions. Since IDP is a comprehensive method, it takes time to unfold in full. We use this method throughout an entire semester or condense it for intensive sessions, such as a three-day or weeklong retreat.

CHAPTER FIFTEEN. HERMENEUTIC OF CREATION: THE FIVE MOVEMENTS OF INTEGRAL DREAM PRACTICE

1. For example, in Chinese philosophy the concept of *Wu* that permeates Taoism is in accord with the *reflexive* function of consciousness—that is, the natural state of being. Although *Wu* can be written in different Chinese characters with different meanings, such as

nonbeing and enlightenment, the term *sudden Wu* relates to a state of consciousness similar to the *reflexive*. "When the absolute Wu corresponds to the unanalyzed principle and causes the principle and wisdom (insight) to be completely without obstruction, this is called the sudden Wu" (Wu, 1986: 74).

2. Carl Jung used Active Imagination to engage with the dream and be in the space of the dreaming mind. In *The Red Book* he immersed himself with the spontaneous arising of his unconscious and extensive dialogues with his inner world. These experiences, no doubt, led him to seek Tibetan cosmology, and study their structure and pattern as visual representations of the mind. In 1938 he visited the monastery of Bhutia Busty near Darjeeling and spoke to Lingdam Gomchen Rinpoche about the structure and meaning of mandala. He learned that the complex mandala is only made by the lama's power of imagination. The lama further explained to Jung that "The true mandala is always an inner image, which is gradually built up through (active) imagination, at such times when psychic equilibrium is disturbed or when a thought cannot be found and must be sought for, because it is not contained in holy doctrine" (1974: 170). Based on his own experience, Jung felt these Eastern symbols were originated in dreams and visions instead of being invented by the lamas. Jung developed Active Imagination as a way of "reentering" into the dream space.

3. Bogzaran developed an integral approach by combining her shamanic training, using drumming, with her scientific study of sleep. She called this method *Shamanic Lucid Dreaming* and has been using it since 1986 (Deslauriers, 1989). She introduced the method at IASD conferences (1988 to 1993) to demonstrate the power of integrating the ancient tradition of shamanic drumming with dream re-entry. For an interview about how the method was developed and called Shamanic Lucid Dreaming, see S. Racicot (1992).

4. Deslauriers presented his model of Dream Indwelling (2001) at the International Association for the Study of Dreams, University of California, Santa Cruz.

5. Dreams have been used for creative problem-solving by many artists and scientists (Barrett, 2001; Garfield, 1974; Glucksman, 2007; Hazarika, 1997; Krippner & Dillard, 1988).

6. Kidd and Kidd (1990) call this movement Experiential Expression.

CHAPTER SIXTEEN. DREAMS IN CREATION: THE URSA MAJOR DREAM

1. In our website, www.integraldreaming.org, we have examples of students using various creative modalities to explore one dream.

2. We have to note that we discourage participants to explore nightmares or deeply traumatic dream experiences while using IDP in groups or classroom settings. We reserve exploring nightmares within individual therapeutic settings as working with nightmares need one-to-one attention. However, unpleasant emotions may arise while exploring any types of dreams.

3. We have created a website (www.integraldreaming.org) to post other examples. We have chosen a dream from a participant in a retreat whose dream is archetypal and we hope her deeply authentic engagement with the process is inspiring to the reader.

4. Our work with dreams has been primarily focused in working and training professionals in various disciplines and students. We hope IDP, although it requires time and engagement from the dreamer, would also speak to the general public.

5. For example, in the experiential part of our courses, we can spend an entire academic semester (CIIS) or quarter (JFKU) exploring one dream; within the therapeutic process, one dream can be explored for an even longer period of time.

6. Even in private practice "biblio-therapy" to educate the client about the field of dream studies can be an essential aspect.

7. In the philosophy of Sri Aurobindo this concept could be linked to the "involution" process.

8. For the purpose of this book, several participants were contacted from different teaching seminars and retreats, but we finally chose Lynne Ehlers from this particular retreat.

9. One can take Lynne's dream and work with the Ullman/Taylor method of "if this was my dream."

10. Surrealists use automatic writing as a way of accessing the Sublime. For further readings on automatic writing refer to: André Breton (1969), *Manifesto of Surrealism*. Or for a brief review refer to a paper by Alan Gullette (1979), "The Theory and Techniques of Surrealist Poetry."

11. Gertrude Stein in *The Autobiography of Alice B. Toklas*.

12. Such as drawing and painting, movement, theater, working with clay, mask making, composing music, writing poetry, and so on.

13. A related existential practice was part of Fariba's trainings in 1988 and taught by existential psychotherapist Bryan Wittine. The original practice, a form of spiritual inquiry, is associated with the Indian sage Bhagavan Sri Ramana Maharishi, who wrote: "For all thoughts the source is the 'I' thought. The mind will merge only by Self-enquiry [*sic*] 'Who am I?' The thought 'Who am I?' will destroy all other thoughts and finally kill itself also. If other thoughts arise, without trying to complete them, one must enquire to whom did

this thought arise. What does it matter how many thoughts arise? As each thought arises one must be watchful and ask to whom is this thought occurring," http://www.sriramanamaharshi.org/teachings.html (June 1, 2010). Fariba's methodological contribution was to apply this particular method to explore dreams.

14. Direct comments by others after reading are not elicited, although dreamers are free to reflect and comment on their own process. Often resonance and synchronicities between the participants create a lively discussion when finding common themes.

15. Pun intended. Referring to Carl Jung's book *Memories, Dreams, Reflections* (1965) and his own reflective process on his dream life in relation to waking.

16. Lynne informed us about this particular image of William Blake. She felt the image strongly spoke to her in relation to her process of integration with the dream. With the request of Lynne we included this image to accompany her description.

17. For this reason we chose to illustrate those practices in this chapter.

18. More examples can be viewed in our website www.integraldreaming.org.

References

Adams, K., & Hyde, B. (2008). Children's grief dreams and the theory of spiritual intelligence. *Dreaming, 18*(1), 58–67.

Aizenstat, S. (2009). *Dream tending*. New Orleans, LA: Spring Journal Books.

Arieti, S. (1976). *Creativity: The magic synthesis*. New York, NY: Basic Books.

Almaas, A. H. (1986). *Essence*. Berkeley, CA: Diamond Books.

Almaas, A. H. (2000). *The point of existence: Transformations of narcissism in self-realization*. Boston, MA: Shambhala.

American Academy of Sleep Medicine. (2008). Four days of REM sleep deprivation affects forebrain, long-term memory in rats. *Science Daily*, February 6. Retrieved July 26, 2008 from http://www.sciencedaily.com/releases/2008/02/080201085713.

Anodea, J. (1996). *Eastern body western mind*. Berkeley, CA: Celestial Arts.

Antrobus, J. (1991). Dreaming: Cognitive processes during cortical activation and high afferent thresholds. *Psychological Review 98*, 96–121.

Antrobus, J. (2000). How does the dreaming brain explain the dreaming mind? *Behavioral and Brain Sciences 23*, 904–907.

Armstrong, K. (2005). *A short history of myth*. Edinburgh, Scotland: Canongate.

Aserinsky, E., & Kleitman, N. (1953). Regularly occurring episodes of eye motility and concomitant phenomena during sleep. *Science 118*, 273–274.

Assagioli, R. (1965). *Psychosynthesis*. New York: The Viking Press.

Aurobindo, Sri. (1970). *The life divine*. Pondicherry, India: Sri Aurobindo Ashram Press.

Aurobindo, Sri. (1989). *Sri Aurobindo: The supermental manifestation and other writings*. First published in *Arya* between 1914–1920. Pondicherry, India: Sri Aurobindo Ashram.

Aurobindo, Sri. (1990). *The life divine*. Wisconsin: Lotus Press.

Balkin, T. J., Braun, A. R., Wesensten, N. J., Jeffries, K., Varga, M., Baldwin, P., Belenky, G., Herscovitch, P. (2002). The process of awakening: A PET study of regional brain activity patterns mediating the reestablishment of alertness and consciousness. *Brain 125*, 2308–2319.

Barasch, M. I. (2000). *Healing dreams: Exploring the dreams that can transform your life*. New York, NY: Penguin Putnam.

Barrett, D. (1993). The committee of sleep: A study of dream incubation for problem solving. *Dreaming 3*(2), 115–122.

Barrett, D. (2001). *The committee of sleep: How artists, scientists, and athletes use dreams for creative problem-solving*. New York, NY: Crown Publishers.

Barrett, D. (2004). *Using hypnosis to work with your dreams*. Presentation at twentieth conference of the International Association for the Study of Dreams. Copenhagen, Denmark.

Barrett, D., & McNamara, P. (Eds.). (2007). *The new science of dreaming*. Westport, CT: Praeger.

Baxter, V., & Kroll-Smith, S. (2005). Normalizing the nap: Blurring the boundaries between public and private space and time. *Current Sociology 53*(1), 33–55.

Baylor G. W., & Deslauriers, D. (1986). Dreams as problem solving: A method of study—Part I: Background and theory. *Imagination, Cognition and Personality 6*(2), 105–118.

Baylor, G. W., & Deslauriers, D. (1987). *Le rêve, sa nature, sa fonction et une méthode d'analyse*. Sillery, Québec, Canada: Presses de l'Université du Québec.

Baylor G. W., & Deslauriers, D. (1989). How are dreams made? Towards a computational model. *Psychiatry Journal of the University of Ottawa 14*(4), 566–71.

Bean, O. (1971). *Me and the orgone*. New York, NY: St. Martin's Press.

Bell, A. J., & Cook, H. (1998). Empirical evidence for a compensatory relationship between dream content and repression. *Psychoanalytic Psychology 15*(1), 154–163.

Bennett, J. (1984). *A study of Spinoza's ethics*. Cambridge, England: Press Syndicate of the University of Cambridge.

Bergson, H. (1912). *An introduction to metaphysics.* Translated by T. E. Hulme. New York, NY: G. Putnam's Sons.

Bergson, H. (1946). *The creative mind: An introduction to metaphysics.* New York, NY: Philosophical Library.

Bertalanffy, K. L. V. (1951). General System Theory: A new approach to unity of science (Symposium), *Human Biology 23,* 303–361.

Blackmore, S. (1984). A postal survey of OBEs and other experiences. *Journal of the Society for Psychical Research 52,* 227–244.

Blagrove, M., Farmer. L., & William, E. (2004). The relationship of nightmare frequency and nightmare distress to well-being. *Journal of Sleep Research 13*(2), 129–136.

Bodian, S. (2007). Field of dreams: An interview with Arnold Mindell. Icarus Project. http://theicarusproject.net/alternative-treatments/interview-with-arnold-mindell.

Bogart, G. (2009). *Dreams and self-healing: Unfolding the symbols of the unconscious.* London, England: Karnac.

Bogzaran, F. (1983). Working with dreams. In J. Taylor, K. Taylor, & J. Van Damm (Eds.), *Coat of many colors* (65–66). San Rafael, CA: Dream Tree Press.

Bogzaran, F. (1989). *Experiencing the divine in lucid dream state.* Master's thesis. Ann Arbor, MI: UMI.

Bogzaran, F. (1990). Painted dream images. In S. Krippner (Ed.), *Dreamtime and dreamwork* (111–112). Los Angeles, CA: Tarcher.

Bogzaran, F. (1990a). Expressive dream art. *Association for the Study of Dreams Newsletter 7*(2), 8–9.

Bogzaran, F. (1991). Dream re-entry and automatic writing. Paper presented at the eighth conference of the International Association for the Study of Dreams, Charlottesville, Virginia.

Bogzaran, F. (1991a). Experiencing the divine in the lucid dream state. *Lucidity Letter 10* (1 & 2), 169–176.

Bogzaran, F. (1991b). *Dream re-entry drumming.* Drumming tape to enhance dream state in waking. (Cassette recording), Robert Rich (studio recording). Reeltime (production). San Francisco, CA: Dream Creations.

Bogzaran, F. (1996). *Images of the lucid mind: A phenomenological study of lucid dreaming and modern paintings.* Ann Arbor, MI: UMI.

Bogzaran, F. (2003). Lucid art and hyperspace lucidity. *Dreaming 13*(1), 29–42.

Bogzaran, F. (2007). Vision beyond surrealism: Wolfgang Paalen and Gordon Onslow Ford. In C.A. Riley, F. Bogzaran, & C. Schwartz, (Eds.), *Surrealism on canvas* (63–74). Roslyn Harbor, NY: Nassau County Museum of Art.

Bogzaran, F. (2011). Contemplating lucid dreaming: East-West views. In S. Kakar (Ed.), *On dreams and dreaming* (120–145). New Delhi, India: Penguin.

Bogzaran, F., & Deslauriers, D. (1989). Theory and practice of dreams. Dream course developed and taught at the John F. Kennedy University, Orinda, California.

Bogzaran, F., & Deslauriers, D. (1990). Dreams, body and maps: Body-oriented dreamwork. Course taught at the Center for Dream Creations, San Francisco, CA.

Bogzaran, F., & Deslauriers, D. (2004). Integral dreaming: A model. Paper presentation, twenty-first conference of the International Association for the Study of Dreams. Copenhagen, Denmark.

Bogzaran, F., & Fowler, M. (2006). Dream education I: The transformative power of dream studies. Paper presentation at the International Association for the Study of Dreams Conference. Bridgewater College, Boston, MA.

Bogzaran, F., & Fowler, M. (2007). Dream education II: The transformative power of dream studies. Paper presentation at the International Association for the Study of Dreams Conference. Sonoma State University, CA.

Bonime, W. (1986). Collaborative dream interpretation. *Journal of the American Academy of Psychoanalysis 14* (1), 15–26.

Bonime, W. (1989). *Collaborative psychoanalysis: Anxiety, depression, dream and personality change*. Cranberry, NJ: Associated University Presses.

Bosnak, R. (1996). *Tracks in the wilderness of dreaming: Exploring interior landscape through practical dreamwork*. New York, NY: Delacorte Press.

Bosnak, R. (2007). *Embodiment: Creative imagination in medicine art and travel*. New York, NY: Routledge.

Bourguignon, E. (1954). Dreams and dream interpretation in Haiti. *American Anthropologist 56*, 262–268.

Braun, A. R., Balkin, T. J., Wesensten, N. J., Carson, R. E., Varga, M., Baldwin, P., Selbie, S., Belenky, G., & Herscovitch, P. (1997). Regional cerebral blood flow throughout the sleep-wake cycle: An H2/15 Pet Study. *Brain 120*, 1173–1197.

Breton, A. (1972). *Manifesto of surrealism*. Translated by Richard Seaver & Helen R. Lane. Ann Arbor, MI: Ann Arbor Paperbacks.

Brunton, M. (2009). The reason of faith: Essay on Karen Armstrong. *Ode Magazine 7* (7), 32–38.

Bulkeley, K. (1994). *The wilderness of dreams: Exploring the religious meanings of dreams in modern Western contexts*. Albany: State University of New York Press.

Bulkeley, K. (1995). *Spiritual dreaming: A cross-cultural and historical journey*. Mahwah, NJ: Paulist Press.

Bulkeley, K. (2000). *Transforming dreams: Learning spiritual lessons from the dreams you never forgot*. New York, NY: John Wiley & Sons.

Bulkeley, K. (2001). *Dreams: A reader on the religious, cultural, and psychological dimensions of dreaming*. New York, NY: Palgrave.

Bulkeley, K. (2006). Sleep and dream patterns of political liberals and conservatives. *Dreaming 16*(3), 223–235.

Bulkeley, K. (2008). *Dreaming in the world's religions: A comparative history*. New York, NY: New York University Press.

Bulkeley, K. (2008a). *American dreamers: What dreams tell us about the political psychology of conservatives, liberals, and everyone else*. Boston, MA: Beacon Press.

Bulkeley, K. (2011). Big dreams: The science of highly memorable dreaming. In S. Kakar (Ed.), *On dreams and dreaming* (1–20). New Delhi, India: Penguin.

Burman, J. T. (2006). Review: R. D. Ellis & N. Newton (Eds.). *Consciousness and emotion: agency, conscious choice and selective perception. Journal of Consciousness Studies 13*(12), 115–119.

Busink, R., & Kuiken, D. (1996). Identifying types of impactful dreams: A replication. *Dreaming 6*(2), 97–119.

Bütz, M. R. (1997). *Chaos and complexity: Implications for psychological theory and practice*. Washington, DC: Taylor and Francis.

Buzzell, L., & Chalquist, C. (2009). *Ecotherapy: Healing with nature in mind*. San Francisco, CA: Sierra Club Books.

Caplan, M., Hartelius, G., & Rardin, M. A. (2003). Contemporary viewpoints on transpersonal psychology. *The Journal of Transpersonal Psychology 35*(2), 143–162.

Capra, F. (1996). *The web of life: A new scientific understanding of living systems*. New York, NY: Anchor Books/ Doubleday.

Cappuccio, F. P., Taggert, F. M., Kandala, N. B., Currie, A., Peile, E., Stranges, S., & Miller, M. A. (2008). Meta-analysis of short sleep duration and obesity in children and adults. *SLEEP 31*(5), 619–626.

Carey B. (2007). An active, purposeful machine that comes out at night to play. Retrieved October 23, 2007 from http://www.nytimes.com/2007/10/23/health/23memo.html?scp=18&sq=&st=nyt.

Cariola, L. A. (2008). A structural and functional analysis of dream narrative. *Dreaming 18*(1), 16–26.

Cartwright, R. (1992). Masochism in dreaming and its relation to depression. *Dreaming 2*(2), 79–84.

Cartwright, R. (2010). *The twenty-four hour mind: The role of sleep and dreams in our emotional life*. New York, NY: Oxford University Press.

Cartwright, R., & Wood, E. (1991). Adjustment disorders of sleep: The effects of a major stressful event and its resolution. *Psychiatry Research 39*, 199–209.

Castonguay, J. G., & Hill, C. (Eds.). (2007). *Insight in psychotherapy*. Washington, DC: APA Books.

Chan, C. W. (1996). The Butterfly Dream. *The Philosopher, Philosophical Society of England 83*(2, Autumn Issue). Retrieved March 26, 2010 from, http://www.the-philosopher.co.uk/butter.htm.

Chaudhuri, H. (1965). *Integral yoga: A concept of harmonious and creative living*. London, England: Unwin Hyman Limited.

Chaudhuri, H. (1973). *Sri Aurobindo: Prophet of life divine*. San Francisco, CA: Cultural Integration Fellowship.

Chaudhuri, H. (1974). *Being, evolution, and immortality*. Wheaton, IL: Theosophical Publishing House.

Chaudhuri, H. (1977). *The evolution of integral consciousness*. Wheaton, IL: Theosophical Publishing House.

Chaudhuri, H., & Spiegelberg, F. (Eds.). (1960). *The Integral philosophy of Sri Aurobindo: A commemorative symposium*. London, England: Allen & Unwin.

Chuang Tzu. (1968). *The complete works of Chuang Tzu*. Translated by Burton Watson. New York, NY: Columbia University Press.

Chuang Tzu. (1991). *Chuang-Tzu: The inner chapters: A classic of Tao*. Translated by A. C. Graham. London, England: Mandala.

Cirelli, C. (2007). Slow-wave activity during sleep affected by quality, intensity of wakefulness. *Science Daily*. Retrieved February 6, 2007 from http://www.sciencedaily.com/releases/2007/02/070201082510.htm.

Clément, P. (2007). Dream imagery as a result of emotions matching with images. *Imagination, Cognition and Personality 27*(3), 245–257.

Clift, J. D., & Clift, W. B. (1992). *Symbols of transformation in dreams*. New York, NY: Crossroads.

Colorado, P. (1988). Bridging Native and western science. *Convergence 21*(2/3), 49–67.

Colorado, P. (1996). Indigenous science. *ReVision: A Journal of Consciousness and Transformation, 18*(3), 6–10.

Combs, A. (2002). *The radiance of being: Understanding the grand integral vision; Living the integral life*. St. Paul, MN: Paragon House.

Combs, A. (2009). *Consciousness explained better: Toward an integral understanding of the multifaceted nature of consciousness*. St. Paul, MN: Paragon House.

Combs, A., & Krippner, S. (1998). Dream sleep and waking reality: A dynamical view of two states of consciousness. In S. Hameroff, A. W. Kaszniak, & A. C. Scott (Eds.), *Toward a science of consciousness: The second Tucson discussions and debates* (478–98). Cambridge, MA: MIT Press.

Conforti, M. (2003). *Field, form, and fate: Patterns in mind, nature, and psyche*. Woodstock, CT: Spring Publications.

Cortright, B. (2007). *Integral psychology: Yoga, growth, and opening the heart*. Albany: State University of New York Press.

Coutinho, S. (2004). *Zhuangzi and early Chinese philosophy: Vagueness, transformation and paradox*. London, England: Ashgate Publishing.

Coutinho, S. (2010). Zhuangzi. *The Internet Encyclopedia of Philosophy*, Retrieved March 23, 2010 from http//www.iep.utm.edu.

Coutinho, S. (2010a). Personal communication with Fariba Bogzaran.

Crook-Lyon, R. E., & Hill, C. E. (2004). Client reactions to working with dreams in psychotherapy. *Dreaming 14*(4), 207–219.

Dalal, A. S. (2004). *The yoga of sleep and dreams: The night-school of sadhana: Selection from the works of Sri Aurobindo and the Mother*. Pondicherry, India: Sri Aurobindo Ashram.

David, S., & Stroumsa, G. G. (1999). *Dream cultures*. New York, NY: Oxford University Press.

Davidson, D., Lee-Archer, S., & Sanders, G. (2005). Dream imagery and emotion. *Dreaming 15*(1), 33–47.

Davis, J. L., Byrd, P., & Rhudy, J. L. (2007). Characteristics of chronic nightmares in a trauma exposed treatment-seeking sample. *Dreaming 17*(4), 187–198.

Dawkins, R. (1976). *The selfish gene*. Oxford, England: Oxford University Press.

de Benedictis, T., Larson, H., Kemp, G., Barston, S., & Segal, R. (2007). *Understanding sleep: Sleep needs, cycles, and stages*. Retrieved January 1, 2008 from http://www.helpguide.org/life/sleeping.htm.

De Koninck J., & Brunette, R. (1991). Presleep suggestion related to a phobic object: Successful manipulation of reported dream affect. *Journal of General Psychology 118*, 185–200.

De Koninck, J., Christ, G., Hebert, G., & Rinfret, N. (1990). Language learning efficiency, dreams and REM sleep. *Psychiatric Journal of the University of Ottawa 15*(2), 91–92.

Delaney, G. (1979). *Living your dreams: Using your sleep to solve problems and to make your best dreams come true*. San Francisco, CA: Harper & Row.

Della Rocca, M. (1996). *Representation and the mind-body problem in Spinoza*. Oxford, England: Oxford University Press.

Dement, W. C. (1972). *Some must watch while some must sleep*. San Francisco, CA: W.H. Freeman.

Dement, W. C., & Vaughan, C. (1999). *The promise of sleep*. New York, NY: Delacorte Press.

Dentan, R. (1987). Ethnographic consideration of the cross-cultural study of dreams. In J. Gackenbach (Ed.), *Sleep and dreams: A sourcebook*. New York, NY: Garland.

De Ridder, D., Van Laere, K., Dupont, P., Menovksy, T., & Van de Heyning, P. (2007). Visualizing out-of-body experience in the brain. *New England Journal of Medicine 357*, 1829–1833.

Deslauriers, D. (1989). A creative journey into dreams with Fariba Bogzaran: Where beauty meets power. *Le Centre D'etude Des Reves De Montreal (The Montreal Center for the Study of Dreams) 3* (3–4), 1–3.

Deslauriers, D. (1990). Organisation narrative suivant le concept de script et rapport emotion-cognition dans les récits de rêve: Étude empirique et differences individuelles. Unpublished doctoral dissertation. Université de Montréal, Québec.

Deslauriers, D. (2000). Dream in the light of emotional and spiritual intelligence. *Advanced Development Journal 9*, 105–122.

Deslauriers, D. (2004). Spiritual intelligence and dream indwelling. Presentation at twentieth conference of the International Association for the Study of Dreams. Copenhagen, Denmark.

Deslauriers, D. (2009). Transcultural strategies for working with dreams. In S. Krippner and D. Joffe Ellis (Eds.), *Perchance to dream: The frontiers of dream psychology*. New York, NY: Nova Science Publishers.

Deslauriers, D. (2011). Dreams at the boundary of self and others: Intersubjective fields, emotions and culture. In S. Kakar (Ed.), *On dreams and dreaming* (88–118). New Delhi, India: Penguin.

Deslauriers, D., & Bogzaran, F. (1991). Creative journey into dreams: Mapping the body connection. Course taught at the California Institute of Integral Studies, San Francisco, CA.

Deslauriers, D., & Bogzaran, F. (1994). Dreams and epiphany. Paper presented at the tenth conference of the International Association for the Study of Dreams. Santa Fe, New Mexico.

Deslauriers, D., & Cordts, J. (1995). Dreams and current concerns: A narrative co-constitutive approach. *Dreaming 5*(4), 247–265.

Dombeck, M. (1991). *Dreams and professional personhood: The context of dream telling and dream interpretation among American psychotherapists*. Albany: State University of New York Press.

Domhoff, G. W. (1996). *Finding meaning in dreams: A quantitative approach*. New York, NY: Plenum Press.

Domhoff, G. W. (2000). *Dreams and parapsychology*. Retrieved May 3, 2010 from http://www.dreamresearch.net/Library/domhoff_2000c.html.

Domhoff, G. W. (2001). A new neurocognitive theory of dreams. *Dreaming 11*(1), 13–33.

Domhoff, G. W. (2003). *The scientific study of dreams: Neural networks, cognitive development, and content analysis.* Washington, DC: American Psychological Association.

Dresler, M., Koch, S. P., Wehrle, R., Spoormaker, V. I., Holsboer, R., Steiger, A., Sämann, P. G., Obrig, H., & Czish, M. (2011). Dreamed movement elicits activation in the sensorimotor cortex. *Current Biology 21*(21), 1833–1837.

Edelman, G. M. (1987). *Neural Darwinism: The theory of neuronal group selection.* New York, NY: Basic Books.

Edelman, G., & Tononi, G. (2000). *A universe of consciousness: How matter becomes imagination.* New York, NY: Basic Books.

Edgar, I. E. (2002). Invisible elites? Authority and the dream. *Dreaming 12*(2), 79–92.

Ehlers, L. (1992). *The alchemical nigredo, albedo, citrinitas and rubedo: Stages of transformation: A case study.* Unpublished dissertation. California School of Professional Psychology, Berkeley, CA.

Ehlers, L. (2000). Sandplay: Kali *Journal of Sandplay Therapy 9*(1), 67–79.

Ehrsson, H. H. (2007). The experimental induction of out-of-body experiences. *Science 317*, 1048.

Ekirch, R. A. (2005). *At day's close: Night in times past.* New York, NY: Norton.

Ellis, R. D., & Newton, N. (2005). *Consciousness and emotion: Agency, conscious choice, and selective perception.* Philadelphia, PA: John Benjamins.

Ewing, K. P. (2003). Diasporic dreaming, identity and self-constitution. In J. Mageo (Ed.), *Dreaming and the self: New perspectives on subjectivity, identity, and emotion.* Albany: State University of New York Press.

Fairbairn, W. R. D. (1952). *An object-relations theory of personality.* New York, NY: Basic Books.

Faraday, A. (1972). *Dream power.* New York, NY: Berkley Medallion Books.

Feinstein, D., & Krippner, S. (1988). *Personal mythology: The psychology of your evolving self.* Los Angeles, CA: Jeremy P. Tarcher.

Ferrer, J. (2002). *Revisioning transpersonal theory: A participatory vision of human spirituality.* Albany: State University of New York Press.

Flanagan, O. (1992). *Consciousness reconsidered.* Cambridge, MA: MIT Press.

Flanagan, O. (2000). *Dreaming souls: Sleep, dreams, and the evolution of the conscious mind.* Oxford, England: Oxford University Press.

Fosse, M. J., Fosse, R., Hobson, J. A., & Stickgold, R. J. (2003). Dreaming and episodic memory: A functional dissociation? *Journal of Cognitive Neuroscience 15*(1), 1–9.

Fosshage, J. L. (1997). The organizing functions of dream mentation. *Contemporary Psychoanalysis 33*(3), 429–458.

Fosshage, J. (2002). A relational self psychological perspective. *Journal of Analytical Psychology 47*, 67–82.

Fosshage, J. L. (2007). The organizing functions of dreaming: Pivotal issues in understanding and working with dreams. *International Forum of Psychoanalysis 16*, 213–221.

Fosshage, J., & Loew, C. A. (Eds.). (1987). *Dream interpretation: A comparative study*. New York, NY: PMA Publishing.

Foulkes, D. (1962). Dream reports from different stages of sleep. *Journal of Abnormal and Social Psychology 65*, 14–25.

Foulkes, D. (1985). *Dreaming: A cognitive-psychological analysis*. Hillside, NJ: Lawrence Erlbaum Associates.

Foulkes, D. (1999). *Children's dreaming and the development of consciousness*. Cambridge, MA: Harvard University Press.

Foulkes, D., & Vogel, G. (1965). Mental activity at sleep onset. *Journal of Abnormal Psychology 70*, 231–43.

Frederickson, B. L., & Losada, M. F. (2005). Positive affect and complex dynamics of human flourishing. *American Psychologist 60*, 678–686.

Freud, S. (1900/1999). *The interpretation of dreams*. Translated by Joyce Crick. New York, NY: Oxford University Press.

Freud, S. (2005/1930). *Civilization and its discontents*. Translated by James Strachey. New York, NY: W. W. Norton & Company.

Frey, A. (2007). *Discerning life with dreams: The triadic relationships between dreams, discernment, and spiritual intelligence*. Doctoral dissertation, California Institute of Integral Studies. Ann Arbor, MI: UMI.

Gackenbach, J. (1989). *Control your dreams*. New York, NY: Harper & Row.

Gackenbach, J. (1991). Frameworks for understanding lucid dreaming: A review. *Dreaming 1* (2), 109–128.

Gackenbach, J. I. (Ed.) (2012). *Video games and consciousness*. NOVA Science publishers.

Gackenbach, J., & LaBerge, S. (1988). *Conscious mind, sleeping brain: Perspectives on lucid dreaming*. New York, NY: Plenum.

Gackenbach, J., & Reiter, S. (2006). Video game structure, preferences, flow and dreams. Paper presentation, twenty-third conference of the International Association for the Study of Dreams. Bridgewater, Boston, MA.

Gadamer, H. G. (Fall 1975). The problem of historical consciousness. *Graduate Faculty Philosophy Journal 5*, 1, 10.

Galvin, F. (1990). The boundary characteristics of lucid dreamers. *Psychiatric Journal of the University of Ottawa 15*(2), 73–78.

Gamwell, L. (Ed.). (2000). *Dreams 1900–2000: Science, art and the unconscious mind.* Ithaca, NY: Cornell University Press.

Garfield, P. (1974; 1995). *Creative dreaming.* New York, NY: Simon & Schuster.

Garfield, P. (1979). *Pathway to ecstasy: The way of the dream mandala.* New York, NY: Holt, Rinehart & Winston.

Garfield, P. (1988). *Women's bodies, women's dreams.* New York, NY: Ballantine.

Garfield, P. (1991). *The healing power of dreams.* New York, NY: Simon & Schuster.

Garfield, P. (2001). *The universal dream key: The 12 most common dream themes around the world.* New York, NY: HarperOne.

Gebser, J. (1986). *The ever-present origin.* Athens: Ohio University Press.

Gendlin, E. T. (1986). *Let your body interpret your dreams.* Wilmette, IL: Chiron Publications.

Gilchrist, S., Davidson, J., & Shakespeare-Finch, J. (2007). Dream emotions, waking emotions, personality characteristics and well-being—A positive psychology approach. *Dreaming 17*(3), 172–185.

Gillespie, G. (1987). Dreamlight: Categories of visual experience during lucid dreaming. *Lucidity Letter 6*(1), 164–168.

Gillespie, G. (2002). Dreams and dreamless sleep. *Dreaming 12*(4), 199–207.

Ginn, V. (1990). *The spirited earth: Dance, myth, and ritual from South Asia to the South Pacific.* New York, NY: Rizzoli International Publications.

Globus, G. (1987). *Dream life, wake life: The human condition through dreams.* Albany: State University of New York Press.

Globus, G. (1995). *The postmodern brain: Advances in consciousness research.* Philadelphia, PA: John Benjamins.

Glucksman, M. L. (2007). *Dreaming: An opportunity for change.* New York, NY: Jason Aronson.

Gordon, D. (2007). *Mindful dreaming.* Franklin Lakes, NJ: Career Press.

Gratton, N., & Séguin, M. (2009). *Les rêves en fin de vie.* Québec, Canada: Flammarion Québec.

Green, C. E. (1968) *Out-of-body experiences.* London, England: Hamish Hamilton.

Grof, S. (1988). *The adventure of self-discovery: Dimensions of consciousness and new perspectives in psychotherapy and inner exploration.* Albany: State University of New York Press.

Grof, S. (1998). *The cosmic game: Explorations of the frontiers of human consciousness*. Albany: State University of New York Press.

Gullette, A. (1979). The theory and techniques of surrealist poetry. University of Tennessee—Knoxville. Retrieved June 28, 2010 from http://alangullette.com/essays/lit/surreal.htm.

Gutheil, E. (1951). *The handbook of dream analysis*. New York, NY: Washington Square Press.

Guzman-Marin, R., Suntsova, N., Bashir, T., Nienhuis, R., Szmusiak, R., & McGinty, D. (2008). Rapid eye movement sleep deprivation contributes to reduction of neurogenesis in the hippocampal dentate gyrus of the adult rat. *Sleep 31*(2), 167–175.

Hall, C. S. (1953). A cognitive theory of dreams. *The Journal of General Psychology 49*, 273–282.

Hall, C. S., & Nordby, V. J. (1972). *The individual and his dreams*. Bergenfield, NJ: Signet.

Hall, C. S., & Van de Castle, R. (1966). *The content analysis of dreams*. New York, NY: Appleton-Century-Croft.

Hartelius, G., Caplan, M., & Rardin, M. A. (2007). Transpersonal psychology: Defining the past, divining the future. *The Humanist Psychologist 35*(2), 1–26.

Hartman, D., & Zimberoff, D. (2008). Dream journey: A new heart-centered therapies modality. *Journal of Heart-Centered Therapies 2*(1), 33–90.

Hartmann, E. H. (1999). *Dreams and nightmares: The new theory on the origin and meaning of dreams*. New York, NY: Plenum Press.

Hartmann, E. (2000). The psychology and physiology of dreaming: A new synthesis. In L. Gamwell (Ed.), *Dreams 1900–2000: Science, Art and the Unconscious Mind*. Ithaca, NY: Cornell University Press.

Hartmann, E. (2008). The central image makes "Big" dreams big: The central image as the emotional heart of the dream. *Dreaming 18*(1), 44–57.

Hazarika, A. (1997). *Daring to dream: Cultivating corporate creativity through dreamwork*. London, England: Response Books.

Hearne, K. M. T. (1978). Lucid dreams: An electrophysiological and psychological study. Unpublished doctoral dissertation, University of Liverpool.

Hegel, G. W. F. (1977). *Phenomenology of spirit*. Translated by A. V. Miller. Oxford, England: Oxford University Press.

Heidegger, M. (1962). *Being and time*. Translated by John Macquarrie &Edward Robinson. London: SMC Press.

Hill, C. E. (Ed.) (2004). *Dream work in therapy: Facilitating exploration, insight, and action*. Washington, DC: American Psychological Association.

Hillman, J. (1979). *The dream and the underworld.* New York, NY: Harper & Row.

Hillman, J. (1997). *Archetypal psychology: A brief account.* Woodstock, CT: Spring Publications.

Hobson, J. A. (1988). *The dreaming brain: How the brain creates both the sense and the nonsense of dreams.* New York, NY: Basic Books.

Hobson, J. A. (1994). *The chemistry of consciousness: How the brain changes its mind.* New York, NY: Little Brown.

Hobson, J. A. (2000). *Dreaming as delirium: How the brain goes out of its mind.* Cambridge, MA: MIT Press.

Hobson, J. A. (2005). *Thirteen dreams Freud never had: The new mind science.* New York, NY: Pi Press.

Hobson, J. A., & McCarley, R. W. (1977). The brain as a dream-state generator: An activation-synthesis hypothesis of the dream process. *American Journal of Psychiatry 134,* 1335–1368.

Hobson, J. A., Pace-Schott, E. F., & Stickgold, R. (2000). Dreaming and the brain: Toward a cognitive neuroscience of conscious states. *Behavioral and Brain Sciences 23*(6), 793–842.

Hunt, H. T. (1989). *The multiplicity of dreams.* New Haven, CT: Yale University Press.

Hunt, H. T. (1989a). A cognitive-psychological perspective on Gillespie's "Lights and lattices": Some relations among perception, imagery, and thought. *Perceptual Motor Skills 68* (2), 631–41.

Hunt, H. T., & Belicki, K. (1989). Lucidity Association Chair, Harry Hunt, interviewed by guest editor Kathryn Belicki. *Lucidity Letter* 8 (1). http://www.spiritwatch.ca.

Hurd, R. (2011). *Sleep paralysis: A guide to hypnagogic visions & visitors of the night.* Los Altos, CA: Hyena Press.

Husserl, E. (1983). *Ideas pertaining to a pure phenomenology and to a phenomenological philosophy.* (second ed.). New York, NY, Vienna: Springer.

Irwin, L. (1996). *The dream seekers: Native American visionary traditions of the Great Plains.* Norman: University of Oklahoma Press.

Irwin, L. (2001). Sending a voice, seeking a place: Visionary traditions among Native women of the Plains. In K. Bulkeley (Ed.), *Dreams: A reader on religious, cultural and psychological dimensions of dreaming.* New York, NY: Palgrave.

Jaenke, K. (2001). *Personal dreamscape as ancestral landscape.* Doctoral dissertation, California Institute of Integral Studies. Ann Arbor, MI: UMI.

Jaenke, K. (2006). Dreaming with the ancestors. *ReVision: A Journal of Consciousness and Transformation 28*(4), 28–35.

Jaenke, K. (2010). Earth dreaming. In C. Chalquist (Ed.), *Rebearths: Conversations with a world Ensouled* (187–202). Walnut Creek, CA: World Soul Books.

Johnson, K. K. (2002). *On the path of the ancestors: Kinship with place as a path of recovery*. Doctoral dissertation, California Institute of Integral Studies. Ann Arbor, MI: UMI.

Johnson, R. (1986). *Inner work: Using dreams and active imagination for personal growth*. San Francisco, CA: Harper & Row.

Johnston, I. (1999). On Freud's Civilization and its discontents. Retrieved April 11, 2008 from http://www.mala.bc.ca/~johnstoi/introser/freud.htm.

Jouvet, M. (1999). *The paradox of sleep: The story of dreaming*. Cambridge, MA: MIT Press.

Jung, C. G. (1972). *The transcendent function*. In *The collected works of C. G. Jung* (67–91). Vol. 8, 2nd edition. Princeton, NJ: Princeton University Press.

Jung, C. G. (1964). *Man and his symbols*. New York, NY: Windfall Books.

Jung, C. G. (1965). *Memories, dreams, reflections*. A. Jaffé (Ed.). New York, NY: Vintage Books.

Jung, C. G. (1974). *Dreams*. Translated by R. F. C. Hull. Princeton, NJ: Princeton University Press.

Jung, C. G. (2009). *The red book*. New York, NY: W.W. Norton & Company.

Kahan, T. L. (1994). Measuring dream self-reflectiveness: A comparison of two approaches. *Dreaming* 4(3), 177–193.

Kahan, T. L. (2001). Consciousness in dreaming: A metacognitive approach. In K. Bulkeley (Ed.), *Dreams: A Reader on the Religious, Cultural, and Psychological Dimensions of Dreaming* (333–360). New York, NY: Palgrave.

Kahan, T. L. (2011). Possible worlds, possible selves: Dreaming and the liberation of consciousness. In S. Kakar (Ed.), *On dreams and dreaming*. New Delhi, India: Penguin.

Kahn, D., Combs, A., & Krippner, S. (2002). Dreaming as a function of chaos-like stochastic processes in the self-organizing brain. *Nonlinear Dynamics, Psychology, and Life Sciences 6*, 311–322.

Kahn, D., & Hobson, J. A. (2005). Theory of mind in dreaming: Awareness of feelings and thoughts of others in dreams. *Dreaming 15*(1), 48–57.

Kakar, S. (Ed.) (2011). *On dreams and dreaming*. New Delhi, India: Penguin.

Kaplan-Williams, S. (1991). *Dreamworking: A comprehensive guide to working with dreams*. San Francisco, CA: Journey Press.

Kearney, R. (2004). *On Paul Ricoeur: The owl of Minerva*. Burlington, VT: Ashgate Publishing.

Keleman, S. (1981). *Your body speaks its mind.* Berkeley: Center Press.

Keleman, S. (2010). Dreams and the body. Center for Energetic Studies. Center Press. Retrieved September 20, 2010 from www.centerpress.com/articles/dreams_and_the_body.html.

Kelzer, K. (1987). The sun and the shadow: My experiment with lucid dreaming. Virginia Beach, VA: A.R.E. Press.

Kelzer, K. (1999). *Deep journey: Experiential psychotherapy with dreams, personal archetypal tales and trance states.* Berkeley, CA: North Atlantic Books.

Kidd, D., & Kidd, J. W. (1990). *Experiential method: Qualitative research in the humanities using metaphysics and phenomenology.* New York, NY: Peter Lang.

Kilborne, B. (1981). Pattern, structure, and style in anthropological study of dreams. *Ethos 9*(2), 165–185.

Knudson, R. M. (2001). Significant dreams: Bizarre or beautiful? *Dreaming 11*(4), 167–177.

Knudson, R. M. (2007). Improvisations on the stage of the dream. Paper presentation, twenty-fourth conference of the International Association for the Study of Dreams. Sonoma State University, Sonoma, California.

Kohut, H. (1977). *The restoration of the self.* New York, NY: International Universities Press.

Koistinen, O., & Biro, J. (2002). *Spinoza: Metaphysical themes.* Oxford, England: Oxford University Press.

Kramer, M. (2007). *The dream experience: A systematic exploration.* New York, NY: Routledge.

Kremer, J. W. (1997). Recovering indigenous mind. *ReVision 19*(4), 32–46.

Kremer, J. W. (2003) Ethnoautobiography as practice of radical presence: Storying the self in participatory visions. *ReVision 25* (2), 5–13.

Kripke, D. F., Garfinkel, L., Wingard, D. L., Klauber, M. R., & Marler, M. R. (2002). Mortality associated with sleep duration and insomnia. *Archives of General Psychiatry 59*, 131–136.

Krippner, S. (1985). Parapsychological research: Past, present, and future. *Psi Research 4* (3/4), 4–35.

Krippner, S. (1987). Dreams and shamanism. In S. Nicholson (Ed.), *Shamanism: An expanded view of reality* (125–132). Wheaton, IL: Quest.

Krippner, S. (Ed.). (1990). *Dreamtime, dreamwork.* Los Angeles, CA: Jeremy Tarcher.

Krippner, S., Bogzaran, F., & de Carvalho, A. P. (2002). *Extraordinary dreams and how to work with them.* Albany: State University of New York Press.

Krippner, S., & Combs, A. (2000). Self-organization in the dreaming brain. *Journal of Mind and Behavior 21*, 399–412.

Krippner, S., & Dillard, J. (1988). *Dreamworking: How to use your dreams for creative problem solving.* New York, NY: Barely Limited.

Krippner, S., & Friedman, H. L. (2010). *Mysterious mind: The neurobiology of psychics, mediums, and other extraordinary people.* Santa Barbara: Praeger.

Krippner, S., & Thompson, A. (1996). A 10-facet model of dreaming applied to dream practices of sixteen Native American cultural groups. *Dreaming 6*(1), 71–96.

Kuiken, D. (1995). Dreams and feeling realization. *Dreaming 5*, 129–157.

Kuiken, D., Lee, M. N., Eng, T. C., & Singh, T. (2006). The influence of impactful dreams on self-perceptual depth and spiritual transformation. *Dreaming 16*, 258–279.

Kuiken, D., & Nielsen, T. A. (1996). Individual differences in orienting activity mediate feelings realization in dreams: Evidence from retrospective movement inhibition. *Dreaming 6*(3), 201–217.

Kuiken, D., & Sikora, S. (1993). The impact of dreams on waking thoughts and feelings. In A. Moffitt, M. Kramer, & R. Hoffman (Eds.), *The functions of dreams* (419–475). Albany: State University of New York Press.

LaBerge, S. (1980). Lucid dreaming: An exploratory study of consciousness during sleep. Unpublished doctoral dissertation, Stanford University.

LaBerge, S. (1985). *Lucid dreaming.* New York, NY: Ballantine.

LaBerge, S. (1990). Lucid dreaming: Psychophysiological studies of consciousness during REM sleep. In R. R. Bootzin, J. F. Kihlstrom, & D. L. Schacter (Eds.), *Sleep and Cognition.* Washington, DC: American Psychological Association.

LaBerge, S. (2000). Lucid dreaming: Evidence and methodology. *Behavioral and Brain Sciences 23*, 962–964.

LaBerge, S., & Rheingold, H. (1990). *Exploring the world of lucid dreaming.* New York, NY: Ballantine Books.

Lamoreaux, J. (2002). *The early Muslim tradition of dream interpretation.* Albany: State University of New York Press.

Langan, T. (1987). Written communication between Langan and James Kidd, Ontario, Canada, February 1987 in Kidd & Kidd (1990). *Experiential Method.* New York, NY: Peter Lang.

Lawrence, W. G. (2005). *Introduction to social dreaming: Transforming thinking.* London, England: Karnac.

Lee, A., & Wilson, M. (2002). Memory of sequential experience in the hippocampus during slow wave sleep. *Neuron 36*(6), 1183–1194.

Lemaitre, G. E. (1941). *From cubism to surrealism*. London: Oxford University Press.

Levitan, L., & LaBerge, S. (1991). In the mind and out-of-body. *Nightlights* 3(2), 1–4.

Lewis, T, Amini, F., & Lannon, R. (2000). *A general theory of love*. New York, NY: Vintage Books.

Li, Y. (2003). Discourse of mid-day napping: A political windsock in contemporary China. In B. Steger & L. Brunt (Eds.), *Night-time and sleep in Asia and the West: Exploring the dark side of life*. New York, NY: Routledge Curzon.

Lian Chew, P. G. (1993). *The Chinese religion and the Baha'i Faith*. Oxford, England: George Ronald Publisher.

Lichtenberg, J. D., Lachmann, F. M., & Fosshage, J. M. (2002). *A spirit of inquiry: Communication in psychoanalysis*. Hillsdale, NJ: The Analytic Press.

Lippmann, P. (1998). On the private and social nature of dreams. *Contemporary Psychoanalysis* *34*(2), 195–221.

Littlewood, W. C., & Roche, M. A. (2004). *Waking up: The work of Charlotte Selver*. Bloomington, IN: AuthorHouse.

Lowen, A. (1975). *Bioenergetics*. London, England: Penguin.

Lyons-Ruth, K., Bruschweiler-Stern, N., Harrison, A. M., Morgan, A. C., Nahum, J. P., Sander, L., Stern, D. N., & Tronick, E. Z. (1998). Implicit relational knowing: Its role in development and psychoanalytic treatment. *Infant Mental Health Journal 19*(3), 282–289.

Mageo, J. (2003). *Dreaming and the self: New perspectives on subjectivity, identity, and emotion*. Albany: State University of New York Press.

Mageo. J. (2004). Towards a holographic theory of dreaming. *Dreaming 14*(2–3), 151–169.

Mahrer, A. R. (1989). *Dreamwork in psychotherapy and self-change*. New York, NY: Norton.

Maitra, S. K. (1968). *The meeting of the East and the West in Sri Aurobindo's philosophy*. Pondicherry, India: Sri Aurobindo Ashram Press.

Mallon, B. (2005). Dreams and bereavement. *Bereavement Care 24*(3), 43–46.

Maquet, P. (2001). The role of sleep in learning and memory. *Science 294*, 1048–1052.

Maquet, P., Peters, J. M., Aerts, J., Delfiore, G., Degueldre, C., Luxen, A., & Franck, G. (1996). Functional neuroanatomy of human rapid-eye-movement sleep and dreaming. *Nature 383*, 163–166.

Maselko, J., Kubzansky, L., Lipsitt, L., & Buka, S. L. (2010). Mother's affection at 8 months predicts emotional distress in adulthood. *Journal of Epidemiology and Community Health*. doi:10.1136/

jech.2009.097873; Retrieved July 26, 2010, from http://jech.bmj.com/search?fulltext=Maselko&submit=yes&x=0&y=0.

Mason, I. Lynn (1995). Electrophysiological correlates of higher states of consciousness during sleep. Maharishi University of Management. Ann Arbor, MI: UMI.

Matheny. D. (2002). *Dreaming: The relationship to self.* Doctoral dissertation, California Institute of Integral Studies. Ann Arbor, MI: UMI.

Maturana, U., & Varela, F. (1987). *The tree of knowledge: The biological roots of human understanding.* Boston, MA: Shambhala.

Mavromatis, A. (1987). *Hypnagogia: The unique state of consciousness between wakefulness and sleep.* London, England: Routledge and Kegan Paul.

Maxfield, M. (1990). Effects of rhythmic drumming of EEG and subjective experience. Unpublished doctoral dissertation, Institute of Transpersonal Psychology, Palo Alto, CA.

McDowell, M. J. (2001). Principle of organization: A dynamic systems view of the archetype-as-such. *The Journal of Analytical Psychology 46*, 637–654.

McGann, M., & Torrance, S. (2005). *Doing it and meaning it: And the relationship between the two.* In R. D. Ellis & N. Newton (Eds.), *Consciousness and emotion: agency, conscious choice and selective perception.* Philadelphia, PA: John Benjamins.

McIntosh, S. (2007). *Integral consciousness and the future of evolution.* St. Paul, MN: Paragon House.

McKenzie, S. (2006). Queering gender: Anima/animus and the paradigm of emergence. *Journal of Analytical Psychology 51*(3), 401–421.

McNamara, P. (2004). *Evolutionary psychology of sleep and dreams.* Westport, CT: Praeger.

McNamara, P., McLaren, D., & Durso, K. (2007). Representation of the self in REM and NREM dreams. *Dreaming 17*(2), 113–126.

McNiff, S. (1981). *The arts and psychotherapy.* Springfield, IL: Charles Thomas Publisher.

Merleau-Ponty, M. (1962). *Phenomenology of perception.* Translated by C. Smith. London, England: Routledge & Kegan Paul.

Meier, C. (1989). *Healing dream and ritual.* Einsiedeln, Switzerland: Daimon Verlag.

Mellick, J. (1996). *The natural artistry of dreams: Creative ways to bring the wisdom of dreams to waking life.* Berkeley: Conari Press.

Meltzer, D. (1984/2009). *Dream life: A re-examination of the psychoanalytic theory and technique.* London, England: Karnac.

Metzner, R. (1998). *The unfolding self: Varieties of transformative experience.* Novato, CA: Origin Press.

Mindell, A. (1982). *Dreambody: The body's role in revealing the self.* Boston, MA: Sigo Press.

Moffitt, A., Kramer, M., & Hoffman, R. (Eds.). (1993). *The functions of dreams.* Albany: State University of New York Press.

Moss, R. (1996). *Conscious dreaming.* New York, NY: Crown Trade Paperback.

Moss, R. (2009). *The secret history of dreaming.* Novato, CA: New World Library.

Narby, J. (1999). *The cosmic serpent: DNA and the origins of knowledge.* Los Angeles, CA: Jeremy Tarcher.

Nielsen, T. A. (2000). Mentation in REM and NREM sleep: A review and possible reconciliation of two models. *Behavioral and Brain Sciences 23* (6), 851–866.

Nielsen, T. A., Kuiken, D., Alain, G., Stenstrom, P., & Powell, R. A. (2004). Immediate and delayed incorporations of events into dreams: Further replication and implications for dream function. *Journal of Sleep Research 13,* 327–336.

Nielsen, T. A., Deslauriers, D., & Baylor, G. W. (1991). Emotions in dream and waking event reports. *Dreaming 1*(4), 287–300.

Nielsen, T. A., & Powell, R. A. (1992). The day-residue and dream-lag effects: A literature review and limited replication of tow temporal studies. *Dreaming 2*(2), 67–77.

Nielsen, T., Zadra, A. L., Simard, V., Saucier, S., Stenstrom, P., Smith, C., & Kuiken, D. (2003). The typical dreams of Canadian university students. *Dreaming 13*(4), 211–235.

Oberkampf, W. L. (August, 2005). Uncertainty quantification using evidence theory. Paper presented at Stanford University (22–23). Sandia National Laboratory, Livermore, CA.

Odin, S. (1981). Sri Aurobindo and Hegel on the involution-evolution of Absolute Spirit. *Philosophy East and West 31*(2), 179–191.

Ogden, T. (2005). *This art of psychoanalysis: Dreaming undreamt dreams and interrupted cries.* New York, NY: Routledge.

Olsen, F. (1999). Dream reentry and on-line chat: An experience of synchronicity and resolving loss in a chat room setting. *Electric Dreams 6*(12).

Ong, R. K. (1985). *The interpretation of dreams in ancient China.* Bochum, Germany: Studienverlag Brockmeyer.

Onslow Ford, G. (1978). *Creation.* Basel, Switzerland: Galerie Schreiner.

Pace-Schott, E. F. (2001). Theory of mind: Social cognition and dreaming. *SRS Bulletin 7,* 33–36.

Palombo, S. R. (1978). *Dreaming and memory: A new information-processing model.* New York, NY: Basic Books.

Pandya, V. (2004). Forest smells and spider webs: Ritualized dream interpretation among Andaman islanders. *Dreaming 14*(2–3), 136–150.

Peat, F. D. (1994). *Lighting the seventh fire: The spiritual ways, healing, and science of the Native American.* New York, NY: Birch Lane Press.

Peay, P. (1999). Interview: At the cutting edge of using psychological concepts in soul work is spiritual teacher Hameed Ali. *Common Boundary*. Retrieved April 1, 2010 from http://www.ahalmaas.com/Articles/common.htm.

Perls, F. S. (1969/1992). *Gestalt therapy verbatim.* Highland, NY: Gestalt Journal.

Persinger, M. A., & Krippner, S. (1989). Dream ESP experiments and geomagnetic activity. *Journal of the American Society for Psychical Research, 83,* 101–116.

Pesant, N., & Zadra, A. L. (2004). Working with dreams in therapy: What do we know and what should we do? *Clinical Psychology Review 24,* 489–512.

Peters, L. (2004). An experiential study of Nepalese Shamanism. In Andrei A. Znamenski (Ed.), *Shamanism* (272–293). New York, NY: Routledge Curzon.

Pierrakos, J. (1987). *Core energetics: Developing the capacity to love and heal.* Mendocino, CA: Life Rhythm.

Purcell, S., Mullington, J., Moffitt, A., Hoffmann, R., & Pigeau, R. (1986). Dream self-reflectiveness as a learned cognitive skill. *Sleep 9*(3), 423–437.

Racicot, A. (1992). Dream creations: A workshop with Fariba Bogzaran and Jessica Allen. *Night Vision: A Dream Journal 3*(3), 18.

Racicot, S. (1992). Shamanic drumming and lucidity: An interview with Fariba Bogzaran. *Night Vision: A Dream Journal 3*(3), 23.

Razali, S. (2003). Hegel, his Dialectics and some of the Hegelians. Retrieved April 3, 2010 from http://humandynamicwholeness.org/Hegel_and_his_Dialectics.html.

Reed, H. (1989). On the marriage of art and science: An interview with Fariba Bogzaran. *Association for the Study of Dreams Newsletter 6* (1), 6–10.

Reich, W. (1979). *The bion experiments: On origins of life.* New York, NY: Farrar, Straus and Giroux.

Reich, W. (1976). *Character analysis.* New York, NY: Pocket Books.

Revonsuo, A. (2000). The reinterpretation of dreams: An evolutionary hypothesis of the function of dreaming. *Behavioral and Brain Science 23,* 877–901.

Ricoeur, P. (1967). *Symbolism of evil.* Boston, MA: Beacon Press.

Ricoeur, P. (1970). *Freud and philosophy: An essay on interpretation.* Translated by D. Savage. New Haven, CT: Yale University Press.

Rogers, N. (April, 1985). Express your self. *AHP Perspective*, 14–15.

Roland, A. (1988). *In search of self in India and Japan: Toward a cross-cultural psychology*. Princeton: Princeton University Press.

Rossi, E. L. (1985/1972). *Dreams and the growth of personality*. (2nd ed.). New York, NY: Brunner/Mazel.

Russell, P. (1998). *Waking up in time*. Novato, CA: Origin Press.

Russo, R. (Ed.) (1987). *Dreams are wiser than man*. Berkeley, North Atlantic Books.

Sabini, M. (Ed.) (2002). *The Nature Writings of C.G. Jung*. Berkeley, CA: North Atlantic Books.

Sabini, M. (2007). Culture dreaming: An arena for societal reflection. *Dreamtime, 24*(1), 16–17, 34–38.

Sabini, M, and Russo, R. (nd). http://dream-institute.org/culture_dreaming_calendar.htm (retrieved 10/18/2010).

Schlitz, M., Vieten, C., & Amorok, A. (2008). *Living deeply: The art and science of transformation in everyday life*. Petaluma, CA: IONS/New Harbinger.

Schredl, M. (2003). Continuity between waking and dreaming: A proposal for a mathematical model. *Sleep and Hypnosis 5*(1), 26–40.

Schredl, M. (2003a). Effects of state and trait factors on nightmare frequency. *European Archives of Psychiatry & Clinical Neuroscience 253*, 241–247.

Schredl, M., Ciric, P., Götz, S., & Wittmann, L. (2004). Typical dreams: Stability and gender differences. *Journal of Psychology 138*, 485–494.

Schredl, M., Nürnber, C., & Weiler, S. (1996). Dream recall, attitude toward dreams, and personality. *Personality and Individual Differences 20*(5), 613–618.

Schredl, M., & Piel, E. (2008). Interest in dream interpretation: A gender difference. *Dreaming 18*(1), 11–15.

Schwartz, S. (2004). What dreaming can reveal about cognitive and brain functions during sleep: A lexico-statistical analysis of dream reports. *Psychologica Belgica 44*(1&2), 5–42.

Schweder, R. (1991). *Thinking through cultures: Expeditions on cultural psychology*. Cambridge, MA: Harvard University Press.

Seligman, M. E. P., & Csíkszentmihályi, M. (2000). Positive psychology: An introduction. *American Psychologist 55*(1), 5–14.

Sen, I. (1986). *Integral psychology*. Pondicherry, India: Sri Aurobindo Ashram Press.

Shafton, A. (1995). *The dream reader: Contemporary approaches to the understanding of dreams*. Albany: State University of New York Press.

Shafton, A. (1995a). Why so few Blacks in the dream movement? *Dream Time*. Retrieved February 11, 2010 from http://www.asdreams.org/magazine/articles/blacks_in_dreamwork.htm.

Shafton, A. (2002). *Dream-singers: The African American way with dreams.* New York, NY: Wiley.

Shirazi, B. (2001). Integral psychology, metaphors and processes of integration. In M. Cornelissen (Ed.), *Consciousness and its transformation* (29–53). Pondicherry, India: SAICE.

Smith, C., & MacNeill, C. (1994). Impaired motor memory for a pursuit rotor task following Stage 2 sleep loss in college students. *Journal of Sleep Research 3*, 206–213.

Smuts, J. C. (1926). *Holism and evolution.* New York, NY: Macmillan.

Solms, M. (1997). *The neuropsychology of dreams: A clinico-anatomical study.* Mahwah, NJ: Erlbaum.

Solms, M. (1999). The new neuropsychology of sleep: Commentary by Mark Solms. *Neuropsychoanalysis 1*, 183–195.

Solms, M. (2000). Dreaming and REM sleep are controlled by different brain mechanisms. *Behavioral and Brain Sciences 23*(6), 793–1121.

Sparrow, S. (1976/1986). *Lucid dreaming: Dawning of the clear light.* Virginia Beach, VA: A.R.E. Press.

Staner, L. (2002). Sleep-wake mechanisms and drug discovery: Sleep EEG as a tool for the development of CNS-acting drugs. *Dialogues in Clinical Neuroscience* 4(4), 342–350.

States, B. O. (1988). *The rhetoric of dreams.* Ithaca, NY: Cornell University Press.

Stein, G. (1933). *The autobiography of Alice B. Toklas.* New York, NY: Harcourt, Brace.

Stern, D. (1985). *The interpersonal world of the infant.* New York, NY: Basic Books.

Stern, D. N. (1998). The process of therapeutic chance involving implicit knowledge: Some implications of developmental observations for adult psychotherapy. *Infant Mental Health Journal 19*(3), 300–308.

Stern, D. N., Bruschweiler-Stern, N., Harrison, A. M., Lyons-Ruth, K., Morgan, A. C., Nahum, J. P., Sander, L., & Tronick, E. Z. (1998). The process of therapeutic change involving implicit knowledge: Some implications of developmental observations for adult psychotherapy. *Infant Mental Health Journal 19*(3), 300–308.

Stickgold, R. (2007). Of sleep, memories and trauma. *Nature Neuroscience 10*(5), 540–542.

Stolorow, R., Brandcraft, B., & Atwood, G. E. (1987). *Psychoanalytic treatment: An intersubjective approach.* Hillsdale, NJ: The Analytic Press.

Suzuki, S. (1970). *Zen mind, beginner's mind.* New York, NY: Weatherhill.

Szmigielska, B., & Holda, M. (2007). Students' views on the role of dreams in human life. *Dreaming 17*(3), 152–159.

Ta-Kao, C. (1948). *Tao te ching.* (Second ed.), Ch. LI. (11). London, England: The Buddhist Society London.

Tandan, M. (2009). *Dreams and beyond: Finding your way in the dark.* New Delhi, India: Hay House.

Tandan, M. (2011). The way leads through yourself to beyond yourself: Dreaming in a Himalayan monastery. In S. Kakar (Ed.), *On dreams and dreaming* (146–167). New Delhi, India: Penguin.

Tharchin, L. R. (2009). *Dream yoga and extraordinary dreams.* Teachings on Karma Lingpa (nd) with Fariba Bogzaran. Paleaku Gardens Peace Sanctuary, The Big Island of Hawaii.

Tart, C. T. (1968). *Altered states of consciousness.* New York, NY: Anchor Books.

Taub-Bynum, B. E. (1984). *The family unconscious.* Wheaton, IL: The Theosophical Publishing House.

Taylor, J. (1983). *Dreamwork: Techniques for discovering the creative power in dreams.* New York, NY: Paulist Press.

Taylor, J. (1992). *Where people fly and water runs uphill: Using dreams to tap the wisdom of the unconscious.* New York, NY: Warner Books.

Tedlock, B. (Ed.). (1992a). *Dreaming: Anthropological and psychological interpretations.* Santa Fe, NM: School of American Research Press.

Tedlock, B. (1987). *Dreaming: Anthropological and psychological interpretations.* Cambridge, MA: Cambridge University Press.

Tedlock, B. (2004). The poetics and spirituality of dreaming: A Native American enactive theory. *Dreaming 14*(2–3), 183–189.

Tedlock, B. (2005). *The woman in the shaman's body: Reclaiming the feminine in religion and medicine.* New York, NY: Bantam.

Tholey, P. (1990). Applications of lucid dreaming. *Lucidity Letter 9*(2), 6–17.

Tonay, V. (1995). The art of dreaming: Using your dreams to unlock your creativity. Berkeley, CA: Celestial Arts.

Tononi, G., & Cirelli, C (2006). Sleep function and synaptic homeostasis. *Sleep Medicine Reviews 10*(1), 49–62.

Ullman, M. (1979). *Working with dreams.* Los Angeles, CA: J. P. Tarcher.

Ullman, M. (1984). Group dreamwork and healing. *Contemporary Psychoanalysis 20,* 120–130.

Ullman, M. (1996). *Appreciating dreams: A group approach.* Thousand Oaks, CA: Sage Publications.

Ullman, M. (1969). Dreaming as metaphor in motion. *Archives of General Psychiatry 21,* 699–703.

Ullman, M., & Krippner, S., with Vaughan, A. (1973). *Dream telepathy: Experiments in Nocturnal ESP.* New York, NY: Macmillan.

Ullman, M., & Zimmerman, N. (1979). *Working with dreams.* New York, NY: Delacorte Press/Eleanor Friede.

University of Wisconsin—Madison (2008, January 21). Brain connections strengthen during waking hours, weaken during sleep. *Science Daily*. Retrieved July 14, 2009 from http://www.sciencedaily.com/releases/2008/01/080120160658.htm.

Van Cauter, E., Leproult, R., & Plat, L. (2000). Age-related changes in slow wave sleep and REM sleep and relationship with growth hormone and cortisol levels in healthy men. *Journal of the American Medical Association 284*(7), 861–868.

Van de Castle, R. (1977). Sleep and dreams. In B. Wolman (Ed.), *Handbook of parapsychology* (473–499). New York, NY: Van Nostrand Reinhold.

Van de Castle, R. (1994). *Our dreaming mind.* New York, NY: Ballantine Books.

Van den Daele, L. (1992). Direct interpretation of dreams: Typology. *The American Journal of Psychoanalysis 52*(4), 307–326.

Varela, F. J., Thompson, E., & Rosch, E. (1991). *The embodied mind: Cognitive science and human experience.* Cambridge, MA: MIT.

Vedfelt, O. (2002). *The dimensions of dreams: The nature, function, and interpretation of dreams.* Philadelphia, PA: Jessica Kingsley Publishers.

Vgontzas, A. N. (2002). *Modest sleep loss increases/alters normal secretion of IL-6, TNF-alpha, cortisol.* eighty-fourth annual meeting of the endocrine society. June. San Francisco, CA.

Von Grunebaum, G. E., & Caillois, R. (1966). *The dream and human societies.* Berkeley, CA: University of California Press.

Voss, U., Holzmann, R., Tuin, I., & Hobson, J. A. (2009). Lucid dreaming: A state of consciousness with features of both waking and non-lucid dreaming. *Sleep 32*(09), 1191–1200.

Waddington, C. H. (1957). *The strategy of the genes: A discussion of some aspects of theoretical biology.* London, England: George Allen & Unwin.

Waggoner, R. (2009). *Lucid dreaming: Gateway to the inner self.* Needham, MA: Moment Point Press.

Wagner, U., Gais, S., Haider, H., Verleger R., & Born, J. (2004). Sleep inspires insight. *Nature 427*(6972), 304–305.

Wallace, A. (2006). *The attention revolution: Unlocking the power of the focused mind.* Somerville, MA: Wisdom Publication.

Wallace, B. W. (1999). *The four immeasurables: Cultivating a boundless heart.* Ithaca, NY: Snow Lion.

Walsh, R., & Vaughan, F. (1993). On transpersonal definitions. *Journal of Transpersonal Psychology 25*(2), 125–182.

Wangyal, T. (1998). *The Tibetan yogas of dreams and sleep.* Ithaca, NY: Snow Lion Publications.

Warren, J. (2007). *The head trip: Adventures on the wheel of consciousness.* New York, NY: Random House.

Washburn, M. (1994). *Transpersonal psychology in psychoanalytic perspective.* Albany: State University of New York Press.

Watson, B. (1968). *The complete works of Chuang Tzu.* New York, NY: Columbia University Press.

Wax, M. L. (1999). The angel of dreams: Towards an ethnology of dream interpreting. *Journal of the American Academy of Psychoanalysis 27*(3), 417–429.

Weaver, J. (1987). Comparison of Reich's concept of orgone and Chinese concept of chi. Lecture in a course on Reichian Psychotherapy. California Institute of Integral Studies, San Francisco, CA.

Welwood, J. (2000). *Toward a psychology of awakening: Buddhism, psychotherapy and the path of personal and spiritual transformation.* Boston, MA: Shambhala.

Wilber, K. (1995). *Sex, ecology, spirituality: The spirit of evolution.* Boston, MA: Shambhala.

Wilber, K. (2000). *Integral psychology: Consciousness, spirit, psychology, therapy.* Boston, MA: Shambhala.

Wilber, K. (2006). *Integral spirituality.* Boston, MA: Shambhala.

Womack, Y. (2003). *Milk of the snow lioness: Numinous presence in spiritually transformative dreams.* PhD dissertation, California Institute of Integral Studies, UMI.

Womack, Y. (2009). *Guardians of the gate: An investigation of numinous presence, "visions of the divine" in dreams.* Koln, Germany: Lambert Academic Publishing.

Woods, R. L., & Greenhouse, H. B. (Eds.). (1974). *The new world of dreams.* New York, NY: Macmillan.

Worthman, C. M., & Melby, M. (2002). Toward a comparative developmental ecology of human sleep. In M. A. Carskadon (Ed.), *Adolescent sleep patterns: Biological, social, and psychological influences* (69–117). New York, NY: Cambridge University Press.

Wu, Y. (1986). *Chinese philosophical terms.* London, England: University Press of America.

Yoo, S., Gujar, N., Hu, P., Jolesz, F. A., & Walker, M. P. (2007). The human emotional brain without sleep: A prefrontal amygdala disconnect. *Current Biology 17*(20), 877–878.

Yu, C. K. (2008). Typical dreams experienced by Chinese people. *Dreaming 18*(1), 1–10.

Zadra, A. L. (1996). Recurrent dreams: Their relation to life events. In D. Barrett, (Ed.), *Trauma and dreams.* Cambridge, MA: Harvard University Press.

Zager, A., Andersen, M. L., Ruiz, F. S., Antunes, I. B., & Tufik, S. (2007). Effects of acute and chronic sleep loss on immune modulation of rats. *American Journal of Physiology: Regulatory, Integrative and Comparative Physiology 293*, 504–509.

Zahavi, D. (2003). *Husserl's phenomenology*. Stanford, CA: Stanford University Press.

Zaleski, C. G. (1994). Attention as a key to Buddhist-Christian dialogue. *Buddhist-Christian Studies 14*, 89–110.

Zangpo, N. (2008). Dream Yoga presented at the course, Lucid dreaming: Consciousness in sleep, John F. Kennedy University, Berkeley, California.

Index